THE BLACK DEATH

THREE DOCTORS AT THE BEDSIDE OF A PLAGUE VICTIM. THE
LATTER IS POINTING TO THE PLAGUE-BOIL UNDER HIS ARMPIT

TURNING POINTS IN HISTORY
General Editor: SIR DENIS BROGAN

THE
BLACK DEATH

1347

BY

GEORGE DEAUX

HAMISH HAMILTON
LONDON

First published in Great Britain, 1969
by Hamish Hamilton Ltd
90 Great Russell Street London WC1
Copyright © 1969 by George Deaux

SBN 241 01514 6

Printed in Great Britain
by Western Printing Services Ltd
Bristol

CONTENTS

LIST OF ILLUSTRATIONS

ACKNOWLEDGMENTS

Thanks are due to the following publishers for permission to quote from the books listed: George Allen & Unwin Ltd. and the Humanities Press, Johannes Nohl's *The Black Death*; the Cambridge University Press, G. G. Coulton's *Medieval Panorama*; J. M. Dent & Sons Ltd., and E. P. Dutton & Co. Inc., (Copyright, 1951, by E. P. Dutton & Co. Inc., Dutton Paperback Edition. Translated by Archibald Colquhoun), the Everyman's Library edition of Alessandro Manzoni's *The Betrothed*; Encyclopaedia Britannica, K. F. Meyers' 'Plague', 1966 edition; Hamish Hamilton Ltd. and Alfred A. Knopf Inc., Albert Camus's *The Plague*.

Chapter I

EARLY WARNINGS

THE FIRST reports came out of the East. They were confused, exaggerated, frightening, as reports from that quarter
of the world so often are: descriptions of storms and earthquakes; of meteors and comets trailing noxious gases that killed
trees and destroyed the fertility of the land; of invasions of rats and
swarms of locusts; and news of a plague that drove its victims screaming through the streets in lunatic frenzy, that struck some so quickly
that they died with the amazement of seeing the first symptoms still
engraved on their faces, a plague so virulent that children fled from
their infected parents and mothers abandoned in horror a baby upon
whom the marks had begun to appear; a plague so deadly that whole
cities were depopulated, the dead left unburied in the streets or
thrown wantonly into rivers and the sea. Some recorded that fleets
of ships drifted about aimlessly, their entire crews dead of plague.

Other more specific reports told of appalling natural catastrophes.
In 1333 a terrible drought and famine afflicted that part of China
watered by the Kiang and Hoai rivers. Soon after, such violent
storms and floods fell upon Kingsai, then the capital of the empire,
that according to tradition over 400,000 people died. There were
strange accounts of violent earthquakes: the mountain Tsincheou
disappeared and enormous clefts appeared in the earth; near Kingsai, it was said, the mountains of Ki-ming-chan utterly fell in and in
their place appeared suddenly a lake more than a hundred leagues in
circumference, where, again, thousands died. In Houkouang and
Ho-nan a drought of five months was followed by vast swarms of
locusts which destroyed crops and hardened the famine. There were
floods in Canton and an unprecedented drought in Tche. And
everywhere in that vaguely defined and fabulously imagined region
which the 14th century knew as 'the East' these disruptions were
followed by a particularly virulent plague.

Later, when Pope Clement VI sought out the causes and origins
of the plague that was then raging in Avignon, he was told that it

1

had spread so rapidly in the East and proved so fatal that the dead
were numbered in millions. A Prague chronicle describes the epidemic in China, India and Persia; and the Florentine historian
Matteo Villani, who took up the work of his brother Giovanni after
he had died of the plague in Florence, relays the account of earthquakes and pestilential fogs from a traveller in Asia: 'A venerable
friar minor of Florence, now a bishop, declared that he was then
in that part of the country at the city of Lamech, where by the
violence [of an earthquake] part of the temple of Mohammed was
thrown down.' And a pestilence followed. A similar incident of
earthquake and pestilential fog was reported from Cyprus, and it was
believed that the wind had been so poisonous that men were struck
down and died from it. Gabrielle de Mussi, a notary of Piacenza,
after a voyage to the Crimea, noted that, 'In the year 1346 in the
eastern parts an immense number of Tartars and Saracens fell
victims to a mysterious and sudden death. In these regions vast
districts, numerous provinces, magnificent kingdoms, cities, castles
and villages, peopled by a great multitude, were suddenly attacked
by the mortality, and in a brief space were depopulated.' It was
recounted to Pope Clement that in China more than thirteen million
had died, that India was depopulated, that Tartary, Mesopotamia,
Syria, Armenia were full of death; that in Caesarea no one remained
alive at all; that in Cairo ten to fifteen thousand died daily; that
in Gaza twenty-two thousand people and nearly all the animals
were dead; that Cyprus lost almost all its inhabitants. The information delivered to the Pope estimated the dead from these catastrophes
in the East at nearly twenty-four million.

Of course these reports are exaggerated. Word of mouth com-
munications from strange and distant places seldom recommend
belief, and the East was extremely remote in the Middle Ages. Nor
were 14th-century writers scrupulously concerned about checking
the accuracy of their information, even where they had the opportunity to do so. This is not to suggest that they were unconcerned
with the discovery and presentation of the truth, but rather that
truth was not yet conceived of as factual accuracy, if indeed facts as
such were of interest at all. Truth in the Middle Ages is somewhat
different to truth as understood by the post-Renaissance world: it is,
one can perhaps say, a more literary truth, a truth which is more
directly personal and more obviously didactic than that of an age
which prides itself on scientific objectivity and detachment. For that
reason, as well as for the fact that there were and are no accurate

population figures for the world, or even always for individual cities, in the 14th century, one must treat with considerable caution the estimates of plague deaths, even those from eye-witnesses. This is a point that must be made, but it must be made with caution in the light of a common tendency to think of the Middle Ages as mankind's dark night of the mind. We are apt to flatter ourselves that we are so much more intelligent now. How is it, we might perhaps ask, that no one ever knew that there is a uniform rate of acceleration for all falling bodies until, as legend has it, Galileo dropped that cannon-ball and grapeshot simultaneously from the bell-tower at Pisa? The answer may be that in the Middle Ages nobody cared. It is reasonable to assume that a heavy body falls faster than a lighter one, and if it is reasonable it is true. It remained for the Renaissance to discover that in the area of natural science what is reasonable is often wrong; in the Middle Ages it was not necessary—it might even have seemed a little strange—to drop cannon-balls off bell-towers. The test of truth was reasonableness, consistency with the teachings of authority, and didactic utility. Thus, like many numberings of the dead from battles, disasters, or demonstrations which, even in our own time, are intended to impress or appal, the figure of twenty-four million may have been simply an arithmetic metaphor for 'a great number of men'.

The important aspect of the early reports of terrestrial and atmospheric disruptions is not their factual accuracy so much as that they fit a pattern of disaster familiar to the age. Wise men would have been apprehensive, recognizing the traditional precursors of even more widespread disaster. And when the calamities that had occurred in the East were repeated in Europe, literate men took careful notice. Simultaneously with the beginning of catastrophic upheavals in the East, Mount Etna erupted in 1333. Three years later troubling and unusual atmospheric phenomena, including frequent and peculiarly severe thunderstorms, harassed inhabitants of northern France. Locusts swarmed over parts of Europe in 1337 and 1338: they are said to have lain a foot high in ponds and wells, their filth dripped from the roofs of houses, at times they were so thick that they darkened the sky and covered the ground for miles around. In 1338 the harvest failed in France. In 1342 there were great floods of the Rhine and elsewhere in France. In 1346 both locusts and mice invaded Germany in huge numbers. There were seismic earthquakes in 1347. In Venice the earth shook so violently that the bells of St. Mark's rang and whole towers and churches collapsed. German accounts speak of a heavy vile-smelling mist which advanced from the East and spread itself over Italy. The English chronicler Knighton wrote that 'many cities in Corinth and Achaia were overturned, and the earth swallowed them. Castles and fortresses were broken, laid low, and swallowed up. Mountains in Cyprus were levelled into one, so that the flow of the rivers was impeded, and many cities were submerged and villages destroyed. Similarly, when a friar was preaching at Naples, the whole city was destroyed by an earthquake. Suddenly, the earth was opened up, as if a stone had been thrown into water, and everyone died along with the preaching friar . . .'

Equally ominous was the astrological evidence of impending disaster. A grand conjunction of the three superior planets, Saturn, Jupiter and Mars, in the sign of Aquarius, took place on March 24, 1345, according to the celebrated physician Guy de Chauliac, who attended the Pope throughout the siege of plague at Avignon. There were disputes about the exact date of this phenomenon but none about its seriousness: no less an authority than Aristotle had regarded the conjunction of Mars and Jupiter to be especially menacing. There was widespread crop failure over all Europe in 1347 and 1348. Food was so scarce in Florence that in 1347 it had to be distributed to the poor. Villani reports that, in April of that year, 94,000 loaves of bread were dispensed daily. Nearly 4,000 are said to have died in the city and the surrounding countryside. Then, too, there had been isolated but sometimes severe outbreaks of plague or some similar disease earlier in the century: in southern France in 1301; in Italy in 1311; again in Italy, Burgundy and Northern Europe in 1316; in Middle Europe in 1335; in upper Italy in 1340 and again in France in 1342.

All in all, the signs were bad. Some sort of disaster was imminent. The earth itself seemed in a state of convulsion, shuddering and splitting, putting forth heavy poisonous winds that destroyed animals and plants and called swarms of insects to life to complete the destruction. There were so many parallel portents in the literature of the Bible, of Greece and Rome, and of the early Church, that only the most ignorant and the most sanguine could have ignored them. But surely none but the most apocalyptically pessimistic would have dared predict the catastrophe about to befall Europe. The accounts of the survivors read like descriptions of the end of the world. Cities were utterly depopulated and their streets silent and empty except for the bodies of the dead and the occasional howling of a terrified dog. Houses stood empty, shutters flapping in the wind. Villages in which everyone had died crumbled into ruin while confused cattle and sheep wandered aimlessly through the grain fields. Crowds of people in panic rushed from their homes into the countryside only to fall by the roads and die huddled in hedges and ditches. Children clung in terror to their dead mothers. Parents deserted their children, and children their parents, at the first signs of sickness. The world was filled with terror. A man who woke healthy could be dead by evening. Infection was everywhere; it could be transmitted by the breath, by the clothes, even by the jewellery of the sick. Many believed that a look could transmit the disease. Others were convinced that the world was being poisoned by a strange international conspiracy with its headquarters in Spain. Some saw demons in the sky. Some were convinced that the very air was foul with pestilence. Men huddled in fear, waiting to die. Some in their frenzy threw themselves into rivers and oceans. Some at the first sign of infection, feeling the fever and swelling, gave up all hope and cast themselves into the burial pits to lie among the corpses until they died. Later generations called it the Black Death and agreed that it was the worst single disaster to befall mankind since the Flood. But to those who endured it during the terrible years 1347 to 1350 it was the Great Mortality, *la Mortalega Grande*, *das grosse Sterben*, or—most simply and terribly—the Death.

The Black Death struck Europe with such ferocious devastation that to many it seemed like the end of the world, and they either fell into despair or set about enjoying their last days. But to some who did not abandon themselves, it was a catastrophe to be dealt with. The doctors searched their texts for causes, cures and preventives. The churchmen sought to understand it in terms of Biblical precedents. The scholars tried to comprehend it in terms of similar disasters described in the literature of antiquity. To many, the most urgent task was to fit the plague into some rational and orderly framework, to find some reasonable precedent for it. If the plague were not to destroy utterly the entire concept of order in the universe, some such precedents had to be found. In a time of such great turmoil and suffering, it must have seemed to many that the very fabric of rational order in nature had been destroyed, and such a destruction may well have seemed a worse disaster than the pestilence itself. In an age oriented towards authority, an age in which empirical knowledge was considered uncertain at best and dangerous at worst, the only place to turn for help was to Biblical sources and ancient authorities. The clergy and the vast majority of men of all classes and degrees of sophistication who depended upon the Church for the interpretation of events were to find their precedents for the Black Death in these sources.

But not only the clergy; medical men also sought guidance in the literature of antiquity. Although the 14th century is not entirely devoid of scientific thought, the idea of natural causation was not well developed or widely held; indeed those who advanced such ideas did so as a revolutionary, and sometimes a dangerously revolutionary, gesture. In any case, the concept of the natural causation of disease was very fundamental. Medicine had advanced little beyond the teaching of Hippocrates and Galen, and it was to these authorities that medical men turned for answers and theories. Even the bravest and most advanced among them, of whom Guy de Chauliac was one, found it necessary to profess frequently their indebtedness to the great men of antiquity to avoid being completely ostracized by the conventional medical fraternity. Natural causation consisted either of disruptions in the body as a result of diet or humours in the case of individual disease, or widespread disruptions of the atmosphere in the case of epidemics; medical men had no clear conception of contagion and were powerless to deal with epidemics. Many believed epidemics to be God's punishment for sinfulness, and the Church encouraged this idea. Jesus himself before commanding a lame man to walk first announced his forgiveness of the victim's sins; on another occasion, he enjoined those whom he had healed to 'sin no more, lest a worse thing befall thee'. But prayers had little effect upon the plague bacillus, and the processions that the Church organized served only to spread infection. Those who saw both the Church and the physicians fail before the onslaught of the plague were tempted in their disillusionment and despair to find cause in the malevolence of men: witches and poisoners who, for whatever reason, were killing them. The preconceptions and expectations of men are a strong influence upon what they actually experience and report. The Biblical and classical sources to which the victims of the plague turned were the only widely accepted points of reference, and these sources encouraged men to reach conclusions that were usually wrong, often strange, and sometimes destructive. But unless the mind could suddenly leap to a vast new insight into the world order, unless, in fact, 14th-century men could actually project themselves *en masse* into the mental frame of Renaissance empiricism, explanations had to be found in the knowledge of the day. And the knowledge of the day derived not from observation but from authority. It is one of the tragedies of the Black Death, as it is one of the tragedies of the world after Hiroshima, that men did not, could not, suddenly and *en masse*, change radically their conception of things. It is one of the triumphs of the period that, in spite of being unable to do so, civilization endured and men moved on to a new order.

So it was to the Bible and classical literature that even medical men first turned for help, and the explanations and answers they found there formed their own explanations and programmes. Confronted with the overwhelming horror of the Black Death, they were to fail miserably and universally, and that failure was to shake the foundations of belief in authority of all sorts. Froissart, a chronicler of the period, wrote a few years later with huge cynicism that it is 'the object of all medical men to gain large salaries'; and Chaucer's comment on the Doctor of Physik among his Canterbury pilgrims is not much kinder. It is possible for us, too, to dismiss the physicians and surgeons of the Black Death as either superstitious quacks or as self-interested charlatans intent on relieving the dying of their wealth. But since so many of them stayed on to die with their patients in countless well-meaning, if futile, gestures of compassion, perhaps one should credit them with dedication and seriousness, even if one cannot commend their preventives and cures, and try to understand the source of their learned ignorance. It is also easy in a secular and scientific age to ridicule or patronize the churchmen, and such a response might be justified if we ourselves had never applied tired traditional remedies to our own dangerous new problems. It is, perhaps, safer to try first to understand. If the pomposity and cowardice of some 14th-century men deserve our condemnation, the ignorance of all deserves our sympathy, or at least our understanding.

It was not only the clergy and the medical fraternity who turned to ancient accounts of plague for guidance. More important, perhaps, for this account, is the fact that the chroniclers, the literary men, and the letter writers, whose eye-witness accounts of the disaster form the bulk of available evidence, turned to these same sources for rhetorical models as well as for explanations. Over and over again we find that men widely separated by distance and sometimes by language, men who could not have been aware of one another's writings, strike upon the same phrase, look at the terror from the same point of view. If there is a common source for these reports, since it is impossible in many cases to discover even the suspicion of a direct influence, it must be sought among these accounts which were available to most literate men. There is, also, another explanation for the remarkable similarity of accounts: it is possible that, confronted with a catastrophe of such proportions, rhetoric is peeled to its bare bones, to the very basis of linguistic structure, and such accounts will always carry the stamp of familiarity. They are similar as one terrified scream is similar to another, as one death rattle resembles all others.

The causes of human suffering are clearly implied in the Bible. Over and over again, in the story of the Fall, of the Flood, of the Tower of Babel, of the destruction of Sodom and Gomorrah, the same lesson is presented: men sin, God grows angry, men suffer. This simplistic explanation of suffering is substantially modified in Job, Ecclesiastes, some of the later prophets, and the New Testament; but the overwhelming impression remains that suffering, like death itself, is man's punishment for disobeying or displeasing God. The many Biblical accounts of plague—the plagues of Pharaoh, the plague of Ashdod, of Sennacherib, of David—all tend to reinforce this idea.

The account in Exodus of the ten plagues of Pharaoh is relevant because it associates a series of disasters which lead finally to the last and most terrible plague, the death of the first-born. The pattern of events is the familiar one: Moses and Aaron at God's command demand freedom from the Pharaoh ; the Pharaoh refuses, and Aaron, again at God's command, brings a plague upon the Egyptians. The first plague is the turning of the waters of the Nile to blood so that 'the fish that was in the river died; and the river stank, and the Egyptians could not drink of the water of the river; and there was blood throughout all the land of Egypt'. The second plague is the invasion of frogs, the third that of lice. It is of interest to note the description of the coming of the lice: 'Aaron stretched out his hand with his rod, and smote the dust of the earth, and it became lice in man, and in beast; all the dust of the land became lice throughout all the land of Egypt', since it makes a connection between atmospheric conditions and insect invasions. There follow the plagues of the flies and the murrain among cattle. The sixth plague is that of boils and that plague, too, begins with a disruption of the atmosphere: 'And they took ashes of the furnace and stood before Pharaoh; and Moses sprinkled it up toward heaven; and it became a boil breaking forth with blains upon man, and upon beast; for the

Lord had promised that the ashes would become small dust in all the land of Egypt.' The seventh plague is that of hail, which 'smote throughout all the land of Egypt all that was in the field, both man and beast; and the hail smote every herb of the field, and brake every tree of the field'. The fearful and destructive storms continue until Pharaoh repents and confesses and acclaims the Lord: 'I have sinned this time: the Lord is righteous, and I and my people are wicked.' But after a brief interval the plagues continue: an invasion of locusts which 'covered the face of the whole earth, so that the land was darkened; and they did eat every herb of the land, and all the fruit of the trees which the hail had left'; and a thick darkness which hung over Egypt for three days.

The final and most terrible plague is that of the death of the firstborn: 'at midnight the Lord smote all the firstborn in the land of Egypt, from the firstborn of Pharaoh that sat on his throne unto the firstborn of the captive that was in the dungeon; and all the firstborn of cattle. And Pharaoh rose up in the night, he, and all his servants, and all the Egyptians; and there was a great cry in Egypt; for there was not a house where there was not one dead.' The Israelites escape the disaster by performing a blood sacrifice, as Moses instructs them: 'Draw out and take you a lamb according to your families, and kill the passover. And ye shall take a bunch of hyssop, and dip it in the blood that is in the basin, and strike the lintel and the two side posts with the blood that is in the basin; and none of you shall go out at the door of his house until the morning.' They are enjoined also to make a feast with the sacrificed lamb in accordance with quite strict instructions that 'they shall eat the flesh in the night, roast with fire, and unleavened bread; and with bitter herbs'. It must not be boiled or eaten raw but roasted well. The Lord's instructions even stipulate that it be eaten 'with your loins girded, your shoes on your feet and your staff in your hand; and ye shall eat it in haste'.

There are several things to note in these familiar passages. First is the universality of the last plague and the manner of its description. The king on his throne and the captive in his cell both suffer the same bereavement and, for the purposes of rhetoric at least, are for the moment equal. It is interesting also to notice that the final disaster is preceded by several specific natural catastrophes. There is now relatively general agreement that these plagues represent merely the seasonal variations to which Egypt is peculiarly liable, magnified by Jewish oral tradition. Even the selectivity of the final plague could be explained by the fact that diseases fall usually with particular severity upon those who are unprotected by the immunity conferred by an earlier epidemic. But these are the qualifications of a modern and sceptical age and hardly those of the 14th century. Men confronted with the terror of the Black Death were impressed by the chain of events leading up to the final plague, and accounts of the coming of the 14th-century pestilence selected from among all the ominous events that must have occurred in the years preceding the outbreak of 1348 those which closely resemble the ten plagues of Pharaoh: disruptions in the atmosphere, storms, unusual invasions of insects, celestial phenomena. There were even, in the 14th century, strange rumours circulated about unknown frogs with tails with which the medical men of the time were unfamiliar. Even stranger are the occasional reports that during the plague loaves of bread when cut open would sometimes bleed. In many such incredible accounts of the plague, and especially of attendant phenomena, one senses the almost hysterical groping of men in the midst of terror for some precedent, no matter how devastating or unbelievable it might be, for their own suffering.

One final point of interest arising from the accounts of the plagues of Pharaoh concerns the preventives and cures: blood sacrifice, dietary control, and, most important of all, repentance and prayer. And it can be noted also that it is a specific person who, by performing a specific act, initiates disaster.

A second plague is mentioned in the book of Numbers. During the period of wandering in the wilderness Korah and others revolted against Moses and Aaron, but as they did so 'the earth opened her mouth, and swallowed them up, and their houses, and all the men that appertained unto Korah, and all their goods'. Some of the children of Israel, disturbed by the harsh fate of Korah, 'murmured against Moses and against Aaron'. Those that did so were punished by the Lord who sent a plague that destroyed 14,700 of them before Aaron arrested it by burning incense as an atonement on the altar. The juxtaposition of earthquake and pestilence in this passage is noteworthy in view of the widespread belief in the 14th century that there was a direct relationship between them. It is also of interest that the plague is dispersed by the burning of incense, since burning aromatic herbs seems to have been one of the most universal of plague remedies.

More information emerges from the description of another plague in I Samuel, the plague of Ashdod. The Philistines defeated the

army of Israel and carried off the ark of the covenant to Ashdod
where it was placed in the temple of the local god, Dagon; but 'the
hand of the Lord was heavy upon them of Ashdod, and he destroyed
them, and smote them with emerods, even Ashdod and the coasts
thereof'. The men of Ashdod associated the ark with this plague
of mysterious swellings and shipped it off to Gath, another Philis-
tine city; but here too, God 'smote the men of the city, both small
and great, and they had emerods in their secret parts'. From Gath
the ark was sent to yet another city, Ekron, but again with the same
result: 'for there was a deadly destruction throughout all the city;
the hand of God was very heavy there. And the men that died not
were smitten with emerods: and the cry of the city went up to
heaven.' The pestilence endured seven months; finally, the priests
and diviners of the Philistines devised a method to end the epidemic. The ark was to be sent back containing 'images of your
emerods and images of your mice that mar the land'. Golden
replicas of the plague swellings and golden mice were made and
placed in the ark, which was then returned to the Israelites. The
method of transporting the ark is of some interest. It was to be sent
in a cart drawn by two cows. If the cows chose to take the coast road
to Beth-shemesh, it would be understood that the pestilence had
come from God, but 'if not, then we shall know that it is not his
hand that smote us: but was a chance thing that happened to us'.
The cows chose the coast road, and the arrival of the ark in Beth-
shemesh was the occasion for great rejoicing. But when the Beth-
shemites dared to look into the ark, even after suitable burnt
offerings had been made, they too were stricken with the plague and
fifty thousand and seventy of them died.

Here, again, the plague is a manifestation of God's displeasure,
but a particularly perplexing one since it falls upon God's chosen
people as well as the Philistines. The idea of contagion and com-
municability being still unborn, the writer reverts to the familiar
explanation: the Israelites also have offended God by looking into
the ark. Perhaps even more relevant is the hint that the plague
might not be the working of God after all, but 'a chance thing that
happened to us': an idea that must be quickly dismissed because it
suggests a world of chaos and anarchic natural forces far more un-
acceptable even than the terrors of a cosmos ruled by a jealous, but
reasonably consistent, God. Since the books of Samuel are thought
to have undergone final revision about the 7th century B.C., this
account must be one of the first to link the plague with mice, or rats,

since mice and rats seem to be seldom distinguished in Biblical literature. It is too much to suppose that the authors of Samuel saw a causal connection. It is more probable that the association is made since mice were a recurring scourge on the land in ancient times, one of the prominent causes of famine; and they are designated in the text as 'mice that mar the land'. But the association of mice and plague is made here and it remained in the minds of men ever after. The description of the plague itself may be one of the earliest instances of an identified epidemic of bubonic plague: it occurred on the sea coast in an area which has even until modern times seen frequent outbreaks of bubonic plague. It first struck a race of maritime traders and spread to inland towns. It lasted seven months. It took two forms, a severe form with early deaths, and a less fatal type characterized by swellings in the groin. But, even with such evidence, it would be foolhardy to attempt a medical diagnosis. The term 'plague' in ancient, and even in quite recent, literature, covers a wide range of infectious diseases. Galen (A.D. 131–201) used the word to signify any epidemic disease causing great mortality; and many epidemics recorded in history as plague do not really refer to the bubonic plague as it is described in modern medical texts. The ancient connotation of the term included diseases such as smallpox, typhus and typhoid fever as well. The Black Death, and even the Great Plague of London in 1665, cannot with absolute certainty be diagnosed as any one disease. It is probable, for instance, that many of the deaths in the London plague would have been attributed by a modern physician to typhus fever.

The cure for the plague of Ashdod as described here is considerably more primitive than the prayers, repentance, and atonement that ended the plagues of Moses and Aaron. It is magic in one of its simplest forms. The sufferers are enjoined to make replicas of the symptoms of their sickness and of the animal associated with it: imitative magic, the essence of which is that an effect can be produced or terminated by imitating it. The same sort of magic was employed by Moses to end the scourge of the 'fiery serpents' which came upon his people (Numbers, xxi): 'And the Lord said unto Moses, Make thee a fiery serpent, and set it upon a pole, and it shall come to pass that every one that is bitten, when he looketh upon it, shall live. And Moses made a serpent of brass and put it upon a pole; and it came to pass, that if a serpent had bitten any man, when he beheld the serpent of brass, he lived.' This sort of magic, and especially the association of serpents with disease, is

very ancient and seems to be almost world-wide: it is found in the
Vedas, in Ovid, in the customs of primitive people from many parts
of the world. Apollonius of Tyana is said to have freed Antioch from
scorpions by making a bronze image of a scorpion and burying it
under a pillar in the middle of the city. In Greek legend Asclepius,
the demigod of medicine, learns the art of healing from a serpent
(although, in Homer's account, he learns from Chiron), and according to Aristophanes in *Plutus* sacred snakes were kept in his temple.
The usual symbol of Asclepius is a serpent coiled on a staff, very
like the brazen serpent of Moses, and the staff with the single coiled
snake is even today a familiar medical symbol. For some reason best
known to themselves, the American Medical Association has chosen
for its symbol the caduceus of Hermes, similar but not identical to
the staff of Asclepius. Hermes, one remembers, is the messenger
who conducts the dead to Hades and is sometimes appealed to as a
protector of thieves.

The association of serpents with disease and with healing and
the magic that invokes the bringer of pestilence to cure it is well-
nigh universal. The agent that brings the misfortune has the power
to end it. The cure for disease is to be found in the disease itself.
Frenzied men in the 14th century, when medicine and religion had
failed them, turned to similar magic. Even today men protect themselves from infectious diseases by injecting themselves with serums
derived from the blood and tissues of other men or animals who
have been infected—with considerably more success than attended
upon some similar experiments of the 14th century. Once again,
however, our recognition of the failures of medieval thinking should
not blind us to the limitations of our own: the complacent rational-
ist must pause before the knowledge that modern magic does
not always work and the magic of the Middle Ages did not always
fail.

Another familiar Biblical plague is that which fell upon the army
of Sennacherib, probably in 701 B.C. at Pelusium, as described in
Isaiah and the second book of Kings. Sennacherib, king of the
Assyrians, laid siege to Jerusalem where he had shut up Hezekiah.
But the curse of the Lord was on him and his army was destroyed
in one blow. 'And it came to pass that night, that the angel of the
Lord went out, and smote the camp of the Assyrians an hundred
fourscore and five thousand; and when they arose early in the
morning, behold, they were all dead corpses.' The brief Biblical
account of this disaster is expanded by a Chaldean chronicler,

Berosus, in a fragment preserved by Josephus in which he attributes the defeat of Sennacherib to pestilence. Herodotus tells that the tradition of this miraculous deliverance lived on in Egypt too. His guide in the temple of Ptah at Memphis told him that a King Sethos despised and neglected the warrior class of the Egyptians and took from them the lands which they possessed under all the previous kings.

> Afterwards, therefore, when Sennacherib, king of the Arabians and Assyrians, marched his vast army into Egypt, the warriors one and all refused to come to his aid. On this the monarch, greatly distressed, entered into the inner sanctuary, and before the image of the god bewailed the fate that impended over him. As he wept he fell asleep, and dreamed that the god came and stood at his side, bidding him be of good cheer, and go boldly forth to meet the Arabian host, which would do him no hurt, as he himself would send those who should help him. Sethos then, relying on the dream, collected such of the Egyptians as were willing to follow him, who were none of them warriors, but traders, artisans, and market people, and with these marched to Pelusium, which commands the entrance into Egypt, and there pitched his camp. As the two armies lay there opposite one another, there came in the night a multitude of field-mice, which devoured all the quivers and bow-strings of the enemy and ate the thongs by which they managed their shields. Next morning they commenced their fight, and great multitudes fell, as they had no arms with which to defend themselves. There stands to this day in the temple of Vulcan a stone statue of Sethos, with a mouse in his hand, and an inscription to this effect: 'Look on me and learn to reverence the gods.'

One does not know quite what to make of this account which depicts Sennacherib attacking the Egyptians under a King Sethos, of whom there is no record in Egyptian history, but there are certain thematic elements of interest. First, of course, is that the Egyptian account of the disaster attributes it to mice, reinforcing the association of mice and pestilence that we have already noted. The second is the location of the battle at Pelusium, a city with a long reputation in the annals of pestilence. Procopius says that Pelusium was the starting point of Justinian's plague, and it was here, too, that one of the crusading armies developed plague. It was also in Pelusium that in 1799 the army of Napoleon was first infected. The eastern and southern coasts of the Mediterranean were the points to which the traders of the East brought their merchandise for exchange with the West. These trade routes from the East, these meeting points of

East and West, were the places where plague would most readily, and actually did, take footing. At Tyre, Sidon, Pelusium, Alexandria and also at Constantinople, the plague was most likely to enter the West. Herodotus particularly records that the Egyptian army was made up, not of soldiers, but of traders and market people, and it is they, rather than armies, who were to be the most frequent transmitters of the Black Death.

There remains to be mentioned one last Biblical plague, the plague of David, which like the others is a punishment for offering offence to God, in this case David's numbering of his people. In retribution for his presumption David is given the choice of enduring seven years of famine, three months of fleeing before his enemies, or three days of pestilence. David chose the pestilence and seven thousand people died. And then, according to the account in I Chronicles, 'God sent an angel unto Jerusalem to destroy it; and as he was destroying, the Lord beheld, and he repented him of the evil, and said to the angel that destroyed: It is enough, stay now thine hand. . . . And David lifted up his eyes, and saw the angel of the Lord stand between the earth and the heaven, having a drawn sword in his hand stretched out over Jerusalem. Then David and the elders of Israel, who were clothed in sackcloth, fell upon their faces.' Then the prophet Gad told David to set up an altar in the threshing-floor of Ornan. When he had set up the altar and offered burnt offerings to God, 'the Lord commanded the angel; and he put up his sword again into the sheath thereof'. Here again, the plague is lifted when the proper propitiatory religious acts are performed: the raising of an altar and the offering of a sacrifice. Here also, as is so frequently the case in these accounts, the angel is the agent by which the Lord spreads the plague. The drawn sword is the specific device by which it falls upon the people, and the sheathing of the sword is the signal for its termination. The metaphor of plague as a blow of the sword or the sting of an arrow is deeply ingrained not only in Biblical literature but in the literature of Greece and Rome as well. Practically all the Hebrew words for plague (*Maggefah*, *Negef*, *Naga*, *Makkah*) indicate a blow. Our English word 'plague' and the German *plage* derive via the Latin *plaga* from a Greek word meaning a blow. The French *fléau*—a flail or a plague—embodies the same idea and is derived from the Latin *flagellum*. The Arabs speak of being 'stung' or 'pricked' with plague.

*

The accounts of plague in the imaginative literature of Greece for the most part confirm the ideas of the Bible. In the first book of the *Iliad* the priest Chryses calls upon Apollo to avenge the ravishing of his daughter; Apollo hears his prayer and

> he came down furious from the summit of Olympus, with his bow and his quiver upon his shoulder, and the arrows rattled on his back with the rage that trembled within him. He sat himself down away from the ships with a face as dark as night, and his silver bow rang death as he shot his arrows in the midst of them. First he smote their mules and their hounds, but presently he aimed his shafts at the people themselves, and all day long the pyres of the dead were burning. For nine whole days he shot his arrows among the people. . .

The plague comes as punishment for sin and it is spread by divine arrows. At first it is epizooic, falling on mules and dogs, and finally epidemic among men. A council is called and Achilles advises that some priest be summoned to say if the Greek host is being punished for failure to make some propitiatory sacrifices, but Calchas informs them that they are being punished rather for flagrant sin, the sin of Agamemnon's carrying off Chryseis. The solution here is to terminate the sin: Chryseis must be sent back and expiation must be made to Apollo with sacrifices. Chryseis is released and 'the son of Atreus bade the people purify themselves; so they purified themselves and cast their filth into the sea. Then they offered hecatombs of bulls and goats without blemish on the seashore, and the smoke with the savour of their sacrifice rose curling up towards heaven.'* Apollo, in this account, like the Lord of the plague of David, is not only the sender of pestilence but the only force to which one can appeal for relief from it.

The plague of Thebes in Sophocles' *Oedipus* is also a punishment for specific sin, in this case, of course, Oedipus's patricide and incest. Sophocles describes a plague that blights the crops and causes murrain among the cattle and disease and death among men. Apollo is appealed to for help and, once again, the solution is the same: the sin must be ended and punished; proper propitiation must be made to the gods.

Of more immediate interest are the accounts of plague in the medical and historical writing of Greece. There is some evidence that the Hippocratic school may have identified bubonic plague. A

---

* *The Iliad of Homer*, trans. Samuel Butler, ed. Louise R. Loomis (New York, 1942), pp. 8–14.

passage in the second Book of the Epidemics says 'fever supervening on buboes is a bad sign, except they be ephemeral: but
buboes supervening on fever is still worse'. But if the Father of
Medicine identified the disease he had little luck in establishing its
cause or finding a cure. Following the Greek physicists, Hippocrates conceived disease to be caused by bodily disturbance, the
result either of the air breathed or of the food and drink taken in.
With this general theory to guide him, he inevitably laid the cause
of epidemic disease chiefly to changes in the atmosphere, to which
all men would be equally exposed. He seemed to recognize the
possibility of atmospheric contamination by putrid effluvia, but it
was the physical change in the atmosphere which was, for him, of
paramount importance. He had no conception of contagion from
man to man, and his criterion for epidemicity, like that of Galen
some five hundred years later, was the incidence of disease on a
large number of people at the same time. Hippocrates attributed pestilence to a distempering of the atmosphere, and quite logically
suggested as a preventive the correction of atmospheric disruptions
by the kindling of large fires. The fires, presumably, would correct
the excessive humidity, and may also have been intended to destroy
by fumigation the effluvia corrupting the air. Hippocrates' example
of kindling fires was to be followed in the 14th century, most
importantly by the papal physican Guy de Chauliac.

Of all the accounts of plague in the literature of Greece by far the
most lucid and the most influential in its effects upon writers and
chroniclers of the Black Death was that of Thucydides, who describes the plague of Athens in 430 B.C. in his *History of the Peloponnesian War*. Each year as the Lacedaemonian army approached,
the inhabitants of Attica sent their sheep and cattle to Euboea and
neighbouring islands and moved, with their property, within the
walls of Athens, where they camped in the vacant spaces of the city
and of the Piraeus. Some found places for themselves in and around
temples, others in the towers and recesses of the city walls, some
lived in tents and sheds, even in tubs, along the long walls. It was in
this overcrowded and beleaguered city that the plague broke out in
the summer of 430 B.C. Here is Thucydides' account of that epidemic:

> In the first days of summer the Lacedaemonians and their allies, with
> two-thirds of their forces as before, invaded Attica, under the com-
> mand of Archidamus, son of Zeuxidamus, king of Lacedaemon, and
> sat down and laid waste the country. Not many days after their arrival

in Attica the plague first began to show itself among the Athenians. It was said that it had broken out in many places previously in the neighbourhood of Lemnos and elsewhere; but a pestilence of such extent and mortality was nowhere remembered. Neither were the physicians at first of any service, ignorant as they were of the proper way to treat it, but they died themselves the most thickly, as they visited the sick most often; nor did any human art succeed any better. Supplications in the temples, divinations, and so forth were found equally futile, till the overwhelming nature of the disaster at last put a stop to them altogether.

It first began, it is said, in the parts of Ethiopia above Egypt, and thence descended into Egypt and Libya and into most of the king's country. Suddenly falling upon Athens, it first attacked the population in Piraeus—which was the occasion of their saying that the Peloponnesians had poisoned the reservoirs, there being as yet no wells there—and afterwards appeared in the upper city, when the deaths became much more frequent. All speculation as to its origin and its causes, if causes can be found adequate to produce so great a disturbance, I leave to other writers, whether lay or professional; for myself, I shall simply set down its nature, and explain the symptoms by which perhaps it may be recognized by the student, if it should ever break out again. This I can better do, as I had the disease myself, and watched its operation in the case of others.

There follows a description of the symptoms of the disease which was characterized by high fever, internal ulceration, and an extremely painful rash. The affected suffered from unquenchable thirst and even plunged themselves into rain tanks in a desperate effort to relieve their thirst and fever.

Meanwhile the town enjoyed an immunity from all the ordinary disorders; or if any case occurred, it ended in this. Some died in neglect, others in the midst of every attention. No remedy was found that could be used as a specific; for what did good in one case, did harm in another. Strong and weak constitutions proved equally incapable of resistance, all alike being swept away, although dieted with the utmost precaution. By far the most terrible feature in the malady was the dejection which ensued when any one felt himself sickening, for the despair into which they instantly fell took away their power of resistance, and left them a much easier prey to the disorder; besides which, there was the awful spectacle of men dying like sheep, through having caught the infection in nursing each other. This caused the greatest mortality. On the one hand, if they were afraid to visit each other, they perished from neglect; indeed many houses were emptied of their inmates for want of a nurse: on the other, if they ventured to do so, death was the consequence. This was especially the case with such as made any pretensions to goodness: honour made them unsparing of themselves in their attendance in their friends' houses, where even the members of the family were at last worn out by the moans of the dying, and succumbed to the force of the disaster. Yet it was with those who had recovered from the disease that the sick and the dying found most compassion. These knew what it was from experience, and had now no fear for themselves; for the same man was never attacked twice—never at least fatally. And such persons not only received the congratulations of others, but themselves also, in the elation of the moment, half entertained the vain hope that they were for the future safe from any disease whatsoever.

An aggravation of the existing calamity was the influx from the country into the city, and this was especially felt by the new arrivals. As there were no houses to receive them they had to be lodged at the hot season of the year in stifling cabins, where the mortality raged without restraint. The bodies of dying men lay one upon another, and half-dead creatures reeled about the streets and gathered round all the fountains in their longing for water. The sacred places also in which they had quartered themselves were full of corpses of persons that had died there, just as they were; for as the disaster passed all bounds, men, not knowing what was to become of them, became utterly careless of everything, whether sacred or profane. All the burial rites before in use were entirely upset, and they buried the bodies as best they could. Many from want of the proper appliances, through so many of their friends having died already, had recourse to the most shameless sepultures: sometimes getting the start of those who had raised a pile, they threw their own dead body upon the stranger's pyre and ignited it; sometimes they tossed the corpse which they were carrying on the top of another that was burning, and so went off.

Nor was this the only form of lawless extravagance which owed its origin to the plague. Men now coolly ventured on what they had formerly done in a corner, and not just as they pleased, seeing the rapid transitions produced by persons in prosperity suddenly dying and those who before had nothing succeeding to their property. So they resolved to spend quickly and enjoy themselves, regarding their lives and riches as alike things of a day. Perseverance in what men called honour was popular with none, it was so uncertain whether they would be spared to attain the object; but it was settled that present enjoyment, and all that contributed to it, was both honourable and useful. Fear of gods or law of man there was none to restrain them. As for the first, they judged it to be just the same whether they worshipped them or not, as they saw all alike perishing; and for the last, no one expected to live to be brought to trial for his offences, but each felt that a far severer sentence had been already passed upon them all and hung ever over their heads, and before this fell it was only reasonable to enjoy life a little.

Such was the nature of the calamity, and heavily did it weigh on the Athenians; death raging within the city and devastation without. . . .*

This account of pestilence seems to be the model for many other records in many other times of epidemic; certainly de Mussi and Boccaccio, whose accounts of the Black Death are among the most complete and the most moving, were aware of Thucydides. Perhaps the first aspect that one notices in his description is that he seems to accept the idea of contagion without any question. The disease which attacked the Athenians is probably not bubonic plague—there is no reference to the characteristic plague swellings—but, according to modern commentators, it was more likely to have been typhus; so Thucydides' analysis of the means of transmission would fit contemporary ideas about the communication of that disease. He does not know, of course, the exact agent of transmission, but he recognizes the conditions that encourage its transmission. In accepting the idea of contagion Thucydides is far in advance not only of the superstitious credulity of some of his fellow-countrymen, but also of the most enlightened medical opinion of his day. We have seen that the Hippocratic school had no inkling of contagion, nor indeed did any medical author give unequivocal support to the idea until Aretaeus of Cappadocia in the second century after Christ. Not even in the 14th century was its concept well established, and over and over again, as in this account by Thucydides, one sees that lay writers, relying upon what they themselves have seen or verified, present a much more accurate and valuable account of the nature of epidemics, the symptoms and means of transmission of disease, than even the most advanced medical writers. Throughout antiquity this seems to have been the case: Levitical ordinances appear to have recognized contagion in the case of leprosy; Aristotle, Lucretius, Vergil, Ovid, Dionysius of Halicarnassus, Livy, Seneca, Plutarch, all seem to have accepted it; but it was not until relatively recent times that science, clutching to its preconceptions in the face of all reported evidence, came to allow the concept. It is not over-surprising that literary men should give the most moving accounts of the plague—one recalls, in addition to Boccaccio, Defoe's account of the plague of London in 1665, Manzoni's tale of

* *History of the Peloponnesian War*, trans. Crawley (New York, 1951 edition), pp. 109–14.

plague in 17th-century Milan, and Camus's story of an imagined plague of Oran in the 1940's—but it is perhaps surprising that in ancient times they should also have given the most medically accurate accounts. One has the feeling, certainly, in the literature of the 14th-century plague, as in the description of the plague of Athens, that men of the time would have been well advised to take their medical theory from literary men and their rhetoric from the physicians: literature would have suffered but the nature of epidemics would have been understood much sooner.

Thucydides is the first to have depicted the corruption and demoralization of a society under the plague, and this theme is to be repeated over and over again in plague accounts. The futility of the physicians, the terrible and merciless advance of the pestilence, the universality of the suffering, the terrors of the disease, the neglect of the dead and the breakdown of family relations, the sacrilegious funeral rites, the pollution of the temples, the lawlessness of men upon whom it is suddenly impressed in the most dramatic way that life and riches are transitory, the neglect of worship by those who see all men regardless of their virtue perishing together, the search for omens and signs to explain the misery, the superstition of total immunity prevalent among those who have recovered, the accusations of poisoning: these themes of human demoralization, of despair, of frenzy are to find expression wherever a writer tries to tell the terror of plague.

Thucydides describes the effect of the epidemic upon the religious feeling of the Athenians. There were some Athenians who put their faith in supplications in the temples and inquiries of oracles; but the lesson of the plague was soon learned: the pious and the impious die together and there is no supernatural intervention that one can count on. The study of pestilence would seem to be inextricably bound up with religion, and the measures of propitiation taken are a clear reflection of the idea of their gods held by the sufferers. For a clearly anthropomorphic god the proper supplication is to approach on bended knee, to cleanse oneself as did the Greeks before Apollo to alleviate the plague of the *Iliad*, and to offer food and drink as a sacrifice. Later with the conception of a god that lives above the earth, the approach may be through the burning of incense, as Aaron offered sacrifice by burning incense on the altar. But always in such a epidemic there lurks the suspicion of the plague sufferers of Ashdod that the disaster is just 'a chance thing that happened to us'. With this suspicion comes real religious doubt. It would be going much too far to suggest that the plague of Athens was the cause of the collapse of the fabric of Greek polytheism; the Persian wars had also taught the lesson that victory is the reward of the strong, not necessarily of the devout. But surely the plague spread doubts. And in the wake of a collapsing faith comes another answer: no, it cannot be just a chance thing that is happening to us. There must be an agent, and if not a god, a man. The Athenian populace ascribed the pestilence to natural causation, but to natural causation of a most direct and obvious sort: the Lacedaemonians must have poisoned the wells. Thucydides does not tell us if the Athenians acted upon this suspicion, and if so, against whom they turned in their search for someone to blame for all that misery. The history of the 14th century is, alas, more complete and more terrible. From the time of the plague of Athens onwards right down to modern times, this phantom of a poisoner and the search for a scapegoat follows in the trail of plague.

Chapter II

ANCIENT PRECEDENTS

NLIKE GREECE, which seems to have been only in-
frequently, if dramatically and disastrously, troubled by
plague, Rome suffered a succession of pestilential epidemics;
and in the accounts left, most importantly by Livy, one can see the
full working out of some of the tendencies apparent in Thucydides'
account. If the plague shook the religious beliefs of the Athenians, it
seems to be inextricably bound up with the very structure of Roman
religion. Livy tells of Tullus Hostilius who scorned religion when
he was well but revived many superstitious practices when he fell
ill during a pestilence in 640 B.C. During another plague in 514 B.C.
Tarquinius Superbus sent his sons to the Greek Delphi to ask the
god how to cure it. He is also credited by Livy for having brought
the Sibylline books, a collection of oracular wisdom from the
prophetesses, or Sibyls, of Greece, to Rome where they were put in
sacred custody to be consulted in times of emergency. These books
recognized the gods and rituals of the Greeks and played an important part in their introduction into the religion of Rome. During
another severe pestilence and drought that ravaged Rome from 435
to 430 B.C. Livy reports that, when appeals to the gods of Rome
proved ineffectual, the worship of Apollo was imported from
Greece, and a temple was erected in his honour in 431 B.C.; from
that time Apollo was appealed to in times of plague until he finally
supplanted the older native gods. In a similar way the cult of
Asclepius came to Rome: in 293 B.C. during a pestilence the magistrates, after consulting the Sibylline books, sent ambassadors to
Epidaurus to demand the serpent of Asclepius. According to a liter-
ally marvellous story, the serpent is said to have presented itself to
the Romans and even to have crawled aboard their galley of its own
accord; upon reaching Rome it leapt overboard and swam to an
island in the middle of the Tiber, where a temple was then erected
to Asclepius. Lucretius, in his *De Rerum Natura*, includes a description of the plague of Athens, heavily influenced by Thucydides, in

order to prepare for his later attack upon the sham of religious superstition, an attack in which he takes account of the somewhat cynical manner whereby the Romans shopped in Greece for their gods.

Among the practices that appeared in Rome as a consequence of the influence of the Sibylline books was the celebration of the *lectisternium*. A festival of Greek origin which the books recommended on the occasion of plague, it consisted of a public banquet of great magnificence which was set before the gods. In addition to the public celebration, domestic feasts were spread throughout the city to which any stranger or passer-by was welcomed. It was important that no discord whatever be heard and even prisoners were liberated to take part in the festival. In this way the people joined in communion with their gods in the hope that the plague would be stayed. In much the same spirit funeral bells were forbidden to be rung in many towns during the raging of the Black Death, and taverns, it is often reported, did a lively business. Another instance of institutionalization of public gaiety as a plague remedy is recounted by Livy. During a plague in 363 B.C., after everything else had failed to appease the gods, scenic plays were brought to Rome from Etruria. The plays were apparently very simple scenic shows in which actors danced together to music without, Livy says, 'any song or imitative gestures', but this appears to have been the beginning of the theatre in Rome; before this the Romans had had only the games of the circus. The plays and the *lectisternium* were perhaps intended most of all to divert the minds of a people ravaged by plague, but they also constitute a kind of public acceptance of the tendency, noted by Thucydides, of men to seek pleasure openly and everywhere in plague-time. Popular amusement had come to be established along with public atonement as an acceptable response to plague. As we shall see, the 14th century repeats this aspect of history with striking similarity.

A far more sinister response to pestilence appeared early in the history of Rome. Dionysius of Halicarnassus leaves the following account of a plague in 473 B.C.:

> In the beginning of the year many prodigies and omens happened, which filled the city with superstition and fear of the gods; and all the augurs and the interpreters of holy things declared that these were signs of divine anger, because some rites had not been performed with sanctity and purity. Not long after, a distemper, supposed to be pestilential, attacked the women, particularly such as were with child, and more of

them died than had ever been known before. For as they miscarried and brought forth dead children, they died together with their infants. And neither supplications at the statues and altars of the gods, nor expiatory sacrifices performed on behalf of the public and of private families gave the women any relief.

Once again the pestilence was attributed to gods, but when the prayers and supplications had no effect, the populace sought other causes. A slave came forward and accused one of the Vestal Virgins, Urbinia, of impurity. Urbinia was tried, convicted, and condemned to be 'whipped with rods, to be carried through the city, and buried alive'. One of the men accused of being her lover killed himself, another was publicly whipped and put to death. After these sacrifices had been performed, 'the distemper, which had attacked the women and caused so great a mortality among them, presently ceased'. This is one of the earliest records of human sacrifice for deliverance from plague. Philostratus tells of another instance as a response to the fear of pestilence. In the first century A.D. the Ephesians summoned Apollonius to come to allay the plague. He gathered the citizens together in a theatre 'where now stands the statue of Averruncus. Here they found an ill-looking old beggar, whom Apollonius ordered them to stone to death, as being the enemy of the gods. As soon as they set to stoning him, fire darted from the old beggar's eyes, so that they knew him for a demon. After they had killed him, Apollonius ordered them to remove the stones from the corpse, and they found instead of a human body a fierce dog vomiting foam, as if mad. . . .'

In both these instances the sacrifice, cruel as it obviously is, has the rough innocence that attends upon such sacrifices among pagan people. In one case, Urbinia failed in her duty to the gods and her failure brought misery upon the city. In the other, the old beggar was identified, and, to the satisfaction of those present at least, proved to be an enemy of the gods. There is a sort of rude justice in their deaths, even if the charges against them are grotesque: a justice which, of course, can only have meaning within the framework of primitive religion. But in instances when religious atonement has totally failed and the populace searches for purely natural causes of its misery, without recognizing any natural causes beyond terrestrial and atmospheric disruptions on the one hand and human malevolence on the other, the possibilities for cruelty and even insanity are greatly increased.

In the historical literature of Rome there are numerous charges of

poisonings; however, unlike the Athenians' suspicions of the
Lacedaemonians with whom they were at war, the Roman charges
seem to have been levelled most generally against members of their
own society who, like Urbinia, were unfortunate enough to have
been dramatically accused, or, like the old beggar, to have simply
been in the wrong place at the wrong time. During a severe epidemic
in 331 B.C. in which a number of the Senate died, a woman slave
brought a charge that the victims had been poisoned and accused
some matrons of mixing and using the poisons against their enemies.
Two patrician women, Cornelia and Sergia, were found actually to
have drugs in their possession; and, although they protested that
the drugs were harmless, they were forced to swallow them. When
they subsequently fell victim to the pestilence themselves, the charge
was considered proved, and Livy reports that one hundred and
seventy other matrons were subsequently tried, found guilty, and
put to death. Similar accusations were made during a plague that
attacked Rome from 183 to 180 B.C. The first reaction was to appease
the gods—Apollo, Asclepius, and Hygieia—by the formation of
processions of suppliants who carried the laurel, sacred to Apollo.
But when, once again, the gods failed to intervene, suspicion of
poisoning arose. In this instance, the accusations resulted in the
condemnation of two thousand people, including Quarta Hostilia,
the wife of the consul who had died of the disease. Another, stranger,
charge appeared during a plague in the reign of Domitian (A.D.
81–96). Dion Cassius reports that, 'Certain individuals poisoned
needles and set to work to prick whomsoever they wished: several
who were pricked died without knowing anything about it: but
some of the scoundrels were denounced and punished; and that
happened not only in Rome, but over all the world. . . .' Dion
Cassius repeats this charge in connection with another plague, that
of A.D. 187 during the reign of Commodus: 'In the reign of Commodus occurred the most violent sickness I have ever known: at
Rome two thousand persons often died in a single day. But many
died, not only in Rome, but in all parts of the empire, in another
manner: scoundrels, poisoning little needles with certain noxious
substances, transmitted the disease in this way for pay. . . .' Ced-
renus, somewhat later, asserted that one person could infect another
simply by looking at him. Thus the tradition was established which
led the 14th century finally to find the cause of plague in poisoners
and demons and to set on the most terrible massacre of Jews that
had yet occurred in the world.

Men seemed ready to accept natural causation for individual maladies; but when disease reached epidemic proportion they saw the hand of a god at work, and when all due sacrifices and propitiation had been made and failed, they looked again for a human scapegoat: always, it would seem, in order to avoid having to accept the suspicion of the men of Ashdod that the disaster was just a chance thing. It was, however, to be the responsibility of Marcus Aurelius to find in the persecution of a religious minority the means of allaying pestilence. During the great Antonine plague, which Galen calls the long plague since it lasted fifteen years and his detractors call Galen's plague because he conspicuously absented himself from Rome until it was over, the Emperor finally, after reinstituting many older religious superstitious practices which included a *lectisternium* that lasted an entire week, decided systematically to persecute Christians whose religion was felt to be an insult to the majesty of the national gods. A Christian chronicler of the period countered the charges by attributing the plague to the persecution which had, in fact, begun in the provinces before the plague broke out: a defence that may well have seemed to many Romans to justify an intensification of the persecutions. The fact that this method failed to stop the disease—Marcus Aurelius himself died of it—did not prevent a later age also from trying it.

Prolonged pestilence generally resulted in the breakdown of normal civic functions and in the corruption of normal human decency. Livy describes the effect of plague upon the Carthaginians in 212 B.C.:

> At last their feelings had become so brutalized by being habituated to these miseries, that they not only did not follow their dead with tears and decent lamentations, but they did not even carry them out and bury them: so that the bodies of the dead lay strewn about, exposed to the view of those who were awaiting a similar fate. And thus the dead were the means of destroying the sick, and the sick those who were in health, both by fear and by the filthy state and the noisome stench of the bodies. Some, preferring to die by the sword, even rushed upon the outposts of the enemy.

And during the pestilence of A.D. 302, in the reign of Maximian, Eusebius reports that the people, suffering also from famine, were finally reduced to eating grass. Dogs fought over the corpses of the dead until men finally slaughtered them wholesale for fear they would go mad and attack the living.

Before the Black Death, the most widespread and devastating

plague to afflict Europe was the plague of Justinian. There are
detailed accounts of its devastation in Antioch, Byzantium, Arles,
Liguria, Auvergne, Narbonne, Marseilles, Rome and Strasbourg;
and it is said to have raged for fifty-two years, moving steadily and
inexorably across Europe from 540 A.D. to 592. These accounts,
most notably those of Procopius, Evagrius and Gregory of Tours,
leave little doubt that it was a bubonic plague, and it is generally
agreed that Procopius is the first to have given a certain and unequivocal description of that disease. As we have seen, Hippocrates
seems to have been familiar with a kind of bubonic plague in its
sporadic, but probably not in its epidemic, form; and Galen also
discusses the relation of buboes to fever. There is moreover a fragment of an account by Rufus of Ephesus, who is thought to have
lived during the time of Trajan (A.D. 98–117), which describes a
plague which 'was accompanied by acute fever, pain, and prostration of the whole body, delirium, and the appearance of large and
hard buboes, which did not suppurate, not only in the accustomed
parts, but also in the groins and armpits'. Rufus goes on to say that
'one can foresee an approaching plague by paying attention to the ill
condition of the seasons, to the mode of living less conducive to
health, and to the death of animals that precedes its invasion'. The
account is preserved by Oribasius, the Christian physician of the
Emperor Julian (A.D. 355–63), in a monumental seventy-volume
text *Synagoguae Medicae*, which is itself preserved only in fragments. Oribasius's work would probably have been best known to
medieval physicians through the *Epitome* of Paul of Aegina, one of
the most celebrated of Byzantine physicians who lived probably at
the end of the 6th or beginning of the 7th century. But it is Procopius's eye-witness account of the plague of Justinian which would
have offered the 14th century its clearest description of the physical
effects of the plague which, in the summer of 1347, was already at
the gates of Europe.

According to Procopius, the epidemic began in Pelusium, the city
already associated with plague in one account of the destruction of
the army of Sennacherib, and spread along routes of trade into
Egypt and into Palestine and finally into the entire world, which
would probably have meant for Procopius from the eastern limits of
Persia to the Atlantic coast. The plague spread slowly but by definite
stages, ravaging one area before it moved on to the next, spreading
usually from a coastal city inland. It took nearly a year to reach
Byzantium, by this account, where it broke out in the spring of

A.D. 542. Although many learned men of the time, following the ancient medical authorities, attributed the disease to atmospheric and terrestrial disruptions, Procopius disagrees. There is not a fragment of evidence to support that theory, he holds, and points out that the plague was universal throughout the world, disregarding differences in climate, in place, in the age and sex or social status or even the health of those which it attacked. The plague, Procopius argues, comes from God and nowhere else. In such an analysis we see again the tragic paradox of man struggling bravely to find the truth within a circumscribing framework of inadequate concepts. On the basis of observation and experience—on, one may almost say, a scientific basis—Procopius discounts the inadequate ancient theories of epidemic, only to fall into greater error himself. It is in such a situation that one comes to recognize the closed circle of the mind, a circle that had expanded considerably by the 14th century, but which still found it necessary to pose the question: Who is responsible for this disaster? It is the question, far more than the answer, that is misleading; in fact, if one accepts the question, then all answers will be wrong. It is much like the question: Who made the universe? One can answer that God made the universe, or that nobody made the universe, but in either case the answer is a theological answer because the question is a theological question. Even so, in recognizing the limitations of Byzantine and later of medieval formulations, it is wisest not to forget our own. Our conception of things is formed often in irreconcilable paradoxes: the notion of a finite but expanding universe, for example, which is just as troubling and irreducible as the ancient oxymoron about God, that He is a 'superluminous darkness of instructive silence'. Tertullian, we are told, accepted Christian doctrine *because* it was absurd. Not all adherents of modern scientific explanations of phenomena are so honest. The pre-Renaissance world got its own incredible answers to its impossible questions, but it also had its indissoluble honesty and its own clear-sighted logic. The errors of man in accounting for natural phenomena are legion, but they are more often the result of an inability to cast off old moulds of thought, old universal field theories, as it were, than in the failure to apply them honestly or logically. Einstein commented that the reason nature answers with contradictions is that we are perhaps asking unanswerable questions.

Procopius describes the physical symptoms of plague in detail. There was first a mild fever without any grave symptoms, after which, in a day or two, buboes appeared, usually in the groin or armpit or behind the ear. Procopius's account is very similar to modern medical descriptions of the prognosis of bubonic plague, which can, of course, take a number of forms. In his record, it is possible to recognize all three forms the disease is known to take: the bubonic, the pneumonic, and the septicaemic. Procopius has no explanation for these different forms except to suggest that they may result from the difference in constitution of the sufferer or else from the will of God. Physicians assumed the source of disease lay in the buboes, an assumption justified by the fact that, in cases of simple suppuration of the bubo, the victim usually recovered, as if some evil humour had passed out of him. In later years, with this same contention, surgeons encouraged suppuration and sometimes performed incisions. Procopius records that many dropped dead from spontaneous vomiting of blood, probably from the lungs as is frequently the case in the pneumonic form of plague. Other descriptions of very rapid death seem to suggest the septicaemic form of plague. Procopius also says the disease took the form of black pustules which broke out all over the body; perhaps there was a simultaneous epidemic of smallpox or spotted fever, as in the case of the Great Plague of London in 1665. Reactions to the disease were as various as the symptoms. Some fell into a deep lethargic depression and simply died of starvation unless food was pressed upon them. Others suffered from a maniacal delirium, struggled with those who attended them, threw themselves out of windows, and in some cases tried to drown themselves in the sea.

In accounting for the spread of the disease Procopius rejects the idea of contagion, as perhaps he was bound to do as a proponent of the theory that the pestilence was a special act of God. He records, along with some later writers, that the physicians and nurses who cared for the sick were not especially afflicted, and on the other hand many who had no contact with the sick died. The epidemic lasted four months in the city and then, as mysteriously as it had come, it left Byzantium; this again is a feature of most of the later European outbreaks. Procopius reports that during the worst time the daily mortality was an appalling ten thousand.

Like many earlier and later chroniclers of plague, Procopius recounts the breakdown of normal civic functions. All work came to a halt in Byzantium and famine gripped the city. After the first, mild onslaught of the disease, when each family buried its dead in accordance with customary practice, funeral rites began to be neglected. At first, as in Thucydides' account, people sometimes threw their dead into graves prepared for others; later the dead simply piled up in the streets. Justinian commissioned his agent Theodorus to bury the dead, but soon all the existing burial grounds were filled. Huge pits were dug around the city wherever space could be found. Finally, in a desperate attempt to clear the city of dead, the roofs were removed from the towers of the city walls in Sycae, the port of Byzantium, and bodies were simply thrown into the towers. When they were filled up the roofs were replaced; but the resulting stench, when the wind blew in from Sycae, was so horrible that the practice was discontinued. As another expedient, corpses were loaded on barges and set adrift out to sea. Under such conditions and the threat of the disease, Procopius says, men turned from their dissolute ways to piety. But if they fell sick and recovered, rather than increasing their piety in thankfulness, they became more dissolute than before under the delusion that nothing could harm them in the future.

As for the course of the disease, Procopius records that it frequently began with hallucinations both visual and auditory. Some people in their sleep and others awake seemed to see evil spirits who struck a part of their body where later pustules and buboes formed. Some heard voices telling them that they had been enrolled already among the dead. Men went to great lengths to avoid these demons, some shutting themselves up in their houses which they refused to leave on any account whatever; others invoked sacred names and experimented with every sort of expiation. The idea of demons as precursors of disease is deeply rooted in the literature of the East and has a particular fascination for writers of the Western Church. The Dark Ages appear to have been fairly enlightened in the matter of demons and witchcraft. Saints Boniface and Agobard had denounced a belief in sorcery as sinful, and Charlemagne had made it a capital crime to execute anyone on a charge of witchcraft. Pope Gregory VII in the 11th century forbade inquisition to be made for sorcerers as the cause of storms and plagues. But by the 14th century the belief in demons was well established again. They were everywhere, even in one's bed, where they were notorious for seducing young women and providing, no doubt, a convenient explanation of inconvenient pregnancy. The *incubus* that so ungallantly attacked women had its counterpart in the *succubus*, a female demon who would mate with men: a nice touch, indicating, perhaps, that in the 14th century the Devil himself despised homosexuality. These were not just country superstitions like the commonly held belief that a wafer consecrated by a priest would bleed with the blood of Christ if one pricked it: theologians also agreed that the *succubi* and *incubi* were real, and warned people against them. Charges of witchcraft touched all levels of society. Even Pope Boniface VIII at the beginning of the 14th century was charged with witchcraft; and in 1317 Pope John XXII executed a number of people for trying to kill him in a plot that involved the use of demons as agents. Among those tortured and finally burned at the stake was the Bishop of Cahors who confessed to having burned a wax effigy of Pope John in the expectation that the Pope himself would suffer. It was believed that Charles VI of France had been driven mad by magic; two sorcerers promised to restore his senses, but when they failed they were beheaded in 1397. The theology faculty of Paris condemned sorcery in 1398, but the condemnation assumed its efficacy and actually tended to increase popular belief in its existence. From the enlightened attitude of the Dark Ages, later centuries became more convinced of the existence of demons and witches and acted against them more harshly. Both Erasmus and Thomas More appear to have accepted the reality of witchcraft. The University of Cologne affirmed it, and the Inquisition moved against witches. Before the mid-15th century punishment was mild, but later authorities took the Biblical injunction seriously: 'Thou shalt not suffer a witch to live.' And many accused of witchcraft were burned.

In describing the plague, the chroniclers of the Church repeatedly write at length about demons as well as mysterious markings on walls, voices from the grave presaging disaster, and improbable celestial phenomena, many of which must have been the result of the sort of delirium the plague sometimes induces. One recalls that Thucydides' account, while recording the mania of sufferers, ignores the content of the hallucinations that must have accompanied the delirium; Christian writers, for their part, are endlessly fascinated by these reports and credit them often alongside observed details as incontestable fact. This dimension of plague is firmly established in the tradition of the 14th century and, like many such reportorial traditions, it is dynamic as well as descriptive, tending to produce the effects it describes. Not only do many writers report extraordinary phenomena but large numbers of men seem actually to have perceived them.

The plague that Procopius described moved westward and its further course is traced by Gregory of Tours (A.D. 540–594). Before the

plague invaded the Auvergne in 567, Gregory reports that three or
four brilliant lights appeared around the sun, which then went into
almost total eclipse in October. The heavens seemed to be on fire
and many strange celestial signs were seen. The following year the
epidemic struck throughout the area, causing so many deaths that
there were soon no coffins available and as many as ten men were
buried in one grave. One Sunday there were three hundred corpses
in the church of St. Peter at Clermont. The victims were seized very
suddenly: 'There grew in the groin or armpit a lesion in the shape
of a serpent, the effect of which was such that men yielded up their
souls on the second or third day, and its violence completely took
away their senses.' Again around Avignon, before the plague broke
out in 590, strange sights were seen in the sky. The earth was as
brightly illuminated at night as in the day. There was a violent
earthquake in June, and the sun endured an almost total eclipse in
August. There were extraordinary violent thunderstorms and the
rivers flooded in the autumn.

At nearly the same time in Italy the plague which cut through
Liguria in 565 had been presaged by the most amazing phenomena.
If one credits Paul the Deacon (A.D. 720–90), whose account was
written long after the event, the plague was foretold by mysterious
marks which appeared on houses, doors, utensils and clothing, and
the more people tried to efface them the more conspicuous they
became. This report of markings on houses and clothes crops up
repeatedly in the reports of the Black Death and of later plagues.
Perhaps the earliest such account is in Leviticus where the Lord
gives Moses the following instructions for the purging of leprosy:
'Then the priest shall command that they empty the house, before
the priest go into it to see the plague, that all that is in the house
be not made unclean: and afterward the priest shall go in to see the
house: And he shall look on the plague, and, behold, if the plague
be in the walls of the house with hollow streaks, greenish or reddish,
which in sight are lower than the wall; Then the priest shall go out
of the house to the door of the house, and shut up the house seven
days. . . .' Johannes Nohl recounts that in Germany in 1501 small
crosses, white, red and the colour of blood, fell upon people's
clothes, and drops of blood were seen on walls; a terrible plague
followed, and those who had seen the crosses usually died. Nohl
quotes from a remarkable letter written from Graz in 1599 by
Johannes Kepler in which the famous German astronomer informs
a friend that his daughter has died of the plague:

Should her father die very shortly it would not come unexpected to him. When a short time ago here and there in Hungary blood-red crosses appeared on the bodies of the people and other blood-red signs on the house-doors, walls, and benches, I was, as far as I know, the first in the town to perceive a little cross on my left foot, the colour of which merged from blood-red to yellow. It appeared on that part of the foot where the back spreads out, right in the middle between the root of the shin and the toes. I should think that this and no other was the place where the nail of the cross was driven into Christ's foot. In some people, as I am informed, there is a mark of a drop of blood on the surface of the hand. Christ's hands were also transfixed. But no one here has anything similar to what I have.

Nohl concludes that sometime in the 18th century the markings were recognized by a naturalist to have been, probably, the excrement of butterflies; so there would seem to be a naturalistic confirmation of at least one manifestation of an ancient tradition. So even this, one of the most incredible of reported harbingers of plague, cannot be automatically rejected as just another example of medieval hysteria. But even if it were only that, we would be brought up short, if we can credit Nohl's account, by the prospect of a man of Kepler's sophistication and objectivity being victimized by the phenomenon at the very end of the 16th century. How much less able were even the most sophisticated men, two hundred and fifty years earlier, to ward off the frenzy and despair that such portents brought?

*

Gregory of Tours' account continues with a description of the plague's effects upon Rome where it struck with special virulence in 590. As has by this time become the custom, he begins with a list of the natural disasters which preceded it: the Tiber flooded in 589 and many old buildings on its banks were destroyed, including the granaries where large stores of grain were ruined. Following the flood a vast number of serpents appeared in the river, some of enormous size; Gregory reports that a dragon of immense proportions floated through the city and down to the sea. The serpents were very likely eels from the mud banks and the dragon, no doubt, the product of over-stimulated imaginations; but nevertheless a severe outbreak of plague followed. What Gregory refers to as *pestilentia, quam inguinariam vocant*, and in other places as *morbus inguinalis*, calling to mind the morbid swellings in the groin so characteristic of the Black Death, was probably the bubonic plague. Once again, the death rate was appalling and normal burial arrangements failed utterly; the dead finally littered the streets and people huddled helplessly in churches hoping for divine protection. Fear increased substantially when on February 8, 590, Pope Pelagius died of the disease.

The selection of a successor to Pelagius lay with the clergy and people of Rome, subject to the confirmation of the Emperor in Constantinople. Almost unanimously they called upon Abbot Gregory to leave the seclusion of his monastery and come to Rome. The pious man, who later was to be Gregory I, the Great—St. Gregory—was most reluctant to accept the summons; and Gregory of Tours, along with his many other biographers, tells that he tried even to intercept the letter of election on its way to Constantinople. But, as the plague still raged, Gregory came to Rome determined to try to appease the wrath of God. From the pulpit of St. John Lateran he preached a memorable sermon, an account of which is left by Gregory of Tours. He urged men to make the suffering an instrument for their conversion and a means of softening their hearts, to be forever ready to die especially in such a time when death could strike at any instant. Gregory implored men to purge away their sins with weeping but not to give up hope, because God does not will the death, but rather the redemption, of sinners. Nor should one despair over the great number of one's sins, for God had given everlasting life even to the dying thief. He recalled that God had spared Nineveh when its people did penance for three days, and proposed for Rome a similar period of prayer and repentance to be followed by a massive procession from each of the seven ecclesiastical districts of Rome to the Church of the Blessed Virgin Mary the Mother of Christ on the fourth day, the festival of St. Mark.

This procession moved through Rome silently except for the chanting of a solemn *Miserere*. The plague struck even as men marched in the hope of alleviating it, and eighty people died before they were able to reach the church of the Mother of Christ. Then a marvellous thing happened. As St. Gregory at the head of his procession reached the Aelian bridge, he saw the Archangel Michael holding a flaming sword, and, as he watched, the angel put the sword back into its sheath, proclaiming that the plague was ended. Neither Gregory of Tours, nor Bede, nor Gregory's biographers, the deacons Paul and John, mention the miracle of the angel, but the legend had appeared by at least the 10th century, written records exist from a German sermon of the 12th or 13th century, and it is recorded in the *Legenda Aurea* which dates from the end of the 13th century. Caxton translates it in the *Golden Legend*:

> And because the mortality ceased not, he ordained a procession in which he did do bear an image of our Lady, which, as is said, St. Luke the Evangelist made, which was a good painter, he had carved it and painted it after the likeness of the glorious Virgin Mary. And anon the mortality ceased, and the air became pure and clear, and about the image was heard a voice of angels that sung this Anthem:

> > Regina Coeli laetare! Alleluia.
> > Quia quem meruisti portare: Alleluia.
> > Resurrexit sicut dixit: Alleluia.

and St. Gregory put thereto

> > Ora pro nobis, deum rogamus: Alleluia.

> At the same time St. Gregory saw an angel upon a castle, which made clean a sword all bloody, and put it into the sheath, and thereby St. Gregory understood that the pestilence of this mortality was passed, and after that it was called the Castle Angel.

The castle is, of course, the Castel San Angelo. The picture carried by St. Gregory in the procession was for a long time believed to be the one still preserved in the church of Santa Maria Maggiore, in Rome, but modern opinion holds that painting, along with several others attributed to Luke, to be no older than the 15th century. For the source of the legend of the angel with a drawn sword one probably has to look no further than I Chronicles for David's vision of the angel with the drawn sword stretched out over Jerusalem. But far from casting doubt upon the vision of St. Gregory, such an identification would, probably, in the 14th century have lent credence to it. It is interesting to note, in passing, that an Italian legend has it that the custom of saying 'God bless you' when a person sneezes began with this plague of St. Gregory. It was thought that those who sneezed were sure to die. It was also believed that yawning preceded death, and men came to make the sign of the cross before their mouths if they yawned.

So a new element was added to the literature and tradition of plague: the legend of the saint who through his miraculous intervention was able to stay the ravages of disease. It was not Gregory, however, but St. Sebastian and St. Roch whom the

14th and later centuries were to venerate specifically as plague saints.

Sebastian was born in the middle of the 3rd century in Narbonne in Gaul. He was of noble birth and as a young man he came to command a company of Praetorian Guards. Although he was secretly Christian and used his position to convert others to his faith, he remained loyal to the interests of the Emperor Diocletian and, it appears, they were also personal friends. Sebastian's position was endangered when two young friends of his, Marcus and Marcellinus, like him both soldiers of noble birth, were accused of having embraced Christianity. They were tortured and led out to die, but on the way to execution their friends and families implored them to recant and save themselves. They were about to do so when Sebastian rushed forward and pleaded with them not to renounce their faith. His speech was so inspiring that not only did the young men change their minds about recanting, but the entire assembly was converted and baptised on the spot. Marcus and Marcellinus were saved, but only for a few months; they were soon put to death along with a great many other Christians. The Emperor, who felt a personal attachment for Sebastian, personally pleaded with him to reject his Christianity; but Sebastian refused, and Diocletian ordered him to be bound to a stake and shot to death with arrows: an inscription tied to the stake with him announced that he was to die only for being a Christian. Sebastian was duly shot full of arrows and left to die, but the arrows had somehow failed to hit a vital spot, and that night the widow of one of Sebastian's martyred friends found him still alive and tended him until he recovered. Undaunted by his previous interview with Diocletian, Sebastian refused the advice of friends to leave Rome and went to the palace gate where he confronted the Emperor once again: this time to plead for the lives of other condemned Christians. Diocletian, showing no more leniency and considerably more efficiency than on the previous occasion, ordered his guards to carry Sebastian to the circus and beat him to death with clubs, which they did. To insure that there should be no more miraculous escapes, it was ordered that his body be thrown into the Cloaca Maxima; but once again a Christian woman recovered it—though this time Sebastian was surely dead—and buried him in the catacombs. Later the church of San Sebastiano was built over the spot.

Although his martyrdom occurred in 288, it was not until the plague of 683 that his cult as protector from pestilence was clearly established. Paul the Deacon, writing about the ravages of that plague in Pavia, says that

> many saw with their own eyes a good and a bad angel passing through the city by night. And whenever at the bidding of the good angel, the bad one, who seemed to carry a lance in his hand, struck so many times with his lance on the door of each house, as many of that household would die on the following day. Then it was revealed to someone that the plague would not cease until an altar was set up to Sebastian, saint and martyr, at the church of San Pietro in Vincoli. This was done, and as soon as the altar was set up, the relics of the martyr-saint Sebastian were brought from Rome, and forthwith the plague ceased.

This association of Sebastian with plague may have been in the first instance purely fortuitous, since devout men in time of plague traditionally asked their own patron saint for help and dedicated altars and chapels, or votive pictures, or perhaps a procession, to him as the price of dispensation. But the association of Sebastian with plague stuck: perhaps because of the story of the attempted martyrdom. Arrows have, from the most ancient times, been linked with plague and the most common effigies of Sebastian show him thus, pierced by arrows. Apollo brought plague upon the Greeks by shooting arrows at them and statues of him, carrying an arrow, were appealed to for relief from the disease. In this sense, Sebastian may be a sort of Christian counterpart of the Greek god. Indeed, many Renaissance paintings of him bear a striking resemblance to paintings of Apollo, perhaps because Apollo is almost always depicted naked and Sebastian is one of the few nude forms permitted to Christian art. He was to become a favourite subject for painters and he is featured on many plague banners of the late Middle Ages.

The pestilence of the late 7th century that saw St. Sebastian established as a plague saint was one of the last great epidemics of the disease to afflict Europe before the Black Death. Bede has left a record of its course in England and reminds us that if some men respond to pestilence with a deepening of their faith, others respond with scepticism. Having discovered that the cross was of little use in stopping epidemics, some men, Bede says, turned again to the old Teutonic gods for help. And during a famine in Ireland in the same century, one hears of another saint, St. Fechin, who is associated with the plague, but in quite another way from Saints Sebastian and Roch. Confronted with widespread famine, the kings summoned the leading clergy and laity to a council to consider the situation.

It was decided that everyone should observe a fast, a solution to famine that seems above reproach. However, a further injunction of the Council is more debatable. In the manner of Dean Swift, who many centuries later suggested that the Irish might solve both the problems of famine and overpopulation by eating their children, the good men enjoined the clergy to use their period of abstinence to pray God to send a plague that would carry off the surplus people of the lower orders and thus solve the problem of famine by reducing the population. St. Gerald disagreed and suggested, at least as a preliminary measure, that one might pray to God to increase the food supply; but clergy and laity, headed by the holy St. Fechin, being in no mood for half-way measures, persisted in the original plan. Any who are doubtful of the efficacy of prayer will be interested to know that the prayed-for plague duly arrived to eliminate many superfluous hungry people. Democrats, and any who may be sceptical of the Almighty's sense of fair play, may find their faith restored by the knowledge that among those divinely designated as superfluous were two kings of Erin and the holy St. Fechin himself, who was among the first to go.

In the 14th century, too, as in earlier and later epidemics, there were some who tried to turn the general evil to their private good; but, if the plague shows up the selfishness and cowardice of some, it gives others the opportunity to demonstrate courage and self-sacrifice. St. Roch was such a man. Europe seems to have been substantially free of plague from the 7th century until the outbreak of the Black Death, a circumstance which may have contributed to the virulence of that attack, the population having exhausted whatever immunity it may be possible to build up. But there were isolated outbreaks, and it was during an epidemic in Rome, early in the 14th century, that one first comes upon reports of the saint most closely associated with bubonic plague, St. Roch. He was born towards the end of the 13th century in Montpellier and from the very first seemed destined for a life of sanctity: a small red mark in the shape of a cross appeared on his breast at birth. He was of noble birth and when his parents died while he was still a boy, he quickly distributed his inherited wealth to the poor and decided to imitate the active virtues of Christ, having rejected the life of the cloister. He set out on foot for Rome but was soon diverted by a plague at Aquapendente. He served the sick there in a hospital and his presence seemed to effect such sure and quick cures that when the plague lifted its end was attributed to his intercession.

St. Roch himself seems to have been as impressed as his patients, and when he heard of a plague in the province of Romagna, he went there to devote himself to the sick in the cities of Cesena and Rimini. From there he went to Rome where, once again, this time for three years, he tended the sick. It is said that he prayed constantly that he might be a martyr in his duties, but for a long time he escaped infection. Finally, however, he succumbed to plague while in Piacenza. He suffered an acute attack attended by fever, an ulcer on his left thigh, and intolerable pain. Unable to keep himself from screaming with the pain, but also unwilling to disturb the other patients in the hospital where he lay, he dragged himself through the streets of Piacenza to a place outside the gates; here he lay down to die alone. However, miraculous aid was available, and he ultimately survived with the help of an angel who dressed his sores, and his faithful dog, who went every day into the city and returned with a loaf of bread for him.

On his recovery, St. Roch returned to Montpellier, but he was older and so wasted with his suffering that he was unrecognized there and subsequently arrested as a spy. He was tried, found guilty, and imprisoned by a judge whom St. Roch recognized as his own uncle; but the saint concealed his identity, believing his suffering to be the will of God, and languished in his dungeon for five years. And then he died. When his jailer entered the cell to find St. Roch dead, he also found the cell filled with a heavenly light and beside the dead saint an inscription that revealed his identity and announced that 'All those that are stricken by the plague, and who pray for aid through the merits and intercession of St. Roch, the servant of God, shall be healed'. His uncle the judge, a decent sort after all, gave him an honourable burial and the whole city mourned his death. St. Roch is believed to have died in 1327 in his thirty-second year, and at Montpellier he was venerated from the first. His veneration spread quickly during the time of the Black Death, but it was not until the 15th century that his cult became really widespread. During the Council of Constance in 1414—it is remembered chiefly for having condemned the reformer Hus to the stake—the plague broke out and the Council was about to disperse when a German monk reminded them of the power of St. Roch. An effigy of the Saint was carried in procession through the city and immediately the plague was stayed. From that time he has been appealed to almost universally in times of plague. So impressed were the Venetians with his power that, during a plague in Venice in 1487, they stole St. Roch's body from Montpellier and built the church of San Rocco to receive it.

The two saints, Sebastian and Roch, commonly figure together in dedicatory plague pictures. The best known such grouping is probably a painting by Titian commemorating the plague of 1512, hanging in the church of Santa Maria della Salute in Venice, itself a plague church: it shows the two saints together with the physician-saints, Damian and Cosmo, before a statue of St. Mark. It is a felicitous combination. Together the two saints represent compassion, courage, and resignation: care and kindness for the suffering of others, courage during one's own suffering, and resignation in the face of a disease which, until our own century, has defied all attempts to cure it.

Men of the 14th century were to need these virtues badly, as in the spring and summer of 1347 the plague advanced upon them, for there was very little else to sustain them. Medical knowledge in its understanding of epidemics had hardly advanced beyond Hippo-crates who attributed disease to personal and atmospheric disrup-tions. There was nothing that could be done about the accumulating natural disasters of earthquake, flood, insect invasions, and strange celestial happenings except to watch them with trepidation. For the mass of men, there was almost as little to be effected in the way of dietary control in a time of widespread crop failure and famine. In any case, the consensus of opinion in the available literature was that in every case, most demonstrable, perhaps, in the plague of Athens, medical men were as helpless as anyone else before the onslaught of plague. Huge fires could be kindled to purge the atmosphere and every sort of personal remedy could, and would, be employed, but all hope in these efforts was to be finally the hope of desperation.

For a disaster as vast as the Black Death was bound to be a sign of God's displeasure, and the only sure help lay in prayers and supplication. But even in such an interpretation of the cause and purpose of plague there was a fearful ambiguity. If suffering is God's way of purifying man, is it pious for a man to try to avoid suffering? In fact the Church taught that the concern of human existence was the preparation for eternal life and that this faulty shell of temporal existence was of no importance. Was it perhaps not impious to devote attention to it at all? Within a religious tradition that had canonized several men and woman solely on the basis of the fact that they had not washed, the answer for many was yes. In 1947 Albert Camus could plausibly present a character,

Father Paneloux, who, during a fictitious plague in modern-day Oran, concludes that it is illogical for a priest to call in a doctor and dies refusing medical attention in accordance with his conviction that 'there is no island of escape in time of plague. No, there is no middle course. We must accept the dilemma and choose either to hate God or to love God. And who would dare to choose to hate Him?' The character and the situation are, to be sure, fictitious, but the dilemma is real, and even more terrible for the 14th century. St. Roch had prayed that he might be a martyr to the disease, and the conviction that if plague is God's disease one *should* die of it was so strong that, centuries later, Christians in Abyssinia are said to have wrapped themselves in the sheets in which men had died of the plague in the hope of contracting it themselves, secure in the knowledge that the disease was a God-sent means of winning eternal life.

Those whose orientation was toward this life and its pleasures, and others who grew disillusioned with the continual failure of prayers and processions, were trapped on the other horn. If only unconsciously recognizing that to save oneself might mean to declare one's hatred for God, they could turn merely to pagan superstitions: to the public amusements and feasts of the Romans, to the strange propitiatory acts and imitative magic of the ancients, to a search for demons to exorcise, and finally to a search for scapegoats. Or they could like Galen, one of the most renowned physicians of them all, simply flee.

Chapter III

THE COMING OF THE DEATH

BY THE mid-14th century the ethno-geographic map of Europe was more or less as it is today; the wanderings of the nations had ceased three hundred years earlier and there was relief from the barbarian invasions following that of the Mongols in the mid-13th century. The Ottoman Turks were pressing from the East and would within another century capture Constantinople; but Western Europe was now relatively secure. Although there were frequent and violent wars, they were for the most part local and short, and men were turning to the elaboration of cities and the development of trade. Several trade routes to the East were open and, in spite of the pressure of the Turks and Tartars, even the Black Sea was secure enough for the Genoese to have developed a trade centre in the Crimea; Kaffa, the present Feodosiya, was important enough to be designated a cathedral city of an extensive diocese by Pope John XXII in a Bull issued in 1316; and by 1346 Kaffa had become a nucleus for much of the trade between Asia and Europe. It was also a military outpost against the onslaught of the Eastern nations.

Kaffa came under siege in 1346, in a manner described by Gabrielle de Mussi, the notary of Piacenza, whose account of the plague in Italy is one of the principal sources of information about the Black Death: 'A place in the East called Tana, situated in a northerly direction from Constantinople and under the rule of the Tartars, to which Italian merchants much resorted, was besieged by a vast horde of Tartars and was in a short time taken.' The Christian merchants expelled from Tana, the present port of Azor on the Sea of Azor, retreated to Kaffa which was more strongly defended. But the Tartars followed and laid siege to Kaffa as well, surrounding the city with a vast army and hammering the walls with their catapults and other instruments of war. The inhabitants of the city were barely able to supply the necessities of life, and these could only be obtained by sea. Suddenly there occurred what must have seemed to

43

the besieged merchants of Kaffa a miraculous intervention. Just as the army of Sennacherib had been destroyed by a plague outside Jerusalem, so the Tartar armies were struck down by, as de Mussi calls it, 'the death.' 'At first,' de Mussi writes, 'the Tartars were paralysed with fear at the ravages of the disease, and at the prospect that sooner or later all must fall victims to it.' But if the Christian defenders of Kaffa counted upon an enemy retreat, their hopes were dashed by the morbid ingenuity of Kipchak Khan Janibeg, the commander of the attacking Tartars. For even if the Khan knew the Biblical story, he was obviously not disposed to apply it to himself. Loading the corpses of his plague-stricken men into the catapults he projected them over the walls of the city and into the midst of its defenders. The Christians, not to be outdone, hauled the bodies back up to the tops of the walls and dumped them into the sea. However, de Mussi continues, 'Soon, as might be supposed, the air became tainted and the wells of water poisoned, and in this way the disease spread so rapidly in the city that few of the inhabitants had strength sufficient to fly from it.' This was the first contact between the Eastern plague and men of Western Europe.

The plague that afflicted both the Tartar army and the Genoese defenders of Kaffa was most probably the same disease that had been reported earlier in the East and been carried westward along the trade routes. It is ironic that trade, which was one of the most important factors in the growth of cities and the dramatic changes in the social and political development of Europe, should also have been the means by which the Black Death entered the continent. From a low ebb between 800 and 1000 when the Mediterranean was 'a Moslem lake', and the dominant position of the landed magnate demonstrated that land and land alone was the source of wealth and power, trading had increased steadily. Byzantium quickly became an important terminus of Asiatic trade routes, and from an early date Naples, Amalfi, Bari and especially Venice, grew rich as they carried Eastern goods from Constantinople to Europe; and by the 11th century Pisa and Genoa had begun to take a sizeable share of the Mediterranean trade. The First Crusade later in the 11th century captured a large area of the Syrian coast, thus assuring the continuing growth of Christian trade in the East, and Bohemond, one of the leading Crusaders, as soon as he declared himself Prince of Antioch promptly gave a trade monopoly there to Genoese merchants. Other Italian cities were quick to seize the opportunity of supplying the new masters of the Syrian coast, and the Crusade, which succeeded in capturing Jerusalem in 1099, opened up trading possibilities even farther afield: east to Damascus, south to Alexandria and Cairo and the Nile valley. From that time on commercial interests triumphed over religious zeal until the Fourth Crusade, largely under the influence of Venetian traders, abandoned the idea of liberating the Holy Land altogether and attacked and captured Constantinople, establishing a Latin Empire which was to last from 1204 until 1261.

Nor did commerce tend only to enlarge the influence of the cities eastward; prosperity also reached inland into Europe. Venetian influence expanded through the valley of the Po and over the Alps; Pisa's prosperity spread to Florence and Lucca and other Tuscan towns; from Genoa and Marseilles money and merchants extended their authority through Provence and up the Rhône valley. In the North, as well, trade with the East had a profound influence on the growth of towns and the character of life generally. Trading posts were established on the west coast of Germany, in England, Scotland and Ireland; and by the end of the 11th century many flourishing communities had grown up in the river valleys of France and western Germany. Hamburg on the Elbe, Cologne and Mainz on the Rhine, and Paris on the Seine were the most important; but there were many others: Cambrai, Ghent, Liège, Verdun, Bruges and, of course, London. The precise nature of commercial operations depended on the locality. In the eastern Mediterranean an important early trade was the export of slaves: Slavs (from which the word 'slave' is derived) captured in the German expansion were sold mainly to the Moslems in Spain. Also iron and timber were exchanged for silk, spices, drugs, precious metals and manufactured articles of decoration and adornment. In the North, there were dealings in furs, honey, and fish. Wine was an early export of Burgundy and the Rhineland; and fustian from Lombardy and woollens from Flanders were circulated far afield. Trade had created a network of roads and population centres throughout Europe. It had also created at least three well-travelled routes to the Orient. The plague, carried from one port to another and spreading inland along the lanes of commerce, was to etch a veritable trader's map of the routes and cities of Europe.

The great commercial routes between Europe and India, China and other Asiatic countries, were clearly described by a Venetian, Marino Sanudo, in a work addressed in 1321 to Pope John XXII. According to Sanudo, Bagdad was the ancient centre of all trade with the East, and to this depot of Oriental merchandise the great caravan routes exclusively led. However, at the time he wrote, the incursion of the barbarian hordes from Central Asia had made over-land traffic perilous, and the most used route—longer, more expen-sive but less dangerous—was by sea from the Indian ports of Mahabar and Cambeth (probably the latter-day Mahe on the Malabar coast and Cambay to the north of Bombay) to ports on the Persian Gulf. From there goods were conveyed either up the river Tigris, or to Aden, at the entrance to the Red Sea. From Aden caravans would make a nine-day journey across the desert to a city Sanudo calls Chus on the Nile, where cargoes were loaded on barges and carried for fifteen days by river to Cairo. From Cairo merchandise was conveyed by canal to Alexandria where, after being heavily taxed by the Sultan, it was transported to Europe.

Goods off-loaded at the mouth of the Tigris passed on to Bagdad and entered Europe along the other two great trade routes. The best known of these, and the shortest by which goods from China and India could be brought to Europe, was from Bagdad over the plains of Mesopotamia and Syria to Lycia, the southernmost part of Asiatic Turkey, where Italian merchants stood ready to buy and ship to European ports. However, according to Sanudo, in 1321 this was the most dangerous route. Another alternative was to follow the Tigris from Bagdad to its sources in Armenia, and from there either to Trebizond and other Black Sea ports, or taking the road from the Caspian, on the other side of the Caucasus Mountains, to the Italian settlements in the Crimea, of which the Genoese-dominated port of Kaffa was the most important. The early accounts of plague in the East offer very substantial evidence that it advanced into Europe along these trade routes. The report made to Pope Clement VI lists among the places hardest hit by the epidemic: India, Mesopotamia, Syria, Armenia and Caesarea, and to the south, Cairo and Gaza. According to de Mussi, it was from Kaffa that it was carried by plague-stricken ships to Italian ports.

In his account of the siege of Kaffa, de Mussi mentions that the city was re-supplied by sea; and, since all vessels from the Mediter-ranean would of necessity have touched at Constantinople, then the great centre of communication between East and West, it was very likely one of these ships from Kaffa that brought the plague to that city, where its devastation is recorded by no less an eye-witness than the Emperor John Cantacuzene. In many instances the Emperor adapts the words of Thucydides in his account, but his description is specific and particular enough to avoid the suspicion that he was anything but an eye-witness, especially as he relates that his own son, Andronicus, died on the third day. 'The young man was not only remarkable for his personal appearance,' he writes, 'but he was endowed in the highest degree with those qualities which form the chief adornment of youth; and everything about him testified that he would have followed nobly in the footsteps of his ancestors.'

Of the epidemic itself, the Emperor notes that it 'traversed almost the entire sea-coasts, when it was carried over the world. For it invaded not only Pontus, Thrace and Macedonia, but Greece, Italy, the Islands, Egypt, Lybia, Judea, Syria, and almost the entire universe'. Cantacuzene was convinced that the disease was incurable and comments that neither regularity of life nor bodily strength was any protection against infection. Medical men were powerless to help and those who received care died as surely as did the poor who had no aid whatever. Agreeing with many other chroniclers of the plague, the Emperor writes that no other disease showed itself during the time of the epidemic, and that any who fell sick ultimately died of that disease; which probably means that all deaths, regardless of the specific cause, were attributed to plague. One of the problems of analysing accounts of the Black Death is the wide variety of symptoms attributed to it: its extreme infectiousness is noted in some accounts, in others it is pointed out that nurses and burial squads were no more affected than any people; in some descriptions the appearance of buboes is almost universal, in others the victims are said to have died before any visible symptoms could appear. Modern clinical definition of the plague takes into account many of these apparent contradictions in recognizing the various forms that the disease can take; but even when contemporary reports tell of reactions that are not recognized by modern medicine as plague-oriented, we today have not necessarily found cause to disbelieve them, for the reason that under the extreme conditions that existed in plague-ridden communities other diseases were almost certainly extant.

In Constantinople some people died suddenly, others during the course of the day after symptoms appeared; some expired, the Emperor writes, after only an hour's suffering. In the cases of those who lived for two or three days, the attack began with a violent fever which deprived the sufferer of his speech and finally rendered him unconscious. Some were attacked first in the lungs, which became inflamed, after which the victim vomited blood. The tongue

became black and congested with blood and the sufferer experienced
a terrible thirst for which there was no relief. Some victims became
extremely restless and unable to sleep. In a great many cases plague
spots broke out over the entire body. All who fell ill suffered a
profound depression and on the appearance of the first symptoms
men lost all hope of recovery and gave themselves up for lost. The
Emperor comments that this despair made them even more susceptible to the ravages of disease and hastened death. But he also
records that some who developed all the symptoms quite surprisingly recovered, and of those who did recover none had another
attack. He seems convinced of the contagious nature of the disease
and notes that those who tended the sick soon became ill themselves
and as a consequence many families died in their entirety.

Cantacuzene believed that the disease afflicting Constantinople
was a very special one, like none other that men had ever suffered;
and he was convinced that it was a chastisement sent by God Himself. This belief was commonly held and many, threatened by the
epidemic, resolved to change their lives. Contrary to the experience
of Procopius during the earlier plague in the city, Cantacuzene says
that it was especially those who had contracted the disease and
recovered who most strenuously devoted themselves to lives of
virtue. A great many people, at the outset of the epidemic, the
chronicler says, distributed their property to the poor, and there
were none who did not, when they were attacked by the sickness,
show a profound sorrow for their faults, so as to appear before
the judgement seat of God with the best possible chance of salvation.

The plague which ravaged Constantinople in 1347 could only have
contributed to the worsening condition of the Eastern Empire. The
Empire had been contracting for centuries, but taxation remained
the backbone of Byzantine administration and, with the increase of
trade, Constantinople had remained the most splendid city of
Christendom. The civilization of the court, an elaborate and corrupt
but nonetheless efficient bureaucracy, the sophisticated and obedient
clergy, all helped to maintain the trappings of grandeur. And the
state had exhibited an enormous resilience. It had weathered the
conquest of the Fourth Crusade, and the last Latin threat to Byzantium had been as early as 1280; Charles of Anjou had planned an
attack which he was unable to mount because of the bitter Sicilian
hostility, which finally came to a head in 1282 with the Sicilian
Vespers and the establishment of the Aragonese house in the

island. But pressure from the Ottomans had continued and they had managed, by 1326, to establish their capital at Brusa in Bithynia, dangerously close to Constantinople. Bitter internal quarrels, and probably the plague of 1347, led to further deterioration of the Empire, until in 1402 its forces were defeated at the battle of Ankara and the Byzantine emperors became, in fact, Ottoman vassals.

*

The Genoese ships from Kaffa continued to spread the disease beyond Constantinople, according to the account of Gabrielle de Mussi, who says that 'the sailors, as if accompanied by evil spirits, as soon as they approached the land, were death to those with whom they mingled'. Sicily was among the many places quickly infected. An account of the plague's ravages of that island has been left by a Franciscan friar, Michael Platiensis of Piazza: 'It happened that in the month of October, in the year of our Lord, 1347, about the beginning of the month, twelve Genoese ships, flying from the divine vengeance which our Lord for their sins had sent upon them, put into the port of Messina, bringing with them such sickness clinging to their very bones that, did anyone speak to them he was directly struck with a mortal sickness from which there was no escape.' There follows a description of the symptoms of the disease sub-stantially the same as that of Cantacuzene. The Sicilian chronicler is also impressed by the infectiousness of the sickness, which was transmitted not only by the breath of the afflicted but even by their clothes and possessions; he notes also the frequent appearance of boils and buboes, of violent fever, and the vomiting of blood. According to him, the disease lasted three days, and on the fourth, at the latest, the victim died. Recognizing the contagiousness of the sickness, the people of Messina took action:

Seeing what a calamity of sudden death had come to them by the arrival of the Genoese, the people of Messina drove them in all haste from their city and port. But the sickness remained and a terrible mor-tality ensued. The one thought in the mind of all was how to avoid the infection. The father abandoned the sick son; magistrates and notaries refused to come and make the wills of the dying; even the priests to hear their confessions. The care of those stricken fell to the Friars Minor, the Dominicans and members of other orders, whose convents were in consequence soon emptied of their inhabitants. Corpses were abandoned in empty houses, and there was none to give them Christian burial. The houses of the dead were left open and unguarded with their jewels, money, and valuables; if anyone wished to enter, there was no one to prevent him. The great pestilence came so suddenly that there was no time to organise any measures of protection; from the very beginning the officials were too few, and soon there were none. The population deserted the city in crowds; fearing even to stay in the environs, they camped out in the open air in the vineyards, whilst some managed to put up at least a temporary shelter for their families. Others, again, trusting in the protection of the virgin, blessed Agatha, sought refuge in Catania, where the Queen of Sicily had gone, and where she directed her son, Don Frederick, to join her. The Messinese, in the month of November, persuaded the Patriarch Archbishop of Catania to allow the relics of the Saint to be taken to their city, but the people refused to permit them to leave their ancient resting place. Processions and pilgrimages were organised to beg God's favour. Still the pestilence raged and with greater fury. Everyone was in too great a terror to aid his neighbour. Flight profited nothing, for the sickness already contracted and clinging to the fugitives, was only carried wherever they sought refuge. Of those who fled some fell on the roads and dragged themselves to die in the fields, the woods, or the valleys. Those who reached Catania breathed their last in the hospitals. At the demand of the terrified populace the Patriarch forbade, under pain of excommunication, the burial of any of these Messina refugees within the city, and their bodies were thrown into deep pits outside the walls. . . . So wicked and timid were the Catanians that they refused even to speak to any from Messina, or to have anything to do with them, but quickly fled at their approach. Had it not been for secret shelter afforded by some of their fellow citizens, resident in the town, the unfortunate refugees would have been left destitute of all human aid.

But the fears of the wicked and timid Catanians were fully justified, and the plague spread in Catania just as it had before in Messina with the same consequences to both individuals and social organizations. There were so many afflicted and the clergy had been so greatly diminished that the Patriarch gave to every priest, even the youngest, all the faculties he himself possessed, both episcopal and patriarchal, for absolving sins. Finally the Patriarch himself, Gerard Otho of the Order of St. Francis, fell victim to the plague. Among others who died was Duke John, who had tried to escape the disease by scrupulously avoiding all contact with anyone whom he thought might be infected; his precautions were of no avail. The account concludes: 'The plague was spread in the same way from Messina throughout Sicily; Syracuse, Girgenti, Sciacca, and Trapani were successively attacked; in particular it raged in the district of Trapani, in the extreme west of the island, which has remained almost without population.' Nor were the other islands in the Mediterranean spared. Villani says that in Sardinia and Corsica two-thirds of the inhabitants died. In Majorca reports of the dead ranged from fifteen to thirty thousand and an ancient tradition holds that eight out of ten people died. Monasteries and convents were particularly affected and in many not one priest was left alive. The Dominicans were so hard hit that they were forced to replenish their ranks by recruiting children.

The Black Death was upon Europe. It was obvious from the havoc the epidemic wrought in Constantinople and in Sicily that measures must be taken, and it was not long before medical men were analysing causes and prescribing cures and preventives. According to J. F. C. Hecker, the first published notice on the plague is by a teacher of Perugia, Gentilis of Foligno, who died himself of the disease in June of 1348. Gentilis, in common with almost all his contemporaries, is deeply influenced by the Arabian doctrines and especially by Galen. He writes that a pestilential atmosphere is responsible for the corruption of the blood in the lungs and in the heart, which is then communicated to the entire body. Thus, following ancient authorities, he prescribes purification of the atmosphere and an appropriate manner of living as both preventive and cure. Huge fires of aromatic woods should be kindled, he said, in the vicinity of both the sick and the healthy. At the beginning of an attack he employed bleeding and purging. The healthy should wash frequently with wine or vinegar, sprinkle their houses with vinegar, and sniff camphor and other volatile substances. But Gentilis, unlike many of his contemporaries, laid little stress upon astrology.

Hecker has preserved another, much more curious, document from the medical faculty of the University of Paris. It is of uncertain date and the exact occasion that called it forth is unknown, but from its reference to the plague in Sicily, it would seem that it must have been prepared before the end of the summer of 1348, before the Black Death was firmly entrenched in the mainland of Europe. The medical faculty of Paris, one of the most celebrated of the 14th century, bestirred itself, in the face of the horrors of the Black Death, to list the causes of the epidemic and to furnish some appropriate regulations with regard to living during its prevalence. The resulting document is a monumental example of authority being wise on command, and of the lengths to which men who are supposed to be wise will go to hide their ignorance under a mass of important-sounding phrases and self-assured prescriptions:

We, the Members of the College of Physicians of Paris, have, after mature consideration and consultation on the present mortality, collected the advice of our old masters in the art, and intend to make known the causes of this pestilence, more clearly than could be done according to the rules and principles of astrology, and natural science; we, therefore, declare as follows:

It is known that in India, and the vicinity of the Great Sea, the constellations which combatted the rays of the sun, and the warmth of the heavenly fire exerted their power especially against the sea, and struggled violently with its waters. (Hence, vapours often originate which envelop the sun, and convert its light into darkness.) These vapours alternately rose and fell for twenty-eight days; but at last, sun and fire acted so powerfully upon the sea, that they attracted a great portion of it to themselves, and the waters of the ocean arose in the form of vapour, thereby the waters were, in some parts, so corrupted that the fish which they contained died. These corrupted waters, however, the heat of the sun could not consume, neither could other water, hail or snow, and dew, originate therefrom. On the contrary, this vapour spread itself through the air in many places on the earth, and enveloped them in fog.

Such was the case all over Arabia, in the port of India; in Crete; in the plains and valleys of Macedonia; in Hungary, Albania and Sicily. Should the same thing occur in Sardinia, not a man will be left alive; and the like will continue, so long as the sun remains in the sign of Leo, on all the islands and adjoining countries to which the corrupted sea-wind extends, or has already extended from India. If the inhabitants of those parts do not employ and adhere to the following, or similar means and precepts, we announce to them inevitable death—except the grace of Christ preserve their lives.

We are of the opinion, that the constellations, with the aid of Nature, strive, by virtue of their divine might, to protect and heal the human race; and to this end, in union with the rays of the sun, acting through the power of fire, endeavour to break through the mist. Accordingly, within the next ten days, and until the seventeenth of the ensuing month of July, this mist will be converted into a stinking deleterious rain, whereby the air will be much purified. Now, as soon as the rain shall announce itself, by thunder or hail, everyone of you should protect himself from the air; and, as well before as after the rain, kindle a large fire of vine-wood, green laurel, or other green wood; wormwood and chamomile should also be burnt in great quantity in the market-places, in other densely inhabited localities, and in the houses.

Until the earth is again completely dry, and for three days thereafter, no one ought to go abroad in the fields. During this time the diet should be simple, and people should be cautious in avoiding exposure in the cool of the evening, at night, and in the morning. Poultry and water-fowl, young pork, old beef, and fat meat, in general, should not be eaten; but on the contrary, meat of a proper age, of a warm and dry, but on no account of a heating or exciting nature. Broth should be taken, seasoned with ground pepper, ginger, and cloves especially by those who are accustomed to live temperately, and are yet choice in their diet. Sleep in the day-time is detrimental; it should be taken at night until sunrise, or somewhat longer. At breakfast, one should drink little; supper should be taken an hour before sunset, when more may be drunk than in the morning. Clear light wine, mixed with a fifth or sixth part of water, should be used as a beverage. Dried or fresh fruits, with wine, are not injurious; but highly so without it. Beet-root and other vegetables, whether eaten pickled or fresh, are hurtful; on the contrary, spicy pot-herbs, as sage and rosemary, are wholesome. Cold, moist, watery food is in general prejudicial. Going out at night, and even until three o'clock in the morning, is dangerous, on account of the dew. Only small river fish should be used. Too much exercise is hurtful. The body should be kept warmer than usual, and thus protected from moisture and cold. Rain-water must not be employed in cooking, and everyone should guard against exposure to wet weather. If it rains, a little fine treacle should be taken after dinner. Fat people should not sit in the sunshine. Good clear wine should be selected and drunk often, but in small quantities, by day. Olive oil, as an article of food, is fatal. Equally injurious are fasting and excessive abstemiousness, anxiety of mind, anger, and immoderate drinking. Young people, in autumn especially, must abstain from all these things, if they do not wish to run a risk of dying of dysentery. In order to keep the body properly open, an enema or some other simple means, should be employed, when necessary. Bathing is injurious. Men must preserve chastity as they value their lives. Everyone should impress this on his recollection, but especially those who reside on the coast, or upon an island into which the noxious wind has penetrated.

One is reminded of the utterances of Presidents and Cabinet ministers faced with the necessity of preserving the appearance of dignified command in the face of an appallingly complex financial or political crisis which they do not understand and over which they can exert little control. The tone of infuriating self-assurance is all too familiar, although it has shifted in our day from the pronouncements of scientists to those of politicians and economists. For 14th-century medical science is rather like 20th-century economic and political science: based largely upon precedent and authority, lacking a well-developed experimental basis, emanating far more often from the sanctuary of the academy than from the rough and dangerous battlefield of experience; while, on the other hand, the barber-surgeons and wandering leeches, like today's politicians, chock-full of practical experience but lacking the good sense to interpret it, operated in terms of homely little analogies and popular superstitions that appealed to, but hardly benefited, the people who paid their fees. Medicine was still in its philosophical phase and its arguments were from analogy, its assurance unassailable and its errors, for that very reason, all the more disastrous. Galen had provided the tone as well as the substance of a good deal of medieval medicine. An admirer of Euclid's methods of proving things, he had tried to make medicine as exact a science as geometry, and in his system everything was explained, all questions were answered, all problems solved. When he had pronounced his last word, there was no further comment to make except, as he said of himself: 'Whoever seeks fame need only become familiar with all that I have achieved.' This overweening confidence, together with many established medical practices, was to be one of the casualties of the Black Death.

In general, the established medical fraternities of the 14th century agreed with the Paris faculty on the causes, prevention and cure of the plague. For a start, there was a long-established association between terrestrial and atmospheric disruptions and plague: Galen held that irregularity of the seasons could bring on an epidemic, in agreement with Hippocrates before him and Avicenna after. Lucretius in *De Rerum Natura* proposed to explain pestilence in terms of his atomic theory: one can see clouds descend from the sky and noxious vapours rise as mists from the land; it is therefore probable, he argues, that pestilence also either comes down from heaven by the medium of clouds or rises up from the earth by the medium of mist. Seneca had associated earthquakes and pestilence in his *Physical Science*. It was also known that the eruption of Vesuvius which destroyed Pompeii had been followed by a plague, attributed by Dion Cassius to the volcanic dust and ashes. As has been noted, there was a violent earthquake in January 1348, which shook Greece, Italy and neighbouring countries. Naples, Rome, Pisa, Bologna, Padua, Venice, among many other cities, had suffered and there were reports from the countryside of whole villages having been wiped out. Knighton imagined that Naples had been totally destroyed. It was generally believed that such disruptions could very

cabis me in equitate tua.

Dutes te tribulatio
ne animam meam et
in misericordia tua di
spertes omnes inimi
cos meos.

Et perdes omnes q
tribulant animam
meam quoniam ego
servus tuus sum.

Gloria patri et filio
et spiritui sancto.

Sicut erat in princi
pio et nunc et semper z
in secula seculorum. amen.

De communicans Ant.

Dne deitra tua nec prcenam
nostram neque inviciam fu
mas et precatus nostris parce do
mine ipso tuo que redemisti
sanguine tuo, ipso ne inci
mum nascens nobis etc.

Photo: Giraudon

GREGORY THE GREAT IN PROCESSION: ST. MICHAEL SHEATHES
HIS SWORD TO SIGNIFY THE END OF THE PLAGUE

ST. ROCH,
THE PLAGUE SAINT

A MEDIEVAL PHARMACY

well unbalance the atmosphere and cause plague, and the Paris faculty, in connecting them with celestial phenomena, were expressing yet another widely held belief.

The Pope's physician, Guy de Chauliac, agreed that the general cause of the plague was a conjunction of planets by which 'the quality of the air and the other elements was so altered, that they set poisonous fluids in motion toward the inward parts of the body, in the same manner as the magnet attracts iron; whence there arose in the commencement fever and the spitting of blood; afterwards, however, a deposition in the form of glandular swellings and inflammatory boils.' Once again it must be emphasized that Guy de Chauliac was probably the greatest medical authority of his time, whose thesis on surgery, written at a time when this was not yet a respectable medical practice, remained the principal text on the subject for centuries after his death. Although he and other surgeons like Henri de Mondeville were the most interesting practitioners of their time, they were slow to obtain recognition from traditional physicians. The University of Paris refused to admit a student to its school of medicine until he had taken an oath never to perform a surgical operation; and even blood-letting, a common 14th-century operation, had to be left to underlings. As a consequence people turned to the barber-surgeons who found this practice so lucrative that they began to abandon shaving and haircutting. By 1365 there were forty such barber-surgeons in Paris. Galen had dissected pigs and apes and concluded that the human skeleton was almost exactly like that of the Barbary ape: nothing more needed to be done. The medical school at Salerno each year publicly dissected a pig, but human dissection was very rare. Guy de Chauliac had studied in Bologna where a cadaver had been dissected as early as 1200, but it was not until 1360, when he persuaded the authorities in Avignon to allow medical schools to dissect the bodies of executed criminals, that there was any sort of systematic study of human anatomy. And yet even such a pioneer was bound firmly to astrology. His great work, the *Chirurgia Magna*, regularly relates the prognosis of a disease to the constellation under which the patient was born. He comments at one place that 'if anyone is wounded in the neck while the moon is in Taurus, the infliction will be dangerous'. Celestial influences were so important that very few medical men were able to ignore them. Galeazzo de Santa Sofia, who treated plague victims in Vienna, agreed that astral influences were the cause of plague. And the list could be continued, because all the sciences, not only medicine, were closely bound up with astrology and taught almost in an occult manner well beyond the 14th century. One of the earliest printed documents is a calendar published at Mainz in 1462 indicating the astrologically best times for blood-letting. And another early text, from 1485, contains the following preface:

> Many a time and oft have I contemplated inwardly the wondrous works of the Creator of the universe: how in the beginning He formed the heavens and adorned them with goodly, shining stars, to which He gave power and might to influence everything under heaven. Also how He formed afterwards the four elements: fire, hot and dry—air, hot and moist, water, cold and moist—earth, dry and cold—and gave to each a nature of its own: and how after this same Great Master of Nature made and formed herbs of many sorts and animals of all kinds, and last of all Man, the noblest of all created things. Therefore I thought on the wondrous order, which the Creator gave these same creatures of His, so that everything, which has its being under heaven, receives it from the stars, and keeps it by their help.

The passage exemplifies something of the state of mind of the Middle Ages. The world was geocentric and man was the final creation of God, His greatest concern and the object of His continuing attention. Although it would seem to us almost insolent to assume that the great siderial movements take place specifically for our edification, it was not at all presumptuous or even illogical for the Middle Ages to think so. Both the clergy and the laity accepted the cosmos as described by Ptolemy, the Alexandrine astronomer of the 2nd century A.D. The earth was the centre of the universe and around it, embedded in eight concentric spheres, moved the planets and the 'fixed' stars, all activated by the ninth sphere, the *primum mobile*. The universe revolved around the earth and the earth was made for man: it followed that celestial movements not only affected man but, if properly interpreted, could instruct him. Not only the cosmos but all society, indeed all objects and even concepts, were similarly arranged in an orderly and hierarchical structure. These theories, derived in the last resort from Platonic and Neo-Platonic sources, and reinforced by elements of Hebrew and Christian thought, fitted and supported the actual social structure with its pyramid of clerical ranks and offices and its stratification of social classes. The whole universe was regarded as a great ladder of ascending entities running unbroken from Hell to the infinite and ultimate unity of God, from the lowest of insects to the angels, from

the simplest of practical concepts to the most exalted philosophical
and theological formulations. In this order each individual and each
concept was both a part of some greater whole and itself a microcosm of inferior creation: in either aspect it was integrally involved
in the 'Great Chain of Being'. And in this series, man held a most
critical place: half-way between the angels and the animals, par-
ticipating in the exalted spiritual nature of the one and the base
physical nature of the other.

Since everything is both a part of the macrocosm and of itself a
microcosm, analogies of all sorts were valid. One could argue logically from one part of the cosmic hierarchy to another: the relations
of a man to God could be described in terms of the duties of a wife
to her husband; the relation of pope to emperor in terms of the
relationship of the heart to the limbs or of the sun to the moon.
Within the framework of such a world view, arguments from analogy
and astrological formulations were not only possible but, once a
correspondence had been established, had all the compulsion of
eternal and inescapable truth. Such reasoning, incontrovertible as it
would have been if only it had had the firm assent of authority, also
had the virtue of being verifiable by observation. After all, one had
only to look to see that the sun, moon, planets and stars did, truly,
move around the earth; and one had only to look to see the social and
ecclesiastical hierarchies which possessed the power, in most cases,
to affirm their unchangeability. A society far more susceptible to
changes of season and the vagaries of weather than our own cen-
trally-heated and refrigerated urban complexes—a society of farmers
fishermen and seafarers—had ample evidence from experience of
the influence of stars upon men: the changing seasons, the relation
of tides to the moon, the lunar periodicity of women, the dependence of agriculture and fishing upon the sky and the weather, and,
of course, the seasonal effect upon epidemics. It is true that, even
in the 14th century, sceptical voices were heard. Nicole Oresme, the
Bishop of Lisieux, who died in 1382, wrote a tract, *De Divinatione*,
against astrologers and soothsayers in which he raised many of the
rational objections: wide belief in an idea does not mean it is true,
the senses can be deceived, even eye-witness accounts should be
treated with scepticism if they contradict our ordinary experience
of nature—but nevertheless he was convinced that there was such a
thing as the evil eye, that if a criminal looked into a mirror he would
darken it, and that the glance of a lynx could penetrate a wall. The
belief in astrology, and consequently a belief in a wide range of

concepts which seem to us utterly untenable, was well-nigh universal, and it should not surprise us to find these ideas intimately bound up with a science as inexact as that of medicine.

In terms of the Great Chain of Being, man's connection with the animals was as firm as his connection with the spiritual beings; and, predictably, medical texts ascribed disease to disruptions in this part of his nature as well as to disruptions in the cosmos. Guy de Chauliac, having asserted that celestial influences were the *causa universalis agens* of the Black Death, continued to specify the *causa particularis patiens*; these specific subordinate causes were 'the diseased state of bodies, the corruption of the fluids, debility, obstruction, and so forth. . . .' Galeazzo de Santa Sofia felt that the disease did not consist so much in the alterations of the four primary qualities—warmth, cold, dryness and moisture—as in the corruption of the air from natural causes. He specifies the corruption of animal and vegetable bodies, and especially the putrefaction of locusts that had died at sea and been thrown up on the beaches.

Although medical theory explained epidemics by the universality of atmospheric disruption, doctors, in the midst of the pestilence, came to recognize the fact of contagion, or at least to act upon it, even if it did not square with doctrine. Some even came to formulate a theory of contagion. The Arab statesman, historian, and physician Ibn al-Khatīb, who observed the Black Death in Granada, wrote in his treatise, *On Plague*:

> The existence of contagion is established by experience, study, and the evidence of the senses, by trustworthy reports on transmission by garments, vessels, ear-rings; by the spread of it by persons from one house, by infection of a healthy sea-port by an arrival from an infected land . . . by the immunity of isolated individuals and . . . nomadic Beduin tribes of Africa. . . . It must be a principle that a proof taken from the Traditions has to undergo modification when in manifest contradiction with the evidence of the perception of the senses.

Guy de Chauliac believed one could even be infected by looking upon someone who had the disease: 'It was so contagious, especially that accompanied by spitting blood, that not only by staying together, but even by looking at one another, people caught it, with the result that men died without attention and were buried without priests.' It seemed that the only thing to do was to follow Galen's example and flee. Chalin de Vinario, also a physician at Avignon, wrote at the time, 'As to approach the patients is coupled with certain danger, there are but few physicians who for an enormous fee expose themselves to so great a peril. In my opinion they are quite right, for many who were not prudent enough to hold back have been involved in the fate of their patients. No one is so blind and senseless that he should care more for the salvation of others than for his own, particularly in the case of so infectious a disease.' But his cynicism may have been the cynicism of despair, for he did not follow his own advice but stayed on at Avignon. So did Guy de Chauliac who writes with an engaging naiveté, 'As for me, to avoid infamy, I did not dare absent myself, but still I was in continual fear.' His fear was justified and he suffered a severe attack of the plague from which he fortunately recovered after six weeks. Both men were convinced the disease was incurable. Vinario declared simply, 'Every pronounced case of plague is incurable.' And Chauliac wrote: 'The disease was most humiliating for the physicians, who were unable to render any assistance, all the more as, for fear of infection, they did not venture to visit the patients, and if they did could do no good and consequently earn no fees, for all infected died with the exception of some towards the end of the epidemic, who escaped, as the boils had been able to mature.'

Nevertheless efforts were made to prevent the infection and to treat it when it appeared. These efforts, for the most part, conformed to the advice of the Paris medical faculty which itself conformed to ancient authority. Preventives consisted mostly of dietary regulations and attempts to purify the atmosphere. Large fires were kindled with green wood that sometimes produced a smoke so heavy that birds died in their nests as a result of it. However, a more conservative opinion held that a thick, moist atmosphere was better since it was more impenetrable to the astral influences that were the primary cause of the disease: and a more eccentric opinion held that the air became 'stiff' and had to be broken up with loud noises: bells were rung, guns were fired, and people set birds flying about in their rooms. Houses were sprinkled with vinegar and other aromatic substances. People were enjoined to sniff volatile substances, just as the Roman Emperor Commodus had been advised to stuff laurel leaves in his nose and ears: Chauliac especially recommended a certain 'poma'. The belief in aromatic substances as a plague preventive persisted long after the Black Death. Daniel Defoe in *A Journal of the Plague Year* says that gunpowder, pitch and sulphur were burned in houses, and that people smoked tobacco as a preventive. He describes a church full of people smelling like an apothecary's shop: '. . . the whole church was like a smelling-bottle; in one corner it was all perfumes, in another, aromatics, balsamics, a variety of drugs and herbs; in another, salts and spirits, as everyone was furnished with their own preservation.' Chauliac and others prescribed Armenian bole internally, a remedy first suggested by Galen, and treacle, apples, and things of savoury flavour to comfort the heart; and aloetic pills for general purgation. Blood-letting was a common preventive, but Galeazzo cautioned that it should be used as a preventive only when the blood was actually unhealthy and when the general health of the patient was reasonably good. Chalin de Vinario also practised blood-letting but in moderation: he would not draw blood from anyone under fourteen.

These preventives differ very little from those proposed by Rufus of Ephesus over thirteen hundred years earlier:

> Should a person foresee that the plague is coming . . . let him observe this—what is the character of the present season, and what that of the whole year, for you will be able thereby to find out the best regimen; such, for example, as if the temperature of the season ought to have been dry, but has become humid; in that case, it will be necessary, by a drying diet, to consume the superabundant moisture. Care also must be had to the belly, and when there is phlegm in the stomach it must be evacuated by emetics. And when a fullness of blood prevails, a vein should be opened. Purgings also by urine, and otherwise by the whole body, are proper. But, if the patient is affected with ardent fever, and has a fiery heat about the breast, it will not be improper to apply cold things to the breast, and to give cold drink, not in small quantities, for it only makes the flame burn more; but in full draughts, so as to extinguish it. But if an ardent fever prevails within, and the extremities are cold, and the skin cold, the hypochondrium is distended, and the stomach sends the matters which have been melted, some upwards, and others downwards; if watchfulness, delirium, and roughness of the tongue, are present; in these cases calefacient remedies are wanted to diffuse the heat all over the body, and every other means ought to be tried, in order to determine the heat from the internal to the external parts. The following proportions may be used: of aloes, two parts; of ammoniac perfume, two parts; of myrrh, one part; pound these in fragrant wine, and give every day to the quantity of half a cyathus. I never knew a person . . . who did not recover after this draught.*

* F. Adams, *The Seven Books of Paulus Aegineta* (London, 1844), I, 277–8. Paul collected the works of Oribasius who had collected fragments of the work of Rufus.

When preventive measures failed and the disease appeared, there was little to do but try to treat the symptoms. Galeazzo applied poultices of mustard and lily-bulbs to inflamed boils and sometimes cauterized them with red-hot iron or, on occasion, gold. Guy de Chauliac used poultices of figs and boiled onions, pounded and mixed with butter, to ripen the buboes. Blood-letting was also practised after the symptoms had appeared. Chalin de Vinario experimented with cupping and tried to moderate inflammation with leeches. When he discovered that most of those who were bled died, he is reported, according to Hecker, to have reserved that treatment for papal courtiers whose pomposity and sensual excesses infuriated him. Both Chauliac and Galeazzo opened the buboes and treated them like ulcers. Incisions were made in the inflammatory boils and they were then burned with red-hot irons, a procedure also recommended by Vinario. Carbuncles were leeched, scarified, and cauterized. Defoe describes such surgery during the plague of London in 1665. It is, of course, the account of a novelist writing about an event to which he was not an eye-witness, but amid the welter of abstract medical speculation about suffering, sometimes the imagined account rings truer, certainly it is more human, than the accounts of the professional attendants upon suffering:

> The pain of the swelling was in particular very violent, and to some intolerable; the physicians and surgeons may be said to have tortured many poor creatures even to death. The swellings in some grew hard, and they applied violent drawing-plasters, or poultices to break them, and if these did not do they cut and scarified them in a terrible manner. In some those swellings were made hard partly by the force of the distemper and partly by their being too violently drawn, and were so hard that no instrument could cut them, and then they burnt them with caustics, so that many died raving mad with the torment, and some in the very operation. In these distresses, some, for want of help to hold them down in their beds, or to look to them, laid hands upon themselves. . . . Some broke out into the streets, perhaps naked, and would run directly down to the river if they were not stopped by the watchman or other officers, and plunge themselves into the water wherever they found it.

All these measures, by the admission of the physicians themselves, were most uncertain. By the time the plague had advanced far enough upon the continent to demonstrate its virulence to those who tried to treat actual patients, the sublime and cloistered confidence of the Paris faculty's prescriptions had wholly evaporated.

Some steps were taken by administrators to confine and isolate the sick and to interrupt the spread of the disease, but these measures were totally inadequate and often misguided. In any case, by the time a sense of urgency was felt among officials it was too late to do anything: the disease was too far advanced to be stopped and the bureaucratic machinery in such disarray that even if effective measures might have been proposed they could not have been carried out. Since the contagious nature of the plague was early recognized, those who could frequently fled from their homes to wherever they felt they might be safer. The sick were often confined to their own houses, but since there were seldom any public programmes for the protection of society, such regulations were left to the individuals themselves to enforce. Families that could not leave an infected area often barricaded themselves in their houses, laying in a store of food and sealing the doors and windows. In many places attempts were made to dispose of the bodies of the dead beyond the walls of the city, but, as was so frequently the case in earlier severe outbreaks, these measures invariably failed under the crushing virulence of the disease. Too often the public measures that were taken give evidence not of planning but of hysterical fear. Chauliac reported that, at Avignon, guards were posted at the gates to allow into the city only those who were well known to them. And later, as true hysteria gripped the population and rumours of poisoners spread everywhere, if powders and salves were found on anyone, the owners, for fear that they were poisons, were forced to swallow them.

The first public regulations were issued in Reggio by Viscount Bernabo on January 17, 1374. Every plague patient was ordered to be taken out of the city into the fields, either to die there or recover. Those who attended the sick had to remain outside the city for ten days before they could associate with any uninfected person. The priests were to examine the diseased and to point out to special commissioners those who were infected, under punishment of confiscation of their property and being burned alive. Finally, none except those officially appointed to look after the sick were allowed to attend plague-patients, again under penalty of death and confiscation of all belongings. In 1383 Marseilles ordered a similar isolation of plague victims for forty days—a quarantine—the number of days being chosen probably because of Biblical influence rather than exact observation of the course of the disease. New ordinances in Reggio in 1399 required the fumigation of houses where the plague had struck and provided for the disinfection of clothing and bedding. But the earliest of these regulations was passed a quarter of a century after the first and most terrible attack.

Clearly inadequate as the medical measures to control the plague were, the helplessness of physicians can only be fully appreciated in the light of modern knowledge of the origin, transmission, prevention and treatment of the disease. It is so virulent and the symptoms so diverse that it is only in the last seventy years that medical science has been able to diagnose and treat it in anything approaching a satisfactory manner. As late as 1869 an eminent French physician declared that the Black Death was a completely new disease unlike anything that had occurred before or since.

In 1892 an article in the *British Medical Journal* reported an epidemic of 'Black Death' in Turkestan, which it distinguished from 'plague', the assumption being, apparently, that this was a very special and horrible disease that largely defied definition or treatment. It was not until Pasteur and Koch discovered the bacterial character of infectious disease that there was any possibility of analysing the real nature and means of transmission of the plague. Lucretius in his atomic theory of infection had faintly foreshadowed the doctrine of particular poisons; and Varro, a contemporary of his, had gone so far as to suggest that disease in animals was caused by living organisms beyond the range of human vision. Nohl quotes from a Jesuit Father, Athanasius Kircher, whose opinion on plague was presented by one Johannes Amerianos in 1667 in a treatise, asserting that 'the plague is nothing but a multitude of small animals and diminutive worms which fly about in the air, and when drawn into the body by the action of breathing they vitiate the blood, impair the spirits and finally gnaw into the flesh and glands. When they fly from an infected body, or, in some other manner, are received by a healthy subject, the plague is spread by them.' The remedy proposed is, characteristically enough, the same as that of Hippocrates, Galen, and the physicians of the 14th century: large fires should be kindled which, Kircher asserts, will burn off the wings and feet of these little plague worms 'so that they can no longer fly about and vitiate the blood of human beings and gnaw their bodies'. A later French physician, Antrechau, supported Kircher's theory of plague worms in 1721, and a German translation of his thesis contains in its introduction this charming admission that there may indeed be such micro-organisms: 'Who can fathom the limits of life in nature? Cannot still more minute (I hardly dare to call them animals) exist which in their composition and condition of life vary as much from the infusoria as these from all animals previously known? The suggestion is offered by the fact that these appear to be pursuing something still more minute which is no longer revealed by the magnifying glass.' During the London plague of 1665, according to Defoe, some were of the opinion that the disease 'might be distinguished by the party's breathing upon a piece of glass, where, the breath condensing, there might living creatures be seen by a microscope, of strange, monstrous, and frightful shapes, such as dragons, snakes, serpents, and devils, horrible to behold'. Others believed the breath of an infected person would kill birds and cause hens to lay rotten eggs. But it was not until 1894, during a terrible epidemic in Hong Kong, that the plague organism *Pasteurella pestis* (known also as *Bacillus pestis* and *Yersinia pestis*) was isolated and identified independently by Alexandre Yersin and Shibasaburo Kitasato.

In 1905 the Plague Research Commission in Bombay established the link between rats and the human disease. Such a connection had been made long ago—one recalls the plague of Ashdod—and Avicenna in the 11th century had clearly associated plague and rats, but it was only in the early years of this century that the Royal Society and the Lister Institute were able to elucidate the whole epidemiology of plague. It was discovered that it is primarily a disease of rodents, and epidemics in humans result from contact with infected rodents, usually rats, or their fleas. The disease normally passes from rodent to flea to rodent; man enters the cycle only accidentally. Although a modified form of the disease called sylvatic plague is endemic in ground squirrels, rats, marmots, prairie dogs, and other rodents in many places, including the western United States, men seldom contract the disease from wild rodents; it is the spread of the disease among domestic rodents in the area of human habitations that creates the conditions favourable for outbreaks among men. When an epizootic reduces the domestic rat population, fleas from the dead animals, failing to find another rodent host, begin to infest men. At first the cases are sporadic, but when other conditions are suitable, large numbers of people may become quickly infected.

The plague bacillus itself, *P. pestis*, is found in the local visicle of a flea bite, in the buboes that are characteristic of one form of the disease, in the blood of septicaemic cases, and in the sputum of pneumonic cases. Post-mortem examinations show large concentrations in the lymph nodes, spleen, bone marrow and liver. Outside the body the bacillus has a low resistance to heat and chemicals, but can remain alive in dried sputum for at least three months and in flea faeces at least five weeks. The bacillus is resistant to cold, and refrigerated cultures have remained active for as long as ten years; in moist soil it may remain infective for as long as seven months. The *P. pestis* is extremely virulent. Laboratory mice have been fatally infected with as few as three to ten bacilli. An infective flea, on the other hand, will disgorge as many as 24,000 organisms in a single bite. It is generally agreed that the virulence of the organism does not diminish in the course of an epidemic: the differences in response to infection are usually attributed to the degree of resistance possessed by the victim. Strains of *P. pestis* from rats, fleas, and men from all parts of the world are biologically identical, and the only sure diagnosis in individual cases is by bacteriological examination and identification of the bacillus. Certain strains of the *P. pestis* can be rendered avirulent for use in active immunization and the manufacture of anti-plague serums, but these strains are somewhat toxic.

The disease in humans is known to take three forms: bubonic, characterized by buboes, or inflammatory swelling of the lymph nodes; pneumonic; and septicaemic. The illness varies greatly among individuals and all degrees of severity have been observed, from a mild indisposition which may hardly be noticed to extreme violence equalled only by fulminating cholera. Mild infections are without exception bubonic; the other types are invariably severe and almost always fatal unless treated. The incubation period is usually three to six days, but has been known to be as short as thirty-six hours and as long as ten days. The onset of the disease is almost always sudden and well-marked.

About three-quarters of all cases are of the bubonic type. A typical case will begin with shivering and occasionally a rigour, followed by a rise in temperature with vomiting, headache, giddiness, intolerance for light, pain in the abdomen, back and limbs. There is usually sleeplessness, apathy, and often delirium, usually of the 'busy' type like delirium tremens. Headache is often very severe. The temperature varies greatly; it is seldom high on the first day, but has been known to rise rapidly to as much as 107. The eyes of the victims are red and inflamed and the tongue is swollen and dry. Prostration is marked, and most patients complain of constipation at first. Diarrhoea is a very grave sign. A severely ill person appears dazed and stupid, staggers, is thick of speech, and looks very much as if he were drunk. None of these symptoms, however, is a positive indication of plague; it is only with the appearance of buboes, usually between the first and the third day, that a positive diagnosis can be made. They form most often in the groin and armpit and usually only on one side of the body. They are extremely painful and patients complain that the pain is 'tearing' or 'cutting' them. If these swellings are not treated they usually form pus and open, but they may subside spontaneously or remain hard. Often small round red spots caused by haemorrhage in the skin appear over the buboes or on the abdomen shortly before death.

Because of the lack of contagion in the bubonic form of plague, it is widely imagined that the disease does not spread directly from man to man. The earliest truly scientific studies of plague, by French physicians in Egypt between 1833 and 1845, came to the same conclusion. The outbreak studied was less severe than many earlier ones, and the doctors determined that the disease was not especially contagious. The fact that it is generally seen, in modern times, in bubonic form, and is most frequently known as 'bubonic plague', adds to the confusion. Anthony Burgess, for instance, in his introduction to the Penguin edition of Defoe's *A Journal of the Plague Year*, states flatly that 'the infection from rat to man was conveyed almost solely by fleas, direct infection of man by man being extremely rare', in contradiction to most of the evidence of direct infection, man to man, which Defoe develops in the text that follows. The fact is that, in its pneumonic form, the disease is highly contagious. When large numbers of bacilli are localized in the lungs and expelled by coughing, and when environmental conditions—cold weather and crowding in poorly ventilated buildings—are favourable, the disease passes directly from man to man.

And it is the pneumonic form of the disease which is most frequently described by eye-witnesses of the old epidemics. It is a much more severe and much more deadly form of the plague. It begins with shivering, difficult and hurried breathing, coughing and spitting. Prostration is great and the course of the illness very rapid. Very soon breathing becomes extremely rapid—forty to sixty respirations a minute—and the face grows dusky. Spittle is soon mixed with blood, and later large amounts of blood teeming with plague bacilli may be coughed up. Temperature is high and irregular and death follows usually in three to four days. The course of the disease in its septicaemic form is even faster. When the plague bacillus is injected directly into the capillaries by the flea bite, or when the bacilli do not localize in the buboes, prostration and cerebral symptoms are particularly marked and violent. Temperature rises quickly to a very high level and the patient may become comatose and die within twenty-four hours. Recovery from both the pneumonic and septicaemic types is rare, and in all forms recovery is slow. Modern clinical evidence supports the contention of many earlier chroniclers of plague, that second attacks are rare.

An indication of the virulence of the disease and its contagiousness in the pneumonic form may be inferred from the extreme precautions recommended to those who must treat its victims: 'Strict isolation of patients in insect-proof rooms is essential. Clothing must be disinfected and disinfected of fleas in a steam sterilizer. All those who come in contact with the patient must wear gloves and gowns. If the infection is pneumonic or suspected of being pneumonic, physicians, nurses and any others in contact with the patient must be protected by complete overalls, gloves, hoods equipped with goggles, and face masks of eight layers of gauze covered by a deflection mask.'*

All three forms of the disease, as has been mentioned, are the result of infection by the same organism, and only a laboratory examination can clearly establish its presence. In isolated cases, diagnosis is difficult because the early symptoms can easily be confused with those of other diseases. Pneumonic plague has been thought to be influenza or lobar pneumonia in outbreaks in California. It has also been confused with typhus and malaria. However, in an epidemic of the disease in its severe form, the plague is relatively easy to identify. Needless to say, in light of the rapid progress of the disease, early diagnosis is essential. Modern treatment employs antibiotics: the first choice is streptomycin, but chloramphenicol, terramycin and aureomycin are also very effective. Where antimicrobial drugs are not available, sulfa drugs can be used both as preventive and cure. Early in the century a horse anti-serum was developed which proved moderately effective, but only after 1940 and the introduction of sulfonamide therapy has there been any really effective attack upon the plague bacillus.

The means of prevention follow logically from the modern knowledge of the disease and its method of transmission; they consist of sanitary measures against fleas and rodents, efforts to increase

* K. F. Meyer, 'Plague', *The Encyclopaedia Britannica*, ed. 1966.

individual resistance to the disease, and the isolation of the sick and handling with the greatest care all infectious materials. Insecticides used early have been known to bring an epidemic under control: a favourite method is to dust rat runs with DDT, a practice which not only kills the fleas on the rats—and sometimes even the rats themselves—but allows the insecticide to be carried to the rats' nests as well. More modern insecticides have proved even more effective than DDT. Since fleas acquire their infection from plague-infected rats, the rats themselves must be poisoned. Buildings and ships should be rat-proofed, and these days funnel-shaped rat-guards midway up the hawsers of moored ships are a common sight; their purpose, of course, is to prevent rats from landing. To increase individual resistance to plague, vaccination techniques have been developed; these do not always prevent infection, but they seem to reduce the seriousness of an attack. Modern medicines, insecticides and pest control measures ensure that no great epidemic of plague in its natural form could again afflict mankind. However, the bacteriological warfare experts of the U.S. Army are reported to have developed a strain of plague bacillus that is resistant to present medicine and control measures. If it should ever be released, the results would be unpredictable but, considering the prognosis of the disease, probably disastrous. The world is full of cruel ironies. Barely have scientists liberated mankind from a scourge as ancient as history than they employ their technical skill to recreate it, in an even more frightening form.

Modern clinical definition of the nature and treatment of plague makes doubly clear the helplessness of the 14th-century physician to understand the disease, much less prevent and treat it. It is hardly surprising then, that men turned to other sources of aid. As we have seen, writers as early as Ovid had believed that, while individual diseases might be the result of natural causes, epidemics were most probably of divine origin. Although it may seem to us that divine and natural causation are mutually exclusive, such a barrier was more easily bridged by a society more religiously oriented than our own. Defoe describes how the London plague could be thought of simultaneously as both a natural disease and a divine visitation, although he himself is convinced that 'no one in this whole nation ever received the sickness or infection but who received it in the ordinary way of infection from somebody, or the clothes or touch or stench of somebody that was infected before'. However, he says:

I reflect upon no man putting the reason of those things upon the immediate hand of God, and the appointment and direction of His providence. . . . But when I am speaking of the plague as a distemper arising from natural causes, we must consider it as it was really propagated by natural means; nor is it at all the less a judgement for its being under the conduct of human causes and effects; for, as the Divine Power has formed the whole scheme of nature and maintains nature in its course, so the same Power thinks fit to let His own actings with men, whether of mercy or judgement, to go on by those natural causes as the ordinary means, excepting and reserving to Himself nevertheless a power to act in a supernatural way when He sees occasion. Now 'tis evident that in the case of an infection there is no apparent extraordinary occasion for supernatural operation, but the ordinary course of things appears sufficiently armed, and made capable of all the effects that Heaven usually directs by a contagion. Among these causes and effects, this of the secret conveyance of infection, imperceptible and unavoidable, is more than sufficient to execute the fierceness of Divine vengeance, without putting it upon supernaturals and miracle.

Such a mingling of divine and natural causation was widely accepted in the Middle Ages, to the extent that medicine and theology were inextricably bound up, the natural world being hardly less mysterious than the supernatural. An anonymous primer for doctors of the period states that the first duty of the physician on entering a house is to ask the relations of the patient if he has confessed and received the holy sacrament, as upon this in the first instance his salvation depended. The patient must then be induced to pray and repent of his sins, or at least promise to do so, since disease is most frequently the consequence of sin. In the 14th century the scruples of Camus's priest about calling in a physician would have been of a somewhat different order, since the physician frequently performed a priestly function, just as the priest performed a medical one: he was as likely to be called in as the doctor to treat an illness, and his prayers and appeals to saints, his intercessions and relics and sacrifices would accompany or supplant the physician's herbs and potions. The situation of the physician was complicated, too, by the fact that the universities were under the jurisdiction of the Church, in whose estimation medicine was a secondary science. Thus when an effective cure was accomplished it was as likely to be attributed to divine intercession as to the skill of the physician; but when a patient died the physician was far more liable to be held responsible than was the priest. There would seem to be no end to the difficulties which faced the physicians in their attempts to treat and diagnose a disease they could not understand. Defoe describes the dilemma of one who had determined that the disease made itself known, before other symptoms appeared, by the smell of the breath, 'but then, as he said, who durst smell to that breath for his information? since, to know it, he must draw the stench of the plague up into his own brain in order to distinguish the smell'.

The obvious failure of medical science to deal effectively with the Black Death did little to recommend public confidence in doctors. Indeed, they began to be treated with great suspicion by a populace that had never really trusted them anyway. Their concern with natural causes brought upon them the ancient and enduring charge of atheism. And worse: rumours circulated that the physicians had actually started the plague in order to get their fees, and, in some instances, it is reported that after the plague had abated medical men were thrown into prison charged with all sorts of crimes against their patients. Most men instead, trusting to traditional authorities, turned even more frantically to the Church. Prayers and sacrifices and processions were conducted with increasing frenzy, culminating in the processions of Flagellants. Some, disillusioned with all authority, fell prey to outrageous quacks and gave themselves over to the most curious practices. Some, in accordance with the old adage that there are more old drunks than old doctors, deliberately pursued the dissolute life; while others, convinced that no one who had a venereal disease ever died of the plague, followed that rumour to its obvious conclusions. Men of a more refined sensibility, but following the same general pattern of thinking, surrounded themselves with objects of art, music, good books, good company, delicate food and fine wines, carefully cultivating the epicurean life in the conviction that if they could banish care they could preserve health.

In the 14th century all manner of quacks, midwives and wandering leeches operated openly, and many terrified sufferers submitted to their remedies and ate, drank and sniffed the most revolting concoctions imaginable. Oliver Wendell Holmes wrote of man's enormous capacity for suffering in pursuit of health: 'There is nothing men will not do, there is nothing they have not done to recover their health and save lives. They have submitted to be half-drowned in water, and half-choked with gases, to be buried up to their chins in earth, to be scarred with hot irons like galley slaves, to be crimped with knives like codfish, to have needles thrust into their flesh, and bonfires kindled on their skins, to swallow all sorts of abominations, and to pay for all this, as if to be singed and scalded were a costly privilege, as if blistering were a blessing and leeches a luxury.' He might well have had in mind the Black Death. Nor was it enough to suffer oneself: the idea spread that a victim could rid himself of the infection by infecting someone else. This belief, which was carried into practice by some frenzied sufferers, coupled with the all-too-common tendency of men in fearful circumstances to look for a human scapegoat upon which to vent the anger and frustration that is the inevitable product of their fear, led to the ultimate panic which demanded human sacrifice and, finally, the mass murder of other men. In light of the barbarities to be committed in the course of the following few years, the pronouncements of the Paris faculty of medicine in 1348 appear moderate and reasonable. They, at least, enjoin no actions that could do any great harm to self or others, even anything particularly painful or unpleasant. They may not have been any value in preventing or curing plague, but the prescriptions had, at least, the virtue of being innocuous.

As one traces the course of the Black Death through Europe the realization grows that this was a very special sort of catastrophe, altogether different from the ravages of war, different even from natural disasters like floods, earthquakes and volcanic eruptions: there was simply nothing dramatic about it for the people who endured it. In the reports of those who lived through it there is a feeling that even the greatest misfortunes, perhaps because they were so widespread, so frequent and of such a duration, became somehow monotonous. In even the most exact descriptions there is a sense of abstraction, perhaps of abstractedness, quite different from accounts of other disasters. There are no great deeds to be detailed, only the story of people numbed by the sense that they are victims of some monstrous and amorphous thing that advances inexorably to crush out everything in its path. Heroism and self-sacrifice are apparent everywhere as are cowardice and depravity, but the accounts of those who endured exhibit the paradoxical combination of reticence and brutality that one sometimes recognizes in the talk of soldiers of inconsequential rank who have been in the line so long that they no longer know or care if their side is winning or losing, or even what those terms mean: those for whom war has become simply an endless course of terror and fatigue mutated to a sort of boredom that destroys everything but the body's motor functions.

Such general horror defies description and beggars rhetoric.

Defoe writes: 'But after I have told you . . . that one man, being tied in his bed, and finding no other way to deliver himself, set the bed on fire with his candle, which unhappily stood within his reach, and burnt himself in his bed; and how another by the insufferable torment he bore, danced and sung naked in the streets, not knowing one ecstasy from another; I say, after I have mentioned these things, what can be added more?' There can be added, and there must be, the statistics, the particular effects upon communities, institutions and ideas; but in the welter of facts, one must try to remember that the disaster was, for those who lived through it, an experience of the most intense and anguished personal suffering coupled with the frustrating suspicion that no help whatsoever was available.

As a corrective to the impersonality of facts and the abstraction of statistics—as a relief too from the accounts of actual witnesses, themselves numbed, it would often seem, by the enormity of the disaster and the monotony of the unspeakable suffering—one must turn occasionally to imaginative literature, with its capacity for presenting the truth, not necessarily in terms of specific particulars of what actually occurred but rather in terms of what might have actually occurred, and almost certainly did, in order to remind ourselves that such a disaster is lived as individual and very particular suffering and frustration by individual and particular men. In this case, one turns to Camus's novel *The Plague*. The scene is a hospital. A child is dying of plague. The doctors and the priest have done everything for him that it is possible to do:

> They had already seen children die—for many months now death has shown no favoritism—but they had never yet watched a child's agony minute by minute, as they had now been doing since daybreak. Needless to say, the pain inflicted on these innocent victims had always seemed to them to be what in fact it was: an abominable thing. But hitherto they had felt its abomination in, so to speak, an abstract way; they had never had to witness over so long a period the death-throes of an innocent child.
>
> And just then the boy had a sudden spasm, as if something had bitten him in the stomach, and uttered a long, shrill wail. For moments that seemed endless he stayed in a queer, contorted position, his body racked by convulsive tremors; it was as if his frail frame were bending before the fierce breath of the plague, breaking under the reiterated gusts of fever. Then the storm-wind passed, there came a lull, and he relaxed a little; the fever seemed to recede, leaving him gasping for breath on a dank, pestilential shore, lost in a languor that already looked like death. When for the third time the fiery wave broke on him, lifting

him a little, the child curled himself up and shrank away to the edge
of the bed, as if in terror of the flames advancing on him, licking his
limbs. A moment later, after tossing his head wildly to and fro, he flung
off the blanket. From between the inflamed eyelids big tears welled up
and trickled down the sunken, leaden-hued cheeks. When the spasm
had passed, utterly exhausted, tensing his thin legs and arms, on which,
within forty-eight hours, the flesh had wasted to the bone, the child lay
flat, racked on the tumbled bed, in a grotesque parody of crucifixion. . . .

Light was increasing in the ward. The occupants of the other nine
beds were tossing about and groaning, but in tones that seemed
deliberately subdued. Only one, at the far end of the ward, was screaming, or rather uttering little exclamations at regular intervals, which
seemed to convey surprise more than pain. Indeed, one had the impression that even for the sufferers the frantic terror of the early phase
had passed, and there was a sort of mournful resignation in their
present attitude toward the disease. Only the child went on fighting
with all his little might. Now and then Rieux took his pulse—less
because this served any purpose than as an escape from utter helplessness—and when he closed his eyes, he seemed to feel its tumult
mingling with the fever of his own blood. And then, at one with the
tortured child, he struggled to sustain him with all the remaining
strength of his own body. But, linked for a few moments, the rhythms
of their heartbeats soon fell apart, the child escaped him, and again
he knew his impotence. Then he released the small, thin wrist and
moved back to his place.

The light on the whitewashed walls was changing from pink to
yellow. The first waves of another day of heat were beating on the
windows. . . . The child, his eyes still closed, seemed to grow a little
calmer. His clawlike fingers were feebly plucking at the sides of the
bed. Then they rose, scratched at the blanket over his knees, and suddenly he doubled up his limbs, bringing his thighs above his stomach,
and remained quite still. For the first time he opened his eyes and gazed
at Rieux, who was standing immediately in front of him. In the small
face, rigid as a mask of greyish clay, slowly the lips parted and from
them rose a long, incessant scream, hardly varying with his respiration,
and filling the ward with a fierce, indignant protest, so little childish
that it seemed like a collective voice issuing from all the sufferers
there. Rieux clenched his jaws, Tarrou looked away. Rambert went
and stood beside Castel, who closed the book lying on his knees.
Paneloux gazed down at the small mouth, fouled with the sordes of
plague and pouring out the angry death-cry that has sounded through
the ages of mankind. He sank on his knees, and all present found it
natural to hear him say in a voice hoarse but clearly audible across that
nameless, never-ending wail:

'My God, spare this child!'

But the wail continued without cease and the other sufferers began to grow restless. The patient at the far end of the ward, whose little broken cries had gone on without break, now quickened their tempo so that they flowed together in one unbroken cry, while the others' groans grew louder. A gust of sobs swept through the room, drowning Paneloux's prayer, and Rieux, who was still tightly gripping the rail of the bed, shut his eyes, dazed with exhaustion and disgust.

When he opened them again, Tarrou was at his side.

'I must go,' Rieux said. 'I can't bear to hear them any longer.'

But then, suddenly, the other sufferers fell silent. And now the doctor grew aware that the child's wail, after weakening more and more, had fluttered out into silence. Around him the groans began again, but more faintly, like a far echo of the fight that now was over. For it was over. Castel had moved round to the other side of the bed and said the end had come. His mouth still gaping, but silent now, the child was lying among the tumbled blankets, a small, shrunken form with the tears still wet on his cheeks.*

* Albert Camus, *The Plague*, trans. Stuart Gilbert (London, 1948), pp. 199–202.

Chapter IV

THE PLAGUE IN ITALY

PLAGUE-RIDDEN SHIPS from Kaffa brought the disease not only to Constantinople and Sicily but also to Italy. As early as January 1348, Genoese ships had carried the infection to their home port and to Venice, and from there the Black Death spread quickly throughout the Italian peninsula. The terrible devastation is recounted in numerous contemporary reports: Gabrielle de Mussi chronicles the progress of the epidemic in Genoa and in his native Piacenza, Agniolo de Tura writes of the devastation in Siena, there are numerous accounts of the ravages in Venice, and others of the terrors in Padua, Orvieto, Rimini and Pisa. In Florence, where the Death took its most terrible toll, there is the account of Matteo Villani and the much more famous one of Boccaccio, who introduces *The Decameron* with a description of the plague. In Parma, the poet Petrarch watched as nearly all his friends died and, as if this were not enough, received from Avignon the report of the death of his famous Laura; he has left in his letters not so much an account of the plague as an anguished personal cry against the injustice and incomprehensibility of such a tragedy. All of these accounts record the same appalling story of death and chaos, of futility, despair and frustration, of the almost total collapse of order and discipline in this unprecedented catastrophe. Some cities lost almost all their inhabitants: in Venice at least three-quarters died, in Florence contemporary accounts say between sixty and a hundred thousand; Hecker, taking the most conservative estimate, concludes that throughout Italy at least half the population died.

There is no complete contemporary account of the effects of the Black Death upon Italy as a whole, since the term had only a vague geographical significance in the 14th century. Although Italy was nominally a part of the Empire, the cities completely dominated the peninsula. In the south were the two kingdoms of Sicily: in the island of Sicily itself the House of Aragon had established itself, and on the mainland power was in the hands of the House of Anjou. In central Italy were the papal states, but the territory was small and the papacy, after the death of Boniface VIII, never regained the political power that it had once held. Benedict XI, who succeeded Boniface, died within the year, and his successor, Clement V, a Frenchman, never set foot in Italy after his coronation. The papacy fell under the influence of French interests and from 1309 to 1377 seven successive popes resided at Avignon, a period known as the Babylonian Captivity. In the absence of the papacy Rome lapsed into anarchy and lawlessness and during the period of the Black Death held very little of the Italian power and wealth. The great city-states of Florence, Milan, Venice and Genoa often treated the Emperor with contempt and vied among themselves for power and wealth. These cities developed a magnificent culture, and Italy became something of a centre of civilization, a role that France had held in the previous century; but there was as yet no feeling of national unity. The accounts of the Black Death in Italy reflect the political situation and are concerned almost exclusively with the effects of the epidemic upon individual cities.

Gabrielle de Mussi, who gave such a vivid account of the plague in Kaffa and in Sicily, continues to relate that some of the ships from Kaffa made for Genoa. A number of the sailors were already sick when the crews landed and de Mussi writes:

Tell, O Sicily, and ye, the many islands of the sea, the judgments of God. Confess, O Genoa, what thou hast done, since we of Genoa and Venice are compelled to make God's chastisement manifest. Alas! our ships enter the port, but of a thousand sailors hardly ten are spared. We reach our homes; our kindred and our neighbours come from all parts to visit us. Woe to us for we cast at them the darts of death! Whilst we spoke to them, whilst they embraced us and kissed us, we scattered the poison from our lips. Going back to their homes, they in turn soon infected their whole families, who in three days succumbed, and were buried in one common grave. Priests and doctors visiting the sick returned from their duties ill, and soon were numbered with the dead. O death! cruel, bitter, impious death! which thus breaks the bonds of affection and divides father and mother, brother and sister, son and wife. Lamenting our misery, we feared to fly, yet we dared not remain.

As soon as the terrible virulence of the disease began to be suspected, the terror increased. People were convinced that even the clothing and possessions of an infected person could communicate the disease; and de Mussi supports this idea with a story of four soldiers who carried away some blankets they had found in a house at Rivarolo, where, he says, the entire community had died of the plague. The soldiers, returning to their camp for the night, slept under their new-found blankets, and in the morning all four were discovered dead. Such rumours circulated freely, and one can only try to imagine the fear they must have caused in people who possessed no idea whatever of the nature of epidemics and found no help in the pronouncements of the most learned medical authorities. Added to the fear that ignorance always provokes, was that of isolation. In towns where all, or nearly all, the population died within a few weeks—and there were many such—there was no way to know that this was not the case throughout the entire world. Although the plague by-passed some towns and cities almost completely, to those who watched their entire community depopulated there was no way of knowing that the end of everything had not come. In Genoa, for instance, it is generally agreed that hardly one-seventh of the population survived. Such devastation coupled with a growing isolation from other cities, an isolation imposed not only by the lack of modern means of communication but by the conscious action of people themselves who feared that any newcomer might bring with him new and even more deadly infection, produced a climate in which the wildest rumours could be believed and the most devastating despair run unchecked.

The conditions of the cities themselves could only have added to the sense of panic as well as to the spread of the sickness. Crowded, unsanitary, no doubt often evil-smelling, they must in themselves have contributed to the feeling of the oppressiveness of the infection. Most of the prosperous cities of the old Roman Empire had declined and the new towns that grew up in the 12th and 13th centuries were founded first to afford protection for their inhabitants. To this end, they were compact and enclosed by walls for safety from attack; streets were narrow and the houses, mostly constructed of wood, were tall, frequently five or six storeys high, so as to crowd the largest number of people into the smallest area. Indeed, at one point, the ancient Roman city of Nimes had shrunk until its inhabitants huddled together inside the walls of the amphitheatre. The upper storeys of houses usually jutted out over the lower ones, so that the narrow, unpaved streets rarely if ever got the sun. In most towns there was no sanitation whatever, and the unlit streets were always muddy and dirty. Although many cities had a water supply, it very rarely reached individual houses and most

families had to obtain water from wells, springs and an occasional
public fountain. Since few houses had privies, most families emptied
their ordure into the yards, or directly into the street where a
stroller would have to dodge the slops poured from windows above
and the swilling hogs and swarming rats below. The market and
church were the only open spaces; there were no amphitheatres or
public baths as in the old Roman cities. Under such circumstances,
it is no wonder that personal hygiene was not well attended to. The
same article of clothing would be worn for months, years, or even
passed on for generations. Nor was this a custom of the poor only;
the aristocracy was not exempted, and if it is reported that the King
of England bathed once a week it is also reported that he frequently
missed the event. Under such conditions it is little wonder that
people were convinced that they could contract the disease from
the stench, or even, as is sometimes described, actually see the
plague coming through the streets as a pale fog.

And yet the Middle Ages was a time of such violent contrasts that
the cities, crowded and unhealthy and frequently unpleasant as they
must have been, provided the locale and stimulus for the magnificent art of the cathedrals, for the painting of Giotto, the Lorenzetti brothers, and a host of *trecento* painters, sculptors and archi-
tects. It is the age, too, of the exquisite art of Dante and Petrarch,
and the lusty ribaldry of Boccaccio. The political history of the
Middle Ages is such a jumble of intrigue, deceit and unveiled personal ambition that to study it is almost to forsake one's hope of
the possibility of human decency; but it is also the age of St.
Francis. The whole epoch is flavoured with this sense of paradox
and extreme contrast. It is an age in which the veneration of the
Virgin knew no bounds, and it is an age that produced some of the
most scurrilous anti-feminist literature of all time. And it was an
era that enjoyed playing with such paradoxes: *Ave* and *Eva*, the
same letters reversed: the source of hope and mercy and the source
of all man's ills. J. Huizinga, in his fascinating study *The Waning of
the Middle Ages*, writes, 'So violent and motley was life, that it bore
the mixed smell of blood and roses. The men of that time always
oscillate between the fear of hell and the most naïve joy, between
cruelty and tenderness, between harsh asceticism and insane attach-
ments to the delights of the world, between hatred and goodness,
always running to extremes.'

The city dweller, even if he had to endure the overcrowding and
lack of sanitation, the continual threat of disease and fire—the

wooden houses were tinderboxes and London had four huge fires in
the 12th century; Rouen burned six times between 1200 and 1225—
enjoyed far greater security than the peasant. By the 14th century
many towns which had grown up around the burg, the fortified
place (hence the terms *bürger*, burgess, *bourgeois*), had expanded,
with the building of walls to enclose the new houses at each stage
of development, to become lively centres of commerce and culture
where the ten per cent of the total population which lived in them
could consider themselves lucky. Town-dwellers had leisure and
freedom unknown to the peasant, and if city life was often oppressive, it was also frequently exciting. There were taverns where men
could drink when they wanted, a privilege almost unknown to the
peasant; guilds and associations of families provided a social life;
there were fairs and festivals and impressive processions; itinerant
preachers and story-tellers brought news and variety to life and
were received with an excitement that a society which gleans its
news and stories mostly from electronic equipment can only dimly
imagine. Huizinga reports that one such preacher, Olivier Maillard,
drew such an enormous crowd for his Lenten sermons at Orléans
that the roofs of surrounding houses were so severely damaged by
the spectators clambering for a vantage point from which to see
and hear him, that a roofer was occupied for the next sixty-four
days repairing them. There was noise and excitement everywhere:
bells rang to announce the hours of prayer, to call the people to
mourn and to rejoice, to announce danger; criers passed through
the streets telling the news. If a man were to lift his eyes from the
filth of the street he was greeted with the splendour of the churches,
a splendour and magnificence which still has its effect upon the
modern visitor to Florence, Siena, Venice, Paris, Chartres, Burgos,
or any of the dozens of cities which are still dominated by their
medieval cathedrals. If the streets were drab, the age itself certainly was not: colour was everywhere, perhaps nowhere more
stunningly than in the churches. The great rose window in Notre
Dame de Paris, or the many-hued light diffused within the Sainte-
Chapelle, has its emotional effect even upon people jaded with over-
exposure to Cinerama-Technicolor extravagances and psychedelic
light shows. Apart from the stained glass, the medieval cathedral is
apt to seem drab to the modern visitor, but to contemporaries they
were filled with colour. The painter completed the work of the
architect and the sculptor: mouldings, vaults, tracery and walls were
decorated in vivid paint and gold. Religious and doctrinal scenes

were depicted on the spaces of church walls, and chivalric incidents were painted on the walls of secular buildings.

And there were always the public executions. The Middle Ages did not accept the ideas which moderate justice today. Men did not trouble themselves with doubts of the criminal's responsibility for his acts or with the suspicion that society was an active force in producing criminal behaviour, which prohibits our taking much pleasure in the spectacle of a man's being punished. A condemned man deserved what he got and huge crowds turned out to see him get it. Executions evoked all the satisfaction of a morality play, and the event was frequently staged with care. Torture, mutilations, and executions would be performed in the market place where frequently a platform would have been erected. For crimes of violence and passion men were sometimes castrated, sometimes had an arm or leg amputated; execution was most frequently by hanging or decapitation. Often the corpse was mutilated and displayed for the edification of all. And the onlookers, untroubled by fears of judicial error or doubts of the condemned man's full responsibility for his crime, would return to their homes wiser and better men, having seen justice done. But if the age was cruel, it was also capable of mercy and compassion. If a condemned man were pardoned, the question of whether he deserved pardon or not was barely relevant, since mercy, like the mercy of God, must be gratuitous. Or if a criminal should endure his punishment with great courage or grace, the susceptible crowd might be moved to tears.

If the age harboured few doubts about the rightness of its judgement in terms of justice, it was not, in fact, a confident age. This very certainty of judgement put individual lives in jeopardy: even the quietest lives were often troubled with endless intrigues and law-suits. Wars were chronic and disease omnipresent. Over everything hung the sense of impending calamity, a terrible feeling of insecurity, and the obsessive fear that the end of the world was imminent. The towns had been built on commerce and commerce produced the wealth that made life in the towns free and exciting; but the very wealth that was the source of much that was good was itself not good. By common consent one of the greatest sins of the Middle Ages was cupidity. *Radix malorum est cupiditas*, preaches Chaucer's Pardoner, and the theme is echoed throughout the Middle Ages. Capitalism had not yet developed to the point where wealth was known by stocks and bonds and bank accounts; it was palpable, there to be seen: gold, fine clothes, horses. The enjoyment of riches was direct and primitive, but it was also productive of doubt and guilt and the object of hatred by those who were less fortunate. There was widespread resentment, even hatred, of the newly-rich bourgeois, a hatred which would be given impetus by the Black Death. In a world so filled with contrast and paradox, every sort of rumour could be credited. There was mystery everywhere. The natural world was poorly understood. An illustration from a 12th-century book about the people of the world shows fabulous creatures: men with their heads growing beneath their shoulders, men with hooves, dog-headed men, an 'Ethiopian' whose lower lip grows over the top of his head and whose enormous foot can be held up for a sun-shade. Monks, we are told, debated fervently how many angels could assemble on the point of a pin; the arguments, of course, were very real and important: either spiritual substances were material or they were immaterial; if they were immaterial then any number could occupy a given space, but if they were material, how much space *did* they occupy? The time is sometimes referred to as an 'Age of Faith' and, in the sense that all Europe assented to the spiritual authority of the Church, this is true; only the most radical reformers dared to question its basic doctrines and these accepted much more than they rejected. Even those few unfortunate eccentrics who class themselves among the Devil's helpers followed Church ritual in the parody of the Black Mass. But it was certainly not a time characterized by confidence and certainty. Insecurity and a fundamental pessimism were among its most pervasive characteristics. It was a world in which anything could happen and anything could be believed; but faith implies doubt: by its very definition faith is the acceptance by an act of will of a concept for which there is inadequate empirical evidence, or as the wags have it, 'Faith is believing what you know isn't so.'

It was into this world of motley and claustrophobic cities, of complex paradoxes and extreme contrasts, of violence and beauty, of deep faith and even deeper insecurity, that the Black Death made its way. In the following accounts one can trace the devastation of the epidemic, the history of death and disorder, but the important history of the plague is perhaps more apparent in that which is not written than in that which is. What men suffer is of interest, but what they think and feel and do about their suffering, the attitude that they assume before the inevitable, is the very stuff of human history. One would like to take the chronicler by the lapel, back him into a corner and demand: 'Yes, but what did you do, what did you feel, what did you think? How did you reconcile this disaster with your general concept of the nature of things?' It is in their failure to provide explicit insights into doubts that the plague must have created in the minds of the writers that the contemporary accounts fall short. But perhaps they only seem to fall short. It is more often in what men do not say than in what they do that one discovers their true thoughts and attitudes. In the abstractedness of some of these accounts—the very absence of the expression of doubts—a sensitive reader may find a revelation of resignation before the inevitable, of striving for objectivity and understanding, of courage before death which has suddenly become not a natural occurrence but an almost palpable force. They reveal a sort of desperate attempt to maintain control of reason and to make some kind of order out of chaos which reveals more about the age than any amount of introspective analysis could ever do. In what is omitted in these accounts one can sometimes sense what is to come: a vast revolution in thought and attitude, a new departure for mankind.

*

Gabrielle de Mussi's account continues to record the terror in Piacenza. Until quite recently it had been believed that de Mussi was himself a passenger on one of the plague-ships from Kaffa; but it is fairly certain that he was, in fact, in Piacenza during 1347, although it would seem from his description of the early attacks of plague that he had access to the accounts of eye-witnesses. In his chronicle of the disease in his native town, however, he provided even more specific details. He continues:

> But as an inhabitant I am asked to write more of Piacenza so that it may be known what happened there in the year 1348. Some Genoese who fled from the plague raging in their city betook themselves higher. They rested at Bobbio, and there sold merchandise they had brought with them. The purchaser and their host, together with all his family and many neighbours, were quickly stricken with the sickness and died. One of these, wishing to make his will, called a notary, his confessor, and the necessary witnesses. The next day all these were buried together. So greatly did the calamity increase that nearly all the inhabitants of Bobbio soon fell a prey to the sickness, and there remained in the town only the dead.
> In the spring of 1348 another Genoese infected with the plague came to Piacenza. He sought out his friend Fulchino della Croce, who took

him into his house. Almost immediately afterwards he died, and the said Fulchino was also quickly carried off with his entire family and many of his neighbours. In a brief space the plague was rife throughout the city. I know not where to begin; everywhere there was weeping and mourning. So great was the mortality that men hardly dared to breathe. The dead were without number, and those who still lived gave themselves up as lost, and prepared for the tomb.

The cemeteries failing, it was necessary to dig trenches to receive the bodies of the dead. It frequently happened that a husband and wife, a father and son, a mother and daughter—nay, whole families —were cast together in the same pit.

It was the same in the neighbouring towns and villages. One Oberto de Sasso, who had come one day from an infected place to the church of the Friars Minor to make his will, called thither a notary, witnesses, and neighbours. All these, together with others, to the number of more than sixty, died within a short space of time. Also the religious man, friar Sifredo de Bardi, of the convent and order of Preachers, a man of prudence and great learning, who had visited our Lord's sepulchre, died with twenty-three other members of his order and convent. Also the learned and virtuous friar, Bertolin Coxadocha, of Piacenza, of the order of Minorites, with four-and-twenty members of his community was carried off. So too of the convent of Augustinian Hermits—seven; of the Carmelites—seven; of the Servites of Mary—four; and more than sixty dignitaries and rectors of churches in the city and the district of Piacenza died. Of nobles, too, many; of young people a vast number.

The account proceeds with the now familiar story of the despair of the sick, abandoned by family and friends, unable to procure help from anyone; the helplessness of the doctors; the fearfulness of the priest called to administer the sacraments; and finally the abandonment of the most rudimentary funeral traditions: no prayers were said, no bells tolled even for the death of the nobility, the perfunctory burial of corpses in a common plague-pit. Houses were desolate and abandoned, but no one dared to enter.

Venice, another port by which the plague entered Italy, was devastated. Hecker estimates that at least three out of every four people there died; Nohl says that fifty patrician families died out completely in 1348. A contemporary account says there were 100,000 deaths in the city, but, as we have seen, all such large, round numbers from medieval sources should be treated with considerable suspicion. In Venice the physicians fled before the epidemic or shut themselves up in their houses and left the care of the sick almost entirely to the surgeons, led by Andrea de Padova, who is credited with saving the lives of over a hundred people. In the absence of the physicians, artisans and even youths tended the sick under the direction of the surgeons and with some degree of success. At first some attempt at organization was made by the Grand Council which on March 30, 1348, appointed three men to act as a Committee of Public Safety. The Committee had burial-pits dug in one of the islands of the lagoon and arranged a service of boats to transport the bodies. But soon, even this broke down. The rich fled; officials either fled or died in such great numbers that the bureaucratic machinery failed. The Great Council could not assemble enough members for the transaction of business; and soon, in a final admission of helplessness, the prisons were thrown open and everyone who could left the city. An anonymous chronicler of the time records his impression of the plague:

> And here I can give my testimony. A certain man bled me, and the blood flowing touched his face. On that same day he was taken ill, and the next he died; and by the mercy of God I have escaped. I note this because, as by mere communication with the sick the plague infected mortally the healthy, the father afterwards avoided his stricken son, the brother his brother, the wife her husband, and so in each case the man in health studiously avoided the sick. Priests and doctors even fled in fear from those ill, and all avoided the dead. In many places and houses when an inmate died the rest quickly, one after another, expired. And so great was the overwhelming number of the dead, that it was necessary to open new cemeteries in every place.

Just as boys had been recruited to serve as physicians, so too they performed sacred offices. The report says that, 'This pestilence did not cease in the land from February till the feast of All Saints, and the offices of the dead were chanted only by the voices of boys; which boys, without learning, and by rote only, sang the office walking through the streets.' Reconstruction of social order in Venice after the plague was an especially formidable task. The Senate had great difficulty in finding doctors to serve again in the city; Gasquet has preserved a letter from a physician, Marco Leon, a native of Venice practising in Perugia. In January 1349 he offered to come to Venice, 'since it has pleased God by the terrible mortality to leave our native place so destitute of upright and capable doctors that it may be said not one has been left'. In order to repopulate the city, the Doge invited foreigners to settle there and promised them the rights of citizenship after two years residence.

In nearby Padua the devastation was nearly as great. A stranger is reported to have brought the disease to the city, and soon the same dismal story is repeated: if one person fell sick in a house, soon the entire family was seized, even the animals; before it had run its course the plague carried off two-thirds of the population of the town. In the Adriatic port of Rimini, the sickness began on May 15, 1348, and lasted until the following December. Here, a chronicler notes, the poor were the first to suffer, but soon the disease was widespread and, once again, two out of every three inhabitants died. In Orvieto, also, the epidemic began in May and lasted until September; when it was over it was found that many families had become extinct. Verona lost three-quarters of its population; Bologna two-thirds. The disease appeared on the opposite coast of the Adriatic at the same time, either spread from northern Italy or perhaps carried there by ships from the East. In Dalmatia, the port of Ragusa was attacked as early as January 13, 1348, and more than 7,000 people are said to have died there. In Spalatro the Archbishop was among the dead, and to add to the terror wolves and other wild animals came down from the mountains and fell upon the city, attacking those who had been spared by the plague.

Rome, which had been so hard hit by plague in ancient times, seems to have suffered less from the Black Death than many other Italian cities. Nevertheless, there remains a monument of the plague in the flight of marble steps leading up to the church of Ara Coeli which was set up by Giovanni di Colonna in October 1348 and designed for use by citizens who, with ropes around their necks and with ashes on their heads, climbed the hill bare-footed to implore the Virgin to end the plague. There is a legend in Rome that, as the panic-stricken people were carrying an effigy of the Virgin from the Ara Coeli to St. Peter's, the statue of the angel on the Castel San Angelo bowed its head to them. Ironically, when Clement VI in 1350 called for a celebration of the Jubilee in Rome, the pestilence broke out more viciously than in 1348 and Hecker reports that not one in one hundred of the many pilgrims escaped.

In Tuscany also the plague raged. In Pisa seven-tenths of the inhabitants died, and many families were completely destroyed. Law and order broke down there, too, and a contemporary chronicle records that the administration of justice became impossible and criminals of every sort roamed freely through the streets. For a considerable time after the plague abated in September 1348 the courts were occupied with disputes over the possessions of the dead.

In Siena the plague raged from April until October and, according
to the *Cronica Senese* of Agnolo di Tura, 80,000 people died in
those seven months. Terror seized the town and people were convinced that the end of the world had come; neither money, power,
nor social position was inducement enough to procure aid or even
porters to carry the dead to the public plague-pits. The chronicler
reports, 'And I, Agnolo di Tura, carried with my own hands my
five little sons to the pit; and what I did many others did likewise.'
The expanding economy of the city was checked and the deaths of
many painters, among them the brothers Pietro and Ambrogio
Lorenzetti, ended the development of the first Sienese school.
Even today the effects of the Black Death may be seen in Siena: the
Duomo, begun in 1339 to the plans of Lando Orefice, was only
partially finished when the plague struck. The transepts had been
built, the foundations of the nave and choir laid, and the walls
partly raised, but money collected for the building was diverted
to the urgent public purposes of aiding the sick and burying the
dead, and the cathedral was never finished according to the original
plans. Splendid as it is, it is a mere fragment of what the Sienese
had intended to erect as a memorial to the glory of their city before
the Black Death.

Florence was so devastated that for a long time the disease itself
was known as 'the plague of Florence'. Estimates of the dead vary
greatly: Villani says three out of every five died, Antoninus, the
Archbishop, estimates the toll at 60,000, Boccaccio says 100,000.
Hecker accepts 60,000; Previté-Orton prefers the figure of at least
half the population. As has already been mentioned, the Florentines
had been weakened by a severe famine in 1347 when, according to
Giovanni Villani, some 94,000 people required aid from the city
and 4,000 died. The famine had followed several bad seasons; and
the incursions of the Free Companies, wandering bands of temporarily unemployed mercenary soldiers, had contributed to the
distress. The economic situation of the city, too, was in a state of
disorganization. The banking houses had been going into liquida-
tion since 1339, and in 1346 the greatest of them fell, the Bardi and
the Peruzzi, dragging down with them a number of lesser houses
and wealthy Florentine families who were their creditors, including
the Villani. Wages and prices had risen steeply, and the whole city
was ripe for disaster and chaos.

Giovanni Villani died in the plague, and his brother Matteo took
up his work, beginning with a description of the effects of the

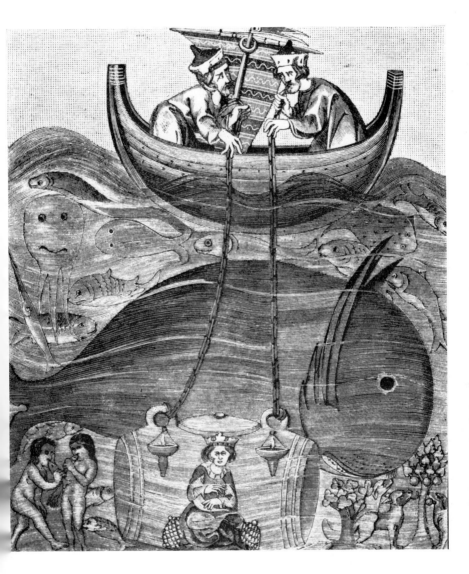

'HOW ALEXANDER LOWERED HIMSELF INTO THE SEA
IN A GLASS BARREL':
AN OUTLANDISH MEDIEVAL CONCEPTION OF THE
NATURAL WORLD

ARLES IN THE MIDDLE AGES:
'OVERCROWDING AND LACK OF SANITATION'

disease. In his estimation the world had not known such a catastrophe since the Flood, and like the Flood, it was sent upon man as
punishment for his sins. His account, like so many others, enlarges
upon the futility of all preventives and remedies and takes notice of
the disease's infectiveness which was such that it could be caught by
simply looking at an afflicted person. Many people fled the city and
those few who remained to help the sick usually fell ill and died
themselves. Villani was appalled by the depravity and demoralization that followed the plague: 'Men gave themselves up to the enjoyment of worldly riches to which they had succeeded' and refused to
work, indulged in idleness and revelry, fickleness of dress, carousing
in taverns. The rich yielded to every whim, but so did the poor who
were convinced that since so many had died there was now an
abundance of wealth for all. The mood of gaiety was so pervasive
that it took the official form of orders forbidding the publishing of
the numbers of plague-dead and the tolling of funeral bells, in
order that the living might not abandon themselves to despair.
Villani blamed the Black Death for the social and moral degeneration and the political anarchy that followed it in Florence.

By far the most famous account of the Black Death can be found
in Giovanni Boccaccio's *Decameron*, where his description of the
the plague in Florence provides both an introduction for a collection of tales and a dramatic framework in which to set them: a
company of young men and women flee the city to the sanctuary of
a palace in the countryside to wait out the epidemic in greater
safety. One may suspect that the evocation of the horrors of the
plague is exaggerated in order to provide dramatic contrast to the
ribald stories that follow, and this suspicion is encouraged by the
obvious influence of Thucydides and by the suggestion of some
critics that Boccaccio himself sat out the plague in Naples and was
thus not a witness to what he describes. But whatever his dramatic
purposes and his source of information, Boccaccio's account agrees
substantially with that of Villani and has the virtue of being considerably more vivid. One of the great literary descriptions of
plague, together with those of Thucydides, Defoe, Manzoni and
Camus, it deserves to be quoted at length, as the most detailed
account of the conditions in a city stricken with the Black
Death. After stating that the disease was sent by God as a punishment for sin, Boccaccio delineates the symptoms and notes that
neither the medicine of the doctors nor the prayers and supplications of the priests had any effect upon it. He then moves on

to the extreme virulence of the disease and the terror it brought to
Florence:

> And this pestilence was the more virulent for that, by communica-
> tion with those who were sick thereof, it gat hold upon the sound, no
> otherwise than fire upon things dry or greasy, whenas they are brought
> very near thereunto. Nay, the mischief was yet greater; for that not
> only did converse and consortion with the sick give the sound infection
> or cause of common death, but the mere touching of the clothes or of
> whatsoever thing had been touched or used of the sick appeared of itself
> to communicate the malady to the toucher. A marvellous thing to hear
> is that which I have to tell and one which, had it not been seen of
> many men's eyes and of mine own, I had scarce dared credit, much less
> set down in writing, though I had heard it from one worthy of belief. I
> say, then, that of such efficience was the nature of the pestilence in
> question in communicating itself from one to another, that, not only
> did it pass from man to man, but this, which is much more, it many
> times visibly did; —to wit, a thing which had pertained to a man sick or
> dead of the aforesaid sickness, being touched by an animal foreign to
> the human species, not only infected this latter with the plague, but in
> a very brief space of time killed it. Of this mine own eyes (as hath a
> little before been said) had one day, among others, experience on this
> wise; to wit, that the rags of a poor man, who had died of the plague,
> being cast out into the public way, two hogs came up to them and
> having first, after their wont, rooted amain among them with their
> snouts, took them in their mouths and tossed them about their jaws;
> then, in a little while, after turning round and round, they both, as if
> they had taken poison, fell down dead upon the rags with which they
> had in an ill hour intermeddled.
>
> From these things and many others like unto them or yet stranger
> divers fears and conceits were begotten in those who abode alive, which
> well nigh all tended to a very barbarous conclusion, namely, to shun and
> flee from the sick and all that pertained to them, and thus doing, each
> thought to secure immunity for himself. Some there were who con-
> ceived that to live moderately and keep oneself from all excess was the
> best defence against such a danger; wherefore, making up their com-
> pany, they lived removed from every other and shut themselves up in
> those houses where none had been sick and where living was best; and
> there, using very temperately of the most delicate viands and the finest
> wines and eschewing all incontinence, they abode with music and such
> other diversions as they might have, never suffering themselves to
> speak with any nor choosing to hear any news from without of death
> or sick folk. Others, inclining to the contrary opinion, maintained that
> to carouse and make merry and go about singing and frolicking and
> satisfy the appetite in everything possible and laugh and scoff at what-

soever befell was a very certain remedy for such an ill. That which they said they put in practice as best they might, going about day and night, now to this tavern, now to that, drinking without stint or measure; and on this wise they did yet more freely in other folk's houses, so but they scented there aught that liked or tempted them, as they might lightly do, for that every one—as he were to live no longer—had abandoned all care of his possessions, as of himself, wherefore the most part of the houses were become common good and strangers used them, whenas they happened upon them, like as the very owner might have done; and with all this bestial preoccupation, they still shunned the sick to the best of their power. In this sore affliction and misery of our city, the reverend authority of the laws, both human and divine, was all in a manner dissolved and fallen into decay for (lack of) the ministers and executors thereof, who, like other men, were all either dead or sick or else left so destitute of followers that they were unable to exercise any office, wherefore every one had licence to do whatever pleased him. . . .

Indeed, leaving be that townsman avoided townsman and that well nigh no neighbour took thought unto other and that kinsfolk seldom or never visited one another and held no converse together save from afar, this tribulation had stricken such terror to the hearts of all, men and women alike, that brother forsook brother, uncle nephew and sister brother and oftentimes wife husband; nay (what is yet more extraordinary and well nigh incredible) fathers and mothers refused to visit or tend their very children, as they had not been theirs. By reason whereof there remained unto those (and the number of them, both males and females, was incalculable) who fell sick, none other succour than that which they owed either to the charity of friends (and of these there were few) or the greed of servants, who tended them, allured by high and extravagant wage; albeit, for all this, these latter were not grown many, and those men and women of mean understanding and for the most part unused to such offices, who served for well nigh nought but to reach things called for by the sick or to note when they died; and in the doing of these services many of them perished with their gain.

Of this abandonment of the sick by neighbours, kinsfolk and friends and of the scarcity of servants arose an usage before well nigh unheard, to wit, that no woman, how fair or lovesome or well-born soever she might be, once fallen sick, recked aught of having a man to tend her, whatever he might be, or young or old, and without any shame discovered to him every part of her body, no otherwise than she would have done to a woman, so but the necessity of her sickness required it; the which belike, in those who recovered, was the occasion of lesser modesty in time to come. . . .

It was then (even as we yet see it used) a custom that the kinswomen and she-neighbours of the dead should assemble in his house and there condole with those who more nearly pertained unto him, whilst his neighbours and many other citizens foregathered with his next of kin before his house, whither, according to the dead man's quality, came the clergy, and he with funeral pomp of chants and candles was borne on the shoulders of his peers to the church chosen by himself before his death; which usages, after the virulence of the plague began to increase, were either altogether or for the most part laid aside, and other and strange customs sprang up in their stead. For that, not only did folk die without having a multitude of women about them, but many there were who departed this life without witness and few indeed were they to whom the pious plaints and bitter tears of their kinsfolk were vouchsafed; nay, in lieu of these things there obtained, for the most part, laughter and jests and gibes and feasting and merry-making in company; which usance women, laying aside womanly pitifulness, had right well learned for their own safety.

Few, again, were they whose bodies were accompanied to the church by more than half a score or a dozen of their neighbours, and of those no worshipful and illustrious citizens, but a sort of blood-suckers, sprung from the dregs of the people, who styled themselves *pickmen* [*becchini*, i.e. gravediggers] and did such offices for hire, shouldered the bier and bore it with hurried steps, not to that church which the dead man had chosen before his death, but most times to the nearest, behind five or six priests, with little light and whiles none at all, which latter, with the aid of the said pickmen, thrust him into what grave soever they first found unoccupied, without troubling themselves with too long or formal a service.

The condition of the common people (and belike, in great part, of the middle class also) was yet more pitiable to behold, for that these, for the most part retained by hope or poverty in their houses and abiding in their own quarters, sickened by the thousand daily and being altogether untended and unsuccoured, died well nigh all without recourse. Many breathed their last in the open street, whilst other many, for all they died in their houses, made it known to the neighbours that they were dead rather by the stench of their rotting bodies than otherwise; and of these and others who died all about the whole city was full. For the most part one same usance was observed by the neighbours, moved more by fear lest the corruption of the dead bodies should imperil themselves than by any charity they had for the departed; to wit, that either with their own hands or with the aid of certain bearers, whenas they might have any, they brought the bodies of those who had died forth of their houses and laid them before their doors, where, especially in the morning, those who went about might see corpses without number; then they fetched biers and some, in default thereof, they laid upon some board or other. Nor was it only one bier that carried two or three corpses, nor did this happen but once; nay, many might have been counted which contained husband and wife, two or three brothers, father and son or the like. And an infinite number of times it befell that, two priests going with one cross for some one, three or four biers, borne by bearers, ranged themselves behind the latter, and whereas the priests thought to have but one dead man to bury, they had six or eight, and whiles more. Nor therefore were the dead honoured with aught of tears or candles or funeral train; nay, the thing was come to such a pass that folk recked no more of men that died than nowadays they would of goats; whereby it very manifestly appeared that that which the natural course of things had not availed, by dint of small and infrequent harms, to teach the wise to endure with patience, the very greatness of their ills had brought even the simple to expect and make no account of. The consecrated ground sufficing not to the burial of the vast multitude of corpses aforesaid, which daily and well nigh hourly came carried in crowds to every church—especially if it were sought to give each his own place, according to ancient usance, —there were made throughout the churchyards, after every other part was full, vast trenches, wherein those who came after were laid by the hundred and being heaped up therein by layers, as goods are stowed aboard ship, were covered with a little earth, till such time as they reached the top of the trench.

Moreover,—not to go longer searching out and recalling every particular of our past miseries, as they befell throughout the city,—I say that, whilst so sinister a time prevailed in the latter, on no wise therefore was the surrounding country spared, wherein (letting be the castles, which in their littleness were like unto the city) throughout the scattered villages and in the fields, the poor and miserable husbandmen, and their families, without succour of physician or aid of servitor, died, not like men, but well nigh like beasts, by the ways or in their tillages or about the houses, indifferently by day and night. By reason whereof, growing lazy like the townsfolk in their manners and customs, they recked not of any thing or business of theirs; nay, all as if they looked for death that very day, studied with all their wit, not to help to maturity the future produce of their cattle and their fields and the fruits of their own past toils, but to consume those which were ready to hand. Thus it came to pass that the oxen, the asses, the sheep, the goats, the swine, the fowls, nay, the very dogs, so faithful to mankind, being driven forth of their own houses, went straying at their pleasure about the fields, where the very corn was abandoned without being cut, much less gathered in; and many, well nigh like reasonable creatures, after grazing all day, returned at night, glutted, to their houses, without the constraint of any herdsman.

To leave the country and return to the city, what more can be said save that such and so great was the cruelty of heaven (and in part, peradventure, that of men) that, between March and the following

July, what with the virulence of that pestiferous sickness and the number of sick folk ill-tended or forsaken in their need, through the fearfulness of those who were whole, it is believed for certain that upward of an hundred thousand human beings perished within the walls of the city of Florence, which, peradventure, before the advent of that death-dealing calamity, had not been accounted to hold so many? Alas, how many great palaces, how many goodly houses, how many noble mansions, once full of families, of lords and of ladies, abode empty even to the meanest servant! How many memorable families, how many ample heritages, how many famous fortunes were seen to remain without lawful heir! How many valiant men, how many fair ladies, how many sprightly youths, whom, not others only, but Galen, Hippocrates or Aesculapius themselves would have judged most hale, breakfasted in the morning with their kinsfolk, comrades and friends and that same night supped with their ancestors in the other world!*

In this tale of unrelieved misery and depravity, there is one bright spot. The Compagnia della Misericordia, established in Florence in 1244 for the service of the sick, remained devoted to its tasks and also helped transport the dead. A picture by Cigoli (1559–1613), now in the church of the Misericordia, shows the brotherhood in their red hoods and gowns gathering up the dead and the dying at the foot of Giotto's tower. Even into the 20th century they continued their service, still wearing robes and hoods masking the entire face except the eyes, but black now instead of red, and driving ambulances instead of carrying hand-litters.

To Boccaccio's account of the plague in Florence must be added that of Petrarch. Petrarch endured the Black Death in Parma and his response to it is quite unlike that of Boccaccio. It is a very personal lamentation, preserved in his letters. The inhabitants of Parma tried to keep the infection out of their city by strictly prohibiting intercourse with people from the already stricken cities of Florence, Venice, Genoa and Pisa; and these measures seem to have had some good effect because the plague did not reach Parma until the beginning of June 1348. However, when it made its appearance, it was no less virulent than in other Italian cities, and in Parma and Reggio an estimated 40,000 died in the space of six months. Petrarch, who was at the time a canon of the cathedral of Parma, had met Laura de Noves at Avignon in his youth; he admired her as a typical Christian mother of a family and she came to be for him a source of poetic inspiration. Laura died at Avignon, a victim of the

* Giovanni Boccaccio, *The Decameron*, trans. John Payne (New York, 1946 edition), pp. 8–17.

plague that was raging there, and Petrarch learned of her death in a letter from a friend which he received in May 1348. Later he expressed the sadness he felt at her death in some lines he wrote on a manuscript of Virgil:

Laura, illustrious by her virtues, and long celebrated in my songs, first greeted my eyes in the days of my youth, the 6th April, 1327, at Avignon; and in the same city, at the same hour of the same 6th April, but in the year 1348, withdrew from life, whilst I was at Verona, unconscious of my loss. The melancholy truth was made known to me by letter, which I received at Parma on the 19th May.

Her chaste and lovely body was interred on the evening of the same day in the Church of the Minorites: her soul, as I believe, returned to heaven, whence it came.

To write these lines in bitter memory of this event, and in the place where they will most often meet my eyes, has in it something of a cruel sweetness, but I forget that nothing more ought in this life to please me, which by the grace of God need not be difficult to one who thinks strenuously and manfully on the idle cares, the empty hopes, and the unexpected end of the years that are gone.

Then, as the plague raged in Parma, the poet wrote to his brother, a religious at Monrieux, who, as the only survivor out of thirty-five, had remained, alone with his dog, to guard and tend the monastery. Petrarch's letter is not entirely free of literary affectation with its rather self-conscious allusions to the classics; but then neither is Boccaccio's account free of the influence of Thucydides. The genuine anguish of Petrarch's letter is just as apparent as is the horror of Boccaccio's account. In both cases the formal framework of rhetoric may have been the only thing available to contain the emotion:

My brother! my brother! my brother! A new beginning to a letter, though used by Marcus Tullius fourteen hundred years ago. Alas! my beloved brother, what shall I say? How shall I begin? Whither shall I turn? On all sides is sorrow; everywhere is fear. I would, my brother, that I had never been born, or, at least, had died before these times. How will posterity believe that there has been a time when without the lightnings of heaven or the fires of earth, without wars or other visible slaughter, not this or that part of the earth, but well-nigh the whole globe, has remained without inhabitants.

When has any such thing been ever heard or seen; in what annals has it ever been read that houses were left vacant, cities deserted, the country neglected, the fields too small for the dead and a fearful and universal solitude over the whole earth? Consult your historians, they are silent; question your doctors, they are dumb, seek an answer from your philosophers, they shrug their shoulders and frown, and with their fingers to their lips bid you be silent.

Will posterity ever believe these things when we, who see, can scarcely credit them? We should think we were dreaming if we did not with our eyes, when we walk abroad, see the city in mourning with funerals, and returning to our home, find it empty, and thus know that what we lament is real.

Oh, happy people of the future, who have not known these miseries and perchance will class our testimony with the fables. We have, indeed, deserved these (punishments) and even greater; but our forefathers also have deserved them, and may our posterity not also merit the same . . .

To turn from public to private sorrows; the first part of the second year is passed since I returned to Italy. I do not ask you to look back any further; count these few days, and think what we were and what we are. Where are now our pleasant friends? Where the loved faces? Where their cheering words? Where their sweet and gentle conversation? We were surrounded by a crowd of intimates, now we are almost alone.

Even after the Black Death had passed on to other lands, general distress persisted in Italy. The social disorganization it had caused was slow to be repaired and famine beset many communities for years after. Law courts were bogged down with the tangled claims of heirs to the fortunes left by the plague's victims; many cities found that competent officials and doctors could not be found to replace those who had died. For years after it had abated, the Black Death was the cause of, and often the excuse for, all sorts of irregularities in government and business. In the countryside land remained uncultivated; in the cities the lavish and dissolute habits of the survivors persisted. As if this were not enough, the pestilence was to recur again and again: there was plague in Europe for thirty-two years of the 14th century, for forty-one years of the 15th, for thirty years of the 16th; and Italy, which lost at least half its inhabitants during the years 1348–50, like the rest of Europe, was not to regain the population that it held before the Black Death until the beginning of the 16th century.

Chapter V

FRANCE, GERMANY, AND THE
REST OF THE CONTINENT

THE FIRST outbreak of the Black Death in France occurred at Marseilles. It is believed to have been brought by Genoese ships turned away from their home port by the inhabitants; the Genoese were already suffering from the plague and beginning to suspect that it had entered their city by way of ships sailing from the East. Although one report says that the first deaths were as early as November 1347, it is generally agreed that the plague was not established in Marseilles until January of the next year. Its ravages in that city were as great as they had been in the Italian ports; a contemporary account says that 57,000 died in Marseilles and the surrounding villages. The clergy was especially hard hit: the Bishop with the entire chapter of the cathedral and nearly all the friars, preachers, and Minorites were reported dead. One chronicler estimates that two-thirds of the inhabitants died and says that after the disease had at last abated the city was nearly uninhabited. Ships loaded with merchandise, but with their entire crews dead, drifted aimlessly in the harbour. In nearby Montpellier the devastation was even greater. Of the twelve magistrates of the city ten died, and the numerous monasteries were almost totally depopulated. An account of the plague in Montpellier has been left by Simon de Covino, a doctor from Paris, who in 1350 set down his recollections in Latin hexameter verse. His analysis of the symptoms coincides with modern clinical definition; he describes the buboes which afflicted many, and also a more virulent form of the disease which attacked the lungs and breathing passages. He also notes the general effect upon the population:

> Faces became pale, and the doom which threatened the people was marked upon their foreheads. It was only necessary to look into the countenances of men and women to read there recorded the blow which was about to fall; a marked pallor announced the approach of the enemy, and before the fatal day the sentence of death was written

unmistakably on the face of the victim. No climate appeared to have any effect upon the strange malady. It appeared to be stayed neither by heat nor cold. High and healthy situations were as much subject to it as damp and low ones. It spread during the colder season of winter as rapidly as in the heat of the summer months.

Covino observed that the contagious nature of the disease was so great that a single breath from an infected person was enough to communicate the disease, and the clothing, and even the furniture in the houses of the afflicted, was thought to be infective. The poor were most severely affected, but everyone suffered; even the doctors, of whom there were a large number, Montpellier having one of the great medical schools of the time, were not spared; indeed, according to Covino, hardly one escaped being infected. The effect upon the morals of the community was as bad as it had been in Florence, and those who were spared gave themselves up to a dissolute and licentious life. As to the number of dead, he says 'that the number of those swept away was greater than those left alive; cities are now depopulated, thousands of houses are locked up, thousands stand with their doors wide open, their owners and those who dwelt in them having been swept away'. The disease quickly spread up the Rhône valley and westward into Languedoc. In Narbonne, where it broke out in the first week of Lent, it killed 30,000; in Arles most of the inhabitants died.

Unlike Italy, France at the time of the Black Death was already well developed as a nation-state. In the previous century, Philip II, known as Philip Augustus, through marriage, conquest and confiscation, had extended the realm from Cherbourg to the Pyrenees. He had amassed a large treasure, paved the streets of Paris and built the Louvre as a fortress to guard the Seine. Philip extended his authority by sending agents, *baillis* and *sénéchaux*, from his court to administer local territories and collect taxes; he was also able to check the power of the nobility and the clergy and establish the Crown as the first power in France. Then, under the rule of Louis IX, Saint Louis, from 1226 until 1270, France reached the height of her medieval glory. Louis crushed a challenge from the barons, and forced the English to pay homage in Poitou, Gascony and Guienne and to relinquish their claims to other French territory. He continued to administer local territories with the *sénéchaux* and *baillis* but added *enquêteurs*, in essence goodwill ambassadors from Court, to whom people could appeal over the heads of the regular administrators. He established a uniform currency for the realm and made improvements in the machinery of government that centralized power. A man of contrasts, he left among his monuments the Saint-Chapelle, built to house a dubious relic of the Crucifixion, and a house built as a refuge for genuine reformed prostitutes. At the very height of his power, he set out on a Crusade in 1270, undeterred by the failure of a similar expedition twenty years earlier, and died of plague in Carthage within the year. At his death, France was the strongest power in Europe; the position of the king was supreme; both the feudal lords and the clergy had been shorn of much of their power; and a real sense of national unity was developing.

Under Philip IV, the Fair, who ruled from 1285 to 1314, the process of centralization of power continued. Justinian's Code of laws of imperial Rome had been rediscovered in the West. Although it had been the subject of study at the law schools in Bologna and Montpellier, it had not been applied to contemporary affairs until Philip's lawyers, building on the Roman theory and interpreting the Code to mean that the King possessed absolute legal prerogatives and that his decrees had the force of law, established for the King an even firmer authority over the feudal barons. His increasing power brought him into direct conflict with the Pope. Philip's military adventures had won to France both Gascony and Flanders, but the aggressive policy required financing, and among other measures taken, Philip required the clergy to vote supplies. Pope Boniface VIII issued a bull, *Clericis laicos*, which insisted that clergy should not be taxed by secular princes. Philip defied the Pope, and in 1302 Boniface issued an even stronger declaration of papal sovereignty in the bull *Unam Sanctam* which asserted flatly that 'it was necessary for salvation that all men should be subject to the Roman Pope'. The answer of a French bureaucrat to Boniface was, 'You may have the right, but we have the power'; and Philip's answer was, in effect, the same. He summoned a general assembly of lords, clergy, knights and *bourgeoisie* and with their support once again defied the Pope. Later this came to be known as the *Etats-Généraux*, Estates-General, named after the three estates of the kingdom—nobles, clergy and commoners—but Philip's assembly was gathered not to offer advice but rather to hear the King's wishes. And in his battle with Boniface, the King's wishes prevailed. The Pope was forced to give way in the matter of taxation when Philip placed an embargo on the export of all gold, silver and jewels, thus depriving the papal treasury of a major source of revenue. The Pope's humiliation was complete when, after his assertion of supreme authority in the *Unam*

Sanctam, Philip prepared to have him deposed. Philip drew up a bill of particulars asserting that Boniface had been illegally elected and charging him with heresy, simony, and immorality. A contingent of troops was sent to bring the Pope to France for trial; they found him an old man of 86, in his birthplace, Anagni, where he had gone to escape the heat of the Roman summer. Philip's troops broke into the old man's bedroom, heaped imprecations upon him, perhaps even manhandled him, and held him prisoner for several days until the people of Anagni rescued him. Sick and humiliated, Boniface died a few weeks later. Philip's victory was complete when, shortly after the death of Boniface, Clement V, one of Philip's councillors, was elected Pope and established himself at Avignon. The papal authority was now solidly under the thumb of the French king.

Ironically, the *Unam Sanctam*, which defined universal papal sovereignty, became a model for secular rulers. In 1324 Marsilius of Padua in his *Defensor Pacis* formally defended the omnipotence of the civil executive, and in England William of Ockham added new arguments to justify the supremacy of princes. By the mid-15th century this supremacy was so firmly established that in Spain and Germany the notion of the divine right of kings was being proclaimed. However, as the political power of the papacy declined, the papal government extended its power as never before over the clergy. The authority of the Curia was greatly extended and soon the papal chancery was the biggest and most efficiently organized bureaucracy in Christendom. By the mid-14th century every Church institution was in obedience to the Pope: it was generally accepted that only the Pope could summon a General Council, although councils had formerly been more important than Popes; the great religious orders were, at least theoretically, amenable to papal control; the universities were usually loyal allies of the Curia. But the 'Babylonian Captivity' of the Popes at Avignon was greeted with suspicion by other countries, and respect, revenue and loyalty to the Church declined. In the absence of normal revenue, the taxes on the clergy were increased and the need to provide more money lead to further demoralization and corruption. Avignon itself became a city of worldly affairs, pleasures and corrupt politics from which the papacy was unable, and sometimes unwilling, to divorce itself. From a small town Avignon grew into a busy city of 80,000 with a sumptuous papal palace and the whole panoply of the immense clerical bureaucracy. Clement VI (1342-52) was a great noble and lived in luxury and splendour in his fortress-palace, scattering money far and wide and emptying the treasury as he made his court a centre of art, letters and learning. The papal court at Avignon grew first luxurious and then avaricious. The entire first year's income of new incumbents was demanded, and the Popes were ruthless in collecting debts. A bishop might remain unburied until the Papacy was satisfied by his successor. But from Avignon the Pope's voice rang with less spiritual authority than it had from Rome, and as the efficiency of its administration increased, the force of papal control over the spiritual affairs of the rest of Europe declined. Men became weary of the disputes between Church and State and disillusioned with the succession of French Popes living at the very border of French territory and under the domination of the French king. This situation, aggravated by the death of so many clergy during the Black Death and the consequent lowering of standards for admission to religious ranks, led to widespread dis-affection, the Great Schism, and ultimately the rise of a completely new protesting religion.

In the years immediately preceding the Black Death French power also declined. When Charles IV, the last male descendant of the Capetian line which had ruled France for over three centuries, died in 1328, the House of Valois was established upon the French throne. The barons of France, in accordance with the opinion of French lawyers that 'custom prohibited the succession of a woman, and consequently, also of her son, to the throne of France', gave the crown to Philip VI of Valois, a nephew of Philip the Fair. Unfor-tunately for France, Edward III of England, whose mother was the daughter of Philip the Fair, added the French fleur-de-lis to the lions on his royal coat of arms and personally lead an invasion force into Normandy, intent upon securing the French crown for himself. Edward's claim to the crown was only one of a number of causes of the Hundred Year's War, but the English incursion from 1337 onwards worked a terrible hardship upon the French. As if the ravages of actual warfare were not enough, between campaigns roving bands of English soldiers and Genoese mercenaries laid waste to large areas of the country. Roaming about like the bar-barians of a previous century, they burned crops and houses and wantonly robbed and killed the inhabitants. Just at the coming of the Black Death, France was further demoralized by the crushing defeat in 1346 at Crécy, where Edward's archers, armed with the long bow which could shoot yard-long arrows at the rate of five or six a minute up to a distance of 400 yards, utterly vanquished a far

superior French force, pouring arrows upon the enemy horsemen
so that, according to Froissart, 'they fell like snow'. In the next year,
Calais was captured by the English; but then, as the Black Death
fell upon both England and France, the war, like so many other
organized activities of men, ground to a temporary halt.

To the papal city of Avignon the plague came early in 1348 with
a viciousness unparalleled elsewhere in France. In the first three
days 1,800 deaths were reported; and during the total seven-month
period that it raged, Gasquet says that 150,000 died in the city and
the surrounding territory, an estimate that must certainly be exaggerated. Even so, the devastation of Avignon was enormous and was
commented upon even in England in another account of that same
year. Although the disease struck the poor, the Jews, and the
Spaniards hardest, no class was spared. The staff of the papal court
was reduced by a quarter: among the dead was Giovanni Cardinal
Colonna, Petrarch's patron. Although many fled the city, Pope
Clement VI remained in Avignon or nearby Valence, where he
secluded himself in his apartment but made some very real efforts to
organize relief: he enjoined doctors to aid the sick, purchased a
large field and had it consecrated as a cemetery, ordained expiatory
processions and penitential litanies, and may even occasionally have
attended them himself. In a bold experiment, the Pope ordered
bodies to be examined—in some cases they were dissected—in the
hope of finding the cause of the disease. Under orders from his
physician Guy de Chauliac, Clement VI was largely confined to his
quarters where he sat between large fires, kindled to purify the air.
The fires may in fact have been of some help in keeping the Pope
free of infection, remembering the plague bacillus's low tolerance
for heat, for, as anyone who has been in Avignon in the summer can
attest, the heat must have been fearsome.

A full description of the Black Death in Avignon is contained
in a letter written by an anonymous canon to his friends in
Bruges. The canon was in the train of a Cardinal on a visit to
the Curia when the plague broke out. His letter is dated April 27,
1348:

> The disease is threefold in its infection; that is to say, firstly, men
> suffer in their lungs and breathing, and whoever have these corrupted,
> or even slightly attacked, cannot by any means escape nor live beyond
> two days. Examinations have been made by doctors in many cities of
> Italy, and also in Avignon, by order of the Pope, in order to discover
> the origin of this disease. Many dead bodies have been thus opened

and dissected, and it is found that all who have died thus suddenly have had their lungs infected and have spat blood. The contagious nature of the disease is indeed the most terrible of all the terrors, for when anyone who is infected by it dies, all who see him in his sickness, or visit him, or do any business with him, or even carry him to the grave, quickly follow him thither, and there is no known means of protection.

There is another form of the sickness, however, at present running its course concurrently with the first; that is, certain aposthumes appear under both arms, and by these also people quickly die. A third form of the disease—like the two former, running its course at this same time with them—is that from which people of both sexes suffer from aposthumes in the groin. This, likewise, is quickly fatal. The sickness has already grown to such proportions that, from fear of contagion, no doctor will visit a sick man, even if the invalid would gladly give him everything he possessed; neither does a father visit his son, nor a mother her daughter, nor a brother his brother, nor a son his father, nor a friend his friend, nor an acquaintance his acquaintance, nor, in fact, does anyone go to another, no matter how closely he may be allied to him by blood, unless he is prepared to die with him or quickly to follow after him. Still, a large number of persons have died merely through their affection for others; for they might have escaped had they not, moved by piety and Christian charity, visited the sick at the time.

To put the matter shortly, one-half, or more than a half of the people at Avignon are already dead. Within the walls of the city there are now more than 7,000 houses shut up; in these no one is living, and all who have inhabited them are departed; the suburbs hardly contain any people at all. A field near 'Our Lady of Miracles' has been bought by the Pope and consecrated as a cemetery. In this, from the 13th of March, 11,000 corpses have been buried. This number does not include those interred in the cemetery of the hospital of St. Anthony, in cemeteries belonging to the religious bodies, and in the many others which exist in Avignon. Nor must I be silent about the neighbouring parts, for at Marseilles all the gates of the city with the exception of two small ones, are now closed, for there four-fifths of the inhabitants are dead.

The like account I can give of all the cities and towns of Provence. Already the sickness has crossed the Rhône, and ravaged many cities and villages as far as Toulouse, and it ever increases in violence as it proceeds. On account of this great mortality there is such a fear of death that people do not dare even to speak with anyone whose relative has died, because it is frequently remarked that in a family where one dies nearly all the relations follow him, and this is commonly believed among the people. Neither are the sick now served by their kindred, except as dogs would be; food is put near the bed for them to eat and drink, and then those still in health fly and leave the house. When a man dies some rough countrymen, called *gavoti*, come to the house, and after receiving a sufficiently large reward, carry the corpse to the grave. Neither relatives nor friends go to the sick, nor do priests even hear their confessions nor give them the Sacraments; but everyone whilst still in health looks after himself. It daily happens that some rich man dying is borne to the grave by these ruffians without lights, and without a soul to follow him, except these hired mourners. When a corpse is carried by all fly through the streets and get into their houses. Nor do these said wretched *gavoti*, strong as they are, escape; but most of them after a time become infected by this contagion and die. All the poor who were wont to receive bread from the rich are dead; that is to say, briefly, where daily in ordinary times there were distributed sixty-four measures of wheat for bread, fifty loaves being made from each measure, now only one measure is given away, and sometimes even a half is found to be sufficient.

And it is said that altogether in three months—that is from January 25th to the present day—62,000 bodies have been buried in Avignon. The Pope, however, about the middle of March last past, after mature deliberation, gave plenary absolution till Easter, as far as the keys of the Church extended, to all those who, having confessed and being contrite, should happen to die of the sickness. He ordered likewise devout processions, singing the Litanies, to be made on certain days each week, and to these, it is said, people sometimes come from the neighbouring districts to the number of 2,000; amongst them many of both sexes are barefooted, some are in sackcloth, some with ashes, walking with tears and tearing their hair, and beating themselves with scourges even to the drawing of blood. The Pope was personally present at some of these processions, but they were then within the precincts of his palace. What will be the end, or when all this has had its beginning, God alone knows. . . .

Some wretched men have been caught with certain dust, and, whether justly or unjustly God only knows, they are accused of having poisoned the water, and men in fear do not drink the water from wells; for this many have been burnt and daily are burnt.

Fish, even sea fish, is commonly not eaten, as people say they have been infected by the bad air. Moreover, people do not eat, nor even touch spices, which have not been kept a year, since they fear they may have lately arrived in the aforesaid ships. And, indeed, it has many times been observed that those who have eaten these new spices and even some kinds of sea fish have suddenly been taken ill.

I write this to you, my friends, that you may know the dangers in which we live. And if you desire to preserve yourselves, the best advice is to eat and drink temperately, to avoid cold, not to commit excess of any kind, and above all, to converse little with others, at this time especially, except with the few whose breath is sweet. But it is best to remain at home until this epidemic has passed. . . .

Know, also, that the Pope has lately left Avignon, as is reported, and has gone to the castle called Stella, near Valence on the Rhône, two leagues off, to remain there till times change. The Curia, however, preferred to remain at Avignon, but vacations have been proclaimed till the feast of St. Michael. All the auditors, advocates, and procurators have either left, intend to leave immediately, or are dead. I am in the hands of God, to whom I commend myself. My master will follow the Pope, so they say, and I with him, for there are some castles near the airy mountains where the mortality has not yet appeared, and it is thought that the best chance is there. To choose and to do what is best may the omnipotent and merciful God grant us all. Amen.

The canon's letter is of especial interest in its mention of two of the phenomena which followed in the wake of the Black Death: the processions of the Flagellants and the persecution of poisoners. Here, for the first time, we find evidence of men turning from the organized propitiations of the Church to individual acts of sacrifice and repentance. The canon's letter says that the Pope witnessed some of the processions; what he thought of them the canon does not say, and probably had no way of knowing. Later, Clement VI was to recognize that the Flagellants posed a real threat to Church authority and denounced them in a bull. Similarly, the accusation that evil men were poisoning the water is the first clear statement of such a suspicion during the Black Death. Guy de Chauliac's account of the plague in Avignon, quoted earlier, confirms the canon's observations: 'Many were in doubt about the cause of this great mortality,' writes the Pope's physician. 'In some places they thought that the Jews had poisoned the world: and so they killed them. In others, that it was the poor deformed people who were responsible: and they drove them out. In others that it was the nobles; and they feared to go abroad. Finally they reached the point where they kept guard in the cities and villages, permitting the entry of no one who was not well known. And if powders and salves were found on anyone, the owners, for fear that they were poisons, were forced to swallow them. . . .' Hideous massacres of Jews had taken place already in southern France and in Spain during previous epidemics of 1320 and 1333, so it is more deplorable than surprising that new persecutions should have been instituted against them. It is pitifully ironical, however, that the Jews of Avignon should have come under suspicion, since, as Hecker reports, the Jewish population of the city was extremely hard hit by the plague; but no doubt the very wretchedness of their condition made the persecutions easier. An insight into the temper of the age may be found in the anonymous canon's passing on from the mention of the burning of poisoners to a discussion of the danger of eating fish, in the very next sentence. Even in the account of Guy de Chauliac, one of the enlightened men of his time, one looks in vain for a clear denunciation of such insanity.

To his everlasting credit, Clement VI extended his personal protection to the Jews at Avignon and, later, when the massacres had reached terrible proportions elsewhere, issued two bulls asserting their innocence and calling upon Christians to refrain from persecuting them. But the Pope himself, enlightened in the matter of poisoners—although the sceptical may feel that his interest in their fate was stimulated more by financial than humanitarian concerns—was not free from superstition: Nohl says that he wore a magical emerald ring on his finger which when turned to the east reduced the possibility of infection, and when turned to the south nullified the effect of any poison that might just possibly be present. Guy de Chauliac's account makes clear that the search for scapegoats extended to 'poor deformed people', perhaps lepers, who were driven forth: the unprotected and miserable of the world once again being suspect for their very helplessness. Perhaps more interesting and indicative of the strenuous proletarian revolutionary fervour that followed the Black Death is the suspicion among the people that the feudal overlords had caused the disease, an early indication of the resentment and suspicion of the rich that grew among the commoners during the Black Death.

The plague raged on in Avignon through the summer and well into the winter months. The mechanism of civil order began to break down, bodies littered the streets and the new burial ground purchased by the Pope was soon full. Finally, Clement was obliged to consecrate the Rhône so that corpses could be sunk in it. There would seem almost no end to the horrors. Baluze in his lives of the Popes of Avignon writes that many 'who were seized with the sickness, being considered certain to die and without any hope of recovery, were carried off at once to the pit and buried. And in this way many were buried alive.'

The plague continued to spread throughout France. It had reached Toulouse in April; in August it appeared in Bordeaux where

Princess Joan, the daughter of Edward III, on her way to marry
Pedro, son of the King of Castile, was suddenly taken sick and died.
It ravaged Lyons and Burgundy during the summer, and by the
early summer of 1348 the Black Death appeared in Paris. The
chronicle of St. Denis reports that the epidemic lasted in France
about a year and a half and that in one day there were 800 deaths in
Paris; he estimates that more than 50,000 people died in Paris and
another 16,000 in the town of St. Denis, and a number of modern
historians accept that figure. The chronicle of the Carmelites at
Rheims says that the death toll in Paris reached 80,000. And no
segment of society was spared: Joan of Burgundy, the wife of King
Philip VI, was among the victims, as was another queen, Joan of
Navarre, daughter of Louis X.

The most complete account of the plague in Paris is contained in
the continuation of the chronicle of Guillaume de Nangis:

> In the same year [1348], both in Paris in the kingdom of France, and
> not less, as is reported, in different parts of the world, and also in the
> following year, there was so great a mortality of people of both sexes,
> and of the young rather than the old, that they could hardly be buried.
> Further they were ill scarcely more than two or three days, and some
> often died suddenly, so that a man today in good health, tomorrow
> was carried a corpse to the grave. . . . And the multitude of people who
> died in the years 1348 and 1349, was so large that nothing like it was
> ever heard, read of, or witnessed in past ages. And the said death and
> sickness often sprung from the imagination, or from the society and
> contagion of another, for a healthy man visiting one sick hardly ever
> escaped death. So that in many towns, small and great, priests retired
> through fear, leaving the administration of the Sacraments to religious,
> who were more bold. Briefly, in many places, there did not remain two
> alive out of every twenty. So great was the mortality in the Hôtel-Dieu
> of Paris that for a long time more than fifty corpses were carried away
> from it each day in carts to be buried. And the devout sisters of the
> Hôtel-Dieu, not fearing death, worked piously and humbly, not out of
> regard for any worldly honour. A great number of these said sisters
> were very frequently summoned to their reward by death, and rest in
> peace with Christ, as is piously believed. . . . It lasted in France the
> greater part of 1348 and 1349, and afterwards there were to be seen
> many towns, country places, and houses in good cities remaining
> empty and without inhabitants.

This writer, whose account dates probably from about 1368, says
that the world had begun to renew itself, but he laments that it has
not changed for the better. 'For people were afterwards more

avaricious and grasping, even when they possessed more of the goods of this world, than before. They were more covetous, vexing themselves by contentious quarrels, strifes, and law-suits. . . . Charity, too, from that time began to grow cold, and wickedness with its attendant, ignorance, was rampant. . . .' He also notes the economic disruptions that followed the Black Death: prices rose until furniture, food and all sorts of other merchandise doubled in price; and servants demanded higher wages. Economic chaos was widespread and, coupled with the suspicion and hatred of the rich which was aggravated if not caused by the Black Death and the drastic reduction of the work-force which is directly attributable to it, led to a series of violent peasant revolts throughout Europe during the rest of the century.

The disease attacked not only cities but the countryside as well; and although the peasants could boast no chroniclers to record their misery, its reality is manifested by the large number of villages that seem to have completely disappeared during the years 1347 and 1350. The living conditions of the peasants were such that should the disease appear in a village it was almost certain to devastate it completely. The peasant's life was hard: it was ordained that he should work. A bishop of the 11th century summed it all up when he mentioned the three classes of society: the nobles who do the fighting, the clergy who do the praying, and the rest of men who do the work. Nor was there any great chance of moving from one class to another; a medieval rhyme states flatly: 'God hath shapen lives three; boor and knight and priest they be.' And until the late Middle Ages when a serf might liberate himself if he could manage to make his way to a town, remain there for a year and a day, and pay his taxes, there was very little opportunity to change one's condition. Little accurate information is available about peasant life before the 13th century, but it is certain that during the long centuries from the decline of Rome until the later Middle Ages, it was dismal and precarious in the extreme. Tertullian, writing in the 3rd century A.D., found that 'delightful farms have now blotted out every trace of the dreadful wastes; cultivated fields have supplanted woods; flocks and herds have driven out wild beasts; sandy spots are sown; rocks and stones have been cleared away; bogs have been drained. Large towns now occupy land hardly tenanted before by cottages. Thick population meets the eye on all sides. We overcrowd the world.' But by the 6th century all that had changed. Paul the Deacon noted of Italy at that time: 'The flocks remained alone in the pastures. You saw villas or fortified places filled with people in utter silence. The whole world seemed brought to its ancient stillness; no voice in the field, no whistling of shepherds. The harvests were untouched. Human habitations became the abode of wild beasts.' The people huddled together in the fortified places for protection, and it was their desire to find some security from the ravaging bands of barbarians that was largely responsible for the manorial system. The early medieval community was a group of squalid cottages around the lord's manor-house, itself perhaps larger but hardly less squalid than the cottages. The system became formalized, and the lord of the manor provided protection and parcelled out land, acting as both a managing director and a commander of the labouring classes. The labourers themselves were divided into several classes which in turn were sub-divided into various degrees. The largest group was known as '*villeins*'—from *villa*, farm—who were free men, born to their condition; they lived on the lord's land, having the use of as much as forty acres of it, and turned over part of the produce to him. Of a lower order were the 'cotters'—from the old Norse *kot*, a cottage—who held smaller amounts of land, sometimes working for the more prosperous *villeins* and sometimes working for the lord for a wage. From one manor to another and from one part of Europe to another the conditions of the servile relationship differed, and every sort of economic and social subjection existed from slavery to relative freedom. But for all, life was hard, and for most there was no hope of change. An extract of dialogue from the *Colloquium* of Aelfric the Grammarian gives an indication of the harsh life: ' "Well, ploughman, how do you work?" "Oh, Sir, I work very hard. I go out in the dawning, driving the oxen to the field and I yoke them to the plough. Be the winter never so stark, I dare not stay at home for fear of my lord; but every day I must plough a full acre or more, having yoked the oxen and fastened the share and coulter to the plough." "Have you any mate?" "I have a boy, who drives the oxen with a goad. He is now hoarse from cold and shouting." "Well, is it very hard work?" "Yes, indeed, it is very hard work." '

Even by the beginning of the 14th century, Europe was still very much the way nature had made it; there were enormous tracts of waste land and agriculture was primitive. Every stage of economic development could be seen, from food gathering to capitalist production. Breeding and raising animals was a principal occupation. Since cotton was unknown except in Sicily and the Levant, sheep were very important, and there were many nomadic sheep herders. Farming, in many areas, was extremely primitive. In eastern Europe the hook plough, which could do little more than scratch the soil, was still in almost universal use. But for many serfs conditions had been steadily improving. The burden of serfdom was disappearing from western Europe and it had not yet fallen heavily on the countries of the north-eastern plain. Population had been steadily increasing during the 13th century and with the increase came an easing of the burdens of peasant life. Many manors by this time had their own church, a smithy, a mill, a carpenter's shop; and although they were most often isolated, there was frequently some exchange of goods with other manors and many people were engaged in 'carrying', since much of the land was owned by the Church and produce had to be carried to the monastery. In addition there were occasional festivals and feudal ceremonies; wandering friars and minstrels brought news and entertainment; on special occasions the men were allowed to sit and drink in the manor hall. And there was the growing opportunity for men to change their condition altogether by escaping to the towns, for as a medieval proverb has it, 'Town air makes free'. But as the life of the serf improved, so did that of the lord. As he began to collect money rather than goods from his serfs, he was able to make substantial improvements in his living conditions, and a greater disparity grew between them. Living conditions in the manor improved for all, but they improved faster and more dramatically for the lord. It is interesting, and perhaps instructive, to note that it is just at this time of improving conditions and, to use the currently popular phrase, rising expectations, that the first serious instances of peasant unrest began to be recorded.

But if peasant life was improving in the first half of the 14th century, it was still a life of hard and continuous work, lived in drab and unsanitary conditions. The average peasant lived in a rude house made of wood or mud, with thatched roof and earth floor, which sheltered his livestock and poultry as well as his family. There was usually a cellar or pit for storing grain and there may have been a small attic, but there were seldom any windows, and where they did exist they were only slits in the wall closed by wooden shutters. The coarse, nearly opaque glass that was available at the time would have been far beyond the means of the peasant: even the rich bourgeois of Paris were filling their windows with waxed cloth or parchment. If there were no windows, a wooden shutter might be fixed over the door to let light in and to let the smoke from the fire out. Furniture was very simple, but might have included such accessories as a spinning wheel, a loom, and some simple copper and tin utensils. The diet was simple, too, consisting primarily of pork, bread and whatever vegetables were in season. There was no fresh meat from Michaelmas to Easter, and the Church enforced a strict Lenten fast. Fishing became an important industry and some land-owners even made artificial lakes in which to breed fish. In France, mustard seems to have been the chief, perhaps the only, condiment; honey served as sweetening, but it was a luxury. Furs were used extensively for dress, and in France linen shirts were utilized widely as undergarments. People slept usually in dark, airless recesses, on straw mattresses and under blankets of fur or feather quilts. And the day was filled with work from sun-up until the light failed. The women cooked, cared for the children and cattle, made clothes and also helped in the field. Life was no easier for the women than for the men. William Langland in *Piers Plowman* describes the life of peasant women in 14th-century England who were

> Charged with children and overcharged by landlords.
> What they may spare in spinning they spend on rental,
> On milk, or on meal to make porridge
> To still the sobbing of children at meal time.
> And they themselves suffer much hunger.
> They have woe in winter time, and wake at midnight
> To rise and to rock the cradle at the bedside,
> To card and to comb, to darn clouts and to wash them,
> To rub and to reel and to put rushes on the paving.
> The woe of these women who dwell in hovels
> Is too sad to speak of or to say in rhyme.

The children worked too, as soon as they were old enough to be of service. Long after the cities found it necessary to establish uniform units of time, peasants followed the ancient practice of dividing the daylight hours into the same number of periods at all seasons, so that although one worked, summer and winter, the same number of 'hours' a day, the hours were longer in summer than in winter. Under such conditions life for most was unpleasant, brutish and short. The peasant's life-span was, on the average, even shorter than that of the lord who so often died prematurely in battle. Famine was endemic; the word Chaucer used most often to mean 'to die' is 'sterven' which shortly came to signify more specifically to die for lack of food, an indication of the frequency of starvation as a cause of death in the 14th century.

Given the terms of life, and the nature of the manorial villages, one is inclined to credit contemporary accounts that speak of the annihilation of rural areas. One chronicler, Gilles Li Muisis, Abbot of St. Martin's, Tournay, describes the devastation in rural France:

> It is impossible to credit the mortality throughout the whole country. Travellers, merchants, pilgrims, and others who have passed through it declare that they have found cattle wandering without herdsmen in fields, town, and waste lands; that they have seen barns and wine-cellars standing wide open, houses empty, and few people to be found anywhere. So much so that in many towns, cities, and villages, where there had been before 20,000 people, scarcely 2,000 are left; and in many cities and country places, where there had been 1,500 people, hardly 100 remain. And in many different lands, both lands and fields are lying uncultivated.

Normandy, Gascony, Poitou and Brittany were ravaged by plague during the summer months. A contemporary account says that in the towns two-thirds of the inhabitants died, and people said that the end of the world had come. Another wave of pestilence moved north. At Amiens 17,000 are said to have died. By the early summer of 1349 the Black Death had made its way into Belgium and Holland. By August it was raging in Tournay where Gilles Li Muisis observed, as had Petrarch before, that what he had seen was so horrible that later ages would hardly be able to believe it. He tells how bodies were carried to the parish churches, first five, then ten, then fifteen, until finally twenty or thirty bodies crowded the churches each day. The bells tolled all day long and a great fear gripped the city. To avert panic, city officials put a stop to the tolling of bells and passed some singular regulations which prohibited more than two people to meet at a funeral and forbade anyone to dress in black. In addition to banishing public shows of grief, the city official set about correcting the morals of the community. There was to be no work done after noon on Saturday and during the entire day Sunday; dice playing and profane swearing were to stop; and any man living with a woman not his wife was enjoined to marry her immediately. The chronicler asserts that the action of the authorities was most beneficial; many who had been living in a state of sin married, swearing diminished markedly, and dice playing was so universally abandoned that the manufacturers of dice turned to making rosaries instead. He does not say if the regulations had any marked effect upon the epidemic. He records that in Tournay more than 25,000 died and that the rich and important people of the community suffered most. But all classes of people suffered, and in many cases, he says, whole families with their dogs and even their cats were stricken. It appears that, in Tournay, the public officials were able to exert firmer control than in many other places; in spite of public dissatisfaction with the regulations, they insisted that plague-dead be buried in special pits outside the city and maintained a restriction on funeral gatherings throughout the course of the epidemic. During a later epidemic the town of Tournay discovered an even more ingenious way to keep off the plague. On the assumption that the major cause was the disruption of the atmosphere, the town officials decided to sponsor pyrotechnic displays to break up the hostile air and set it right, and to this end at dawn and sunset cannon and blunderbusses were shot off.

It is impossible to say with any kind of certainty what the total mortality in France might have been during these years of the plague. Froissart estimated that one-third of the population of the world died, and from the accounts of the ravages in individual cities, it would seem that his estimate is justified at least for France. Previté-Orton estimates the population of France at the beginning of the Hundred Years' War at twelve million; other modern historians go as far as twenty million. The obvious conclusion, incredible as it may seem, is that somewhere between four and seven million people died in France between 1348 and 1350.

The rest of Europe fared no better than France and Italy. From Flanders, where the plague was reported at Tournay, the epidemic spread into Holland. As in so many other places, its effects were especially devastating among the religious communities. A chronicler reported from Holland that people expired while walking in the streets, and in the Monastery of Fleurchamps there were eighty deaths, while in the Abbey of Foswert, a monastery for both men and women, 207 monks, nuns and lay brothers and sisters died. Farther south, the disease had spread from Italy and from France into Austria, Hungary and Switzerland. After attacking Padua and Verona, the plague moved up the valley of the Etsch and made its appearance in Trent on June 22, 1348. From there it spread up the Brenner Pass in the Tyrolese Alps and was reported in Muhldorf in Bavaria by the end of June, where a contemporary reports that 1,400 of 'the better class of inhabitants' died. In Carinthia and Bavaria the accounts repeat the devastation seen elsewhere: whole towns were depopulated and entire families destroyed. In November 1348, the plague attacked Neuberg in Styria where, according to the Neuberg Chronicle:

> Since this deadly pestilence raged everywhere, cities became desolate which up to this had been populous. Their inhabitants were swept off in such numbers that such as were left, with closed gates, strenuously watched that no one should steal the property of those departed. . . . The pest in its wandering came to Carinthia, and then so completely took possession of Styria, that people, rendered desperate, walked about as if mad. From so many sick pestilential odours proceeded, infecting those visiting and serving them, and very frequently it happened that when one died in a house all, one after the other, were carried off. . . . As a consequence of this overwhelming visitation cattle were left to wander in the fields without guardians, for no one thought of troubling himself about the future; and wolves coming down from the mountains to attack them, against their instincts, and as if frightened by something unseen, quickly fled into the wilds again. Property, too, both moveable and immoveable, which sick people leave by will, is carefully avoided by all, as if it were sure to be infected.

The plague reached Vienna early in the summer of the following year, 1349, but its virulence had not abated. The daily death toll in the city mounted from five or six hundred to 960, and one eyewitness says 1,200 died in a single day. The dead were buried in huge pits outside the city, each of which contained 6,000 corpses. Contemporary accounts estimate that between one- and two-thirds of the population died; Nohl gives the figure of 100,000 but it seems unlikely that the total population of Vienna was as much as 100,000 in 1349. One chronicler says that 'because of the odour, and horror inspired by the dead bodies, burials in the church cemeteries were not allowed; but as soon as life was extinct the corpses were carried out of the city to a common burial-place called "God's acre". There the deep and broad pits were quickly filled to the top with the dead.' The excited and superstitious populace personified the plague as the Pest-Jungfrau, who was seen flying through the air above the city in the form of a blue flame; she had only to raise her hand to infect a victim, and there were reports of this Plague-Virgin's blue flame rising out of the mouths of the dying. Others saw the plague poison descend upon the city as a ball of fire. One such sighting was called to the attention of a bishop who hurriedly exorcized it; it fell harmlessly to the earth and a stone statue of the Madonna was set up in the street to mark the place where it fell.

From Vienna as from Avignon came reports of the processions of Flagellants, for by this time the movement had gained considerable momentum. Among the less spectacular measures taken to control the disease were ordinances segregating the sick. The doors and windows of infected houses were nailed up, but soon, as the dead actually began to litter the streets, these measures were abandoned.

The Black Death attacked Hungary and Poland at the same time as it appeared in Austria and with the same results. Towns were left totally depopulated; in Hungary many of the nobility died; in Poland Hecker says that three-quarters of the population were carried off. A chronicler in Prague is of the opinion that the extremely cold winter delayed the arrival of the disease in Bohemia, but it appeared at last in the spring of 1350 with its familiar virulence. Switzerland endured the epidemic during 1348 and 1349. It seems to have advanced into that country along the great highway over the Alps through the St. Gothard Pass where it attacked Momo, Gallarete, Varese and Bellinzona, and then passed down the Rhine Valley. Another wave of pestilence passed into Switzerland from France following the Rhône. It attacked Berne and appeared in the area of Lucerne in March 1349, where in the city itself over 3,000 died. Zurich, Constance and Basle were contaminated during that same winter. It was in Switzerland, at Chillon on the Lake of Geneva, that the first organized massacre of the Jews occurred in September and October 1348. The fear of well-poisoners reached hysterical proportions there and hysteria spread quickly.

The epidemic advanced up the Rhine and by December 1349 its presence in Cologne is reported. In Germany, also, the devastation was great; but, as always, the estimates of the dead in the chronicles are most probably wild guesses. In Weimar 5,000 are said to have died; in Limburg, 2,500; in Bremen, 7,000; in Pomerania and Holstein two-thirds of the population; and in Schleswig four-fifths. In Erfurt, after the churchyards were filled, huge pits were dug and 12,000 people were buried in them. In Lübeck 9,000 died, and the citizens, according to Nohl, were seized by a mass hysteria. Taking leave of life willingly, they renounced all worldly possessions and heaped money and property upon the churches and monasteries. When the monks, fearing that the goods carried the infection, refused the offerings, the citizens crowded around the closed gates and the walls of the monasteries and threw money over the walls. The devastation in the countryside was as great as in the cities. Hecker says that 200,000 small country towns in Germany were

bereft of all their inhabitants; and Nohl prints the following account
from a German chronicler:

> Savage wolves roamed about in packs at night and howled round the
> walls of the towns. In the villages they did not slake their thirst for
> human blood by lurking in secret places, as was otherwise their wont,
> but boldly entered the open houses and tore the little ones from their
> mothers' sides; indeed they did not only attack children, but even
> armed men and overcame them. To the contemporaries they seemed no
> longer wild animals but demons. Other quadrupeds forsook their
> woods, and in herds approached the vicinity of human habitations, as
> if aware of the extraordinary conditions. Ravens in innumerable flocks
> flew over the towns with loud croaking. The kite and the vulture were
> heard in the air, and other unusual migratory birds appeared. But on
> the houses the cuckoos and owls alighted and filled the night with their
> mournful lament. The field-mice had lost all fear and took up their
> abode among human beings.

Hecker offers 1,224,434 as the total number of dead in Germany as
a result of the Black Death, but the exact figure recommends belief
even less than the round numbers of the contemporary chronicles.

Nor was Spain spared. The Black Death appeared there early in
1348, first at Almeria and then in Barcelona where whole quarters
of the city were desolated and four of the five councillors of the city
died. By May its grip was upon Valencia where 300 people a day
are reported to have been buried. Spain suffered as did the rest of
Europe, not only from the ravages of the disease but from the
demoralization and disorganization that followed it. Gilles Li Muisis
includes in his account of the Black Death in Tournay a report of
the pestilence in Spain he had received from a pilgrim to Com-
postella. The pilgrim and a companion, on their return, passed
through Galicia and stopped for the night at a town he calls Sal-
vaterra at the foot of the Pyrenees. The town, the pilgrim reported,
was so hard hit by the plague that not one in ten of its people
remained alive. Still the pilgrim managed to find a place for the
night with a man who, with two daughters and one servant, had
managed to survive, although all the rest of his family were dead.
The account continues: 'After supping with the host, he settled with
him for his entertainment, intending to start on his journey at
daybreak, and went to bed. Next morning rising and wanting something from those with whom they had supped, the travellers could
make no one hear. Then they learnt from an old woman they found
in bed that the host, his two daughters, and servant had died in the

night. On hearing this the pilgrims made all haste to leave the place.' The Black Death's royal victims included Alfonso XI of Castile who died of plague while besieging Gibraltar in 1350. The Queen of Aragon, too, had been one of the earliest of victims. But for the King, Peter IV, the Ceremonious, of Aragon, the Black Death worked some good to compensate for his loss. During a war with the unruly nobles of Aragon and Valencia, he was captured and held in Valencia; but the Black Death caused such havoc among his captors that he was able to escape, gather his forces and overthrow his enemies at the battle of Epila in July 1348.

The epidemic seems to have entered Scandinavia by way of England, where the plague raged during the summer and autumn of 1349. One report says that a ship left London with a cargo of wool early in the summer of 1349; the plague had infected the crew and while the ship was still at sea all hands died. Driven about by the winds and currents the death ship came ashore at Bergen, and from there the disease spread quickly over all Norway. In Drontheim, the Archbishop and all but one of his chapter died, and the sole survivor was nominated Archbishop. Another account says that the Bishop of Oslo was the only bishop to survive the Black Death. Hecker says that only one-third of the population of Norway survived. Many villages were completely depopulated and grown over by forests, and much of the land reverted to wilderness. In Sweden the plague appeared in 1350 and the King, Magnus II, announced its coming to his people in a letter which says that 'God for the sins of man has struck the world with this great punishment of sudden death. By it most of the people in the land to the west of our country are dead. It is now ravaging Norway and Holland, and is approaching our kingdom of Sweden.' The King then commands his people to eat nothing on Fridays but bread and water, or at most bread and a little ale, to walk to their parish churches in their bare feet, and to carry holy relics around the cemeteries. When the Black Death arrived in the capital city, the streets are reported to have been strewn with corpses. Among the dead were Håken and Knut, the King's brothers. The immediate effect of the plague was to increase the power of the surviving nobles, mainly those of Swedish extraction, over the greatly depleted population; the steady political decline of Norway had begun.

A death toll of twenty-five million is often given for the plague in Europe. Hecker arrives at this number by assuming a total population before the Black Death of 105 million and an overall mortality of one in four. But it should be clear that no estimate of population or rate of mortality can be made with any certainty. It is beyond question, however, that the death toll was enormous and that the population of Europe, which for nearly three centuries had been steadily increasing, was sharply reduced and remained almost stagnant until the close of the Middle Ages. But for all its devastation on the continent, it was in England that the plague raged with its greatest ferocity, carrying off, in the space of little more than a year, close to half of the total population.

Chapter VI

THE DEATH IN ENGLAND

THE BLACK DEATH advanced upon an England prosperous and flushed with victory. Edward III's triumph over the French at Crécy was followed in 1347 by the capture of Calais, and when he landed at Sandwich in October 1347 he was greeted with the greatest enthusiasm. Walsingham wrote that 'a new sun seemed to have arisen over the people, in the perfect peace, in the plenty of all things, and in the glory of such victories. There was hardly a woman of any name who did not possess spoils of Caen, Calais and other French towns across the sea'. England was enjoying a period of unparalleled prosperity, and the great ladies dressed in their fine new clothes and ornaments from the spoiled cities of France to attend spectacular tournaments arranged to celebrate the foundation of the Order of the Garter which the King had instituted to perpetuate the memory of his military successes. The Leicester cloisterer Knighton describes the time:

> In those days there arose a huge rumour and outcry among the people, because when tournaments were held, almost in every place, a band of women would come as if to share the sport, dressed in divers and marvellous dresses of men—sometimes to the number of forty or fifty ladies, of the fairest and comeliest (though I say not, of the best) among the whole kingdom. Thither they came in party-coloured tunics, one colour or pattern on the right side and another on the left, with short hoods that had pendants like ropes wound round their necks, and belts thickly studded with gold or silver—nay, they even wore, in pouches slung across their bodies, those knives which are called *daggers* in the vulgar tongue; and thus they rode on choice war-horses or other splendid steeds to the place of tournament. There and thus they spent and lavished their possessions, and wearied their bodies with fooleries and wanton buffoonery, if popular report lie not . . .

The conquest of Calais gave the English an important debarkation point on the continent to which wool from the flourishing new industry could be shipped to Flanders for manufacture and from which the fine new clothes Knighton complains of could be sent to England. But, ironically, the same ships that brought new trade and prosperity from Calais also brought the infective rats and fleas and the bacillus of the Black Death. Knighton, predictably, attributes the disease to God's anger at the intemperance of the fine ladies: 'But God in this matter, as in all others, brought marvellous remedy; for He harassed the places and times appointed for such vanities by opening the floodgates of heaven with rain and thunder and lurid lightning, and by unwonted blasts of tempestuous winds. . . . That same year and the next came the general mortality throughout the world.'

It was very probably a ship from France that first brought the plague into English ports. A monk of Malmesbury wrote, 'In the year of our Lord 1348, about the feast of the Translation of St. Thomas [July 7], the cruel pestilence, terrible to all future ages, came from parts over the sea to the south coast of England, into a port called Melcombe, in Dorsetshire.' Galfrid le Baker agrees that the plague entered the country first through a seaport in Dorset, and there are other contemporary accounts that report the plague's entry by way of Melcombe Regis, or Weymouth, which at the time was a port of some importance, having furnished Edward III with twenty ships for his siege at Calais while Bristol furnished only twenty-two and London twenty-five. There is no report of the effects of the disease in the port itself, but there are many descriptions of its ravages in Devon, Dorset, Somerset and Cornwall. Gasquet produces evidence to show that the date of July 7 is too early for the plague to have established itself in England, but there is no question that by the end of summer 1348 it had a firm hold on the western counties. A contemporary record says that summer and autumn were extremely wet and cold with rain almost every day from mid-July until Christmas. Such conditions may have lowered resistance to the disease and made transmission easier, but whatever the reasons, it struck with terrible ferocity. Robert of Avesbury, the Registrar of the Court of Canterbury at the time, wrote that 'it passed most rapidly from place to place, swiftly killing ere mid-day many who in the morning had been well, and without respect of persons (some few rich people excepted), not permitting those destined to die to live more than three, or at most four, days. On the same day twenty, forty, sixty and very often more corpses were committed to the same grave'. By mid-winter the plague had a firm grip on Dorset. It spread along the coast and Bridport, East

Lulworth, Tynham, Langton and Wareham had all begun to suffer by November. By the end of the month, the disease appeared in Shaftesbury. Poole, which was important enough to have furnished four ships to the King for his attack on Calais, was so laid waste that it did not entirely recover for the next 150 years.

The effects of the disease were especially devastating in Somerset. In August 1348, Ralph of Shrewsbury, the Bishop of Bath and Wells, had tried to prepare his diocese for the possibility of such a disaster by circulating letters which ordered processions and stations every Friday in all churches to beg God for protection from the 'pestilence which had come from the East into the neighbouring kingdom', probably France. The letter also granted an indulgence of forty days to anyone who gave alms, fasted and prayed, in order to avert God's anger. By January of the next year the plague had killed so many clergy in Somerset that the Bishop issued another letter of advice to his people. The letter leaves no doubt as to the terrible mortality of the epidemic and its widespread effect not only on population but upon the whole structure of the religious organization:

The contagious nature of the present pestilence, which is ever spreading itself far and wide, has left many parish churches and other cures, and consequently the people of our diocese, destitute of curates and priests. And inasmuch as priests cannot be found who are willing out of zeal, devotion, or for stipend to undertake the care of the foresaid places, and to visit the sick and administer to the Sacraments of the Church (perchance for dread of the infection and contagion), many, as we understand, are dying without the Sacrament of Penance. These, too, are ignorant of what ought to be done in such necessity, and believe that no confession of their sins, even in a case of such need, is useful or meritorious, unless made to a priest having the keys of the Church. Therefore, desiring, as we are bound to do, the salvation of souls, and ever watching to bring back the wandering from the crooked paths of error, we, on the obedience you have sworn to us, urgently enjoin upon you and command you—rectors, vicars, and parish priests—in all your churches, and you deans, in such places of your deaneries as are destitute of priests, that you at once and publicly instruct and induce, yourselves or by some other, all who are sick of the present malady, or who shall happen to be taken ill, that *in articulo mortis*, if they are not able to obtain any priest, they should make confession of their sins (according to the teaching of the apostle) even to a layman, and, if a man is not at hand, then to a woman. We exhort you, by the present

letters, in the bowels of Jesus Christ, to do this, and to proclaim publicly in the aforesaid places that such confession made to a layman in
the presumed case can be most salutary and profitable to them for the
remission of their sins, according to the teaching and the sacred
canons of the Church.

The Bishop's letter is of considerable interest. It takes note of the
fact that priests were not available to administer to their parishes
and strongly implies that some had deserted their posts out of fear
of the disease. Such criticism of the clergy was also voiced by continental chroniclers. The behaviour of the parish priests during the
plague had a considerable effect upon subsequent popular attitudes
to the clergy. More importantly, the Bishop quietly, and probably
quite unconsciously, introduces the beginning of a revolution in the
Church. One may confess to a layman. Faith takes the place of the
Sacrament, not only here and there, but among the multitude.

During the winter months the plague was at its height in Somerset. The Bishop of Bath and Wells remained in his manor until the
disease abated in May 1349, preparing letters of institution for the
priests that came to fill the benefices abruptly left vacant. Gasquet
has made an exhaustive search of English ecclesiastical records and
is able, for many dioceses, to state the exact number of benefices
filled during the plague and to compare that with the average numbers for the years preceding 1349. These figures are extremely
valuable and present a far more accurate source of information
about the mortality than the round numbers and percentages given
by the chroniclers. The mortality among the clergy may be inferred
from them, and they also give some indication of the mortality
among the population in general. Perhaps surprisingly they confirm
the estimates of chroniclers that close to half died. However, even
these records must be treated with caution. For one thing, the
records were kept only for the beneficed clergy. For another, as the
letter of the Bishop of Bath and Wells implied, not all vacancies
were due to death. And for a third, priests ran special risks and their
death-rate may have been higher than average. Even with these
reservations, however, the increase in the number of vacancies was
so great during the plague years as to erase any doubt about the
extent of the catastrophe. In Somerset the average number of
inductions to livings in the months immediately before the coming
of the plague was less than three, but in December it had risen to
thirty-two. In 1349, against a previous yearly average of thirty-five,
the Bishop instituted 232 clergy to vacant livings. In some instances

three or four men were appointed to the same benefice within the space of a few months. The abbey at Glastonbury lost nearly half its members; at Bath, before the outbreak, the community at the priory consisted of thirty monks under Prior John de Ford, but after the plague and until its final dissolution in the 16th century it never again had more than sixteen. In England, generally, the sad tale was repeated over and over again: nearly half the clergy died, in some areas a far higher percentage.

In Bristol, the devastation was terrible. Knighton says of Bristol that 'people died as if the whole strength of the city were seized by sudden death'. A later historian confirms this: 'Here in Bristol in 1348 the plague raged to such a degree that the living were scarce able to bury the dead. The Gloucestershire men would not suffer the Bristol men to have access to them. At last it reached Gloucester, Oxford and London; scarce the tenth person was left alive, male or female. At this period the grass grew several inches high in High Street and Broad Street. . . .' English cities were no more sanitary than continental ones, and the crowded and unhealthy conditions favoured the rapid spread of disease. In Bristol at the time streets were extremely narrow, so narrow in fact that no vehicle could be used in them and all goods had to be carried by pack horses and porters. In parts of the city the ground was honeycombed with cellars for storing wine, salt and other merchandise. Refuse from the houses was carried off, if it was carried off, by a central ditch in the street. In Bristol, as in so many other places, the cemeteries were finally unable to hold all the dead and new burial plots had to be established.

The disease appeared in Devon and Cornwall at about the same time as it appeared in Somerset. The records of the diocese of Exeter, which comprised these two counties, indicate that the number of livings instituted in January 1349 was nearly as great as the average number for the preceding years; and during the rest of the year the register groups the vacancies by months, rather than by years as had previously been the case. The average number of livings annually rendered vacant in these two counties was thirty-six prior to the plague; in 1349 there are recorded 382. Gasquet estimates that some 346 of these vacancies may be attributed to deaths from the plague, the rest probably were the result of resignations of benefices that, due to the large number of dead, had become too poor to provide maintenance. The scribe who kept the diocese record, in listing the vacancies, omits the customary phrase 'vacant *per mortem*', and one wonders if he did so because it was simply understood that death was the cause, or perhaps in embarrassment at the increasing frequency of hasty resignations and outright desertions.

The deaths which impoverished the parishes and led to the resignation of some clergy had a similar effect upon the other great medieval institution, the manor. Everywhere throughout England the deaths of tenants drastically reduced the value of land. Workers who could no longer pay the previous rents and taxes moved on, in hope of earning the higher wages that came to be paid for the services of a radically diminished work-force. In 1350, the Black Prince was forced to remit a quarter of the rents of the tenants in the district of Tintagel 'for fear that they should through poverty depart from their holding'. Further evidence of the effect of the disease is provided by the receiver of the revenues of the Prince of Cornwall who wrote in 1353 that the estates remained in a deplorable condition and that he 'has not been able to let [the lands], nor to raise or obtain anything from the said lands and tenements, because the said tenements for the most part have remained unoccupied, and the lands lain waste for want of tenants [in the place of those] who died in the mortal pestilence lately raging in the said county'. From Tintagel, too, there comes definite evidence of the defection of the clergy, who too often, like the workers, moved on to more profitable territory: a contemporary record notes that the 'fifty shillings previously paid each year as stipend to the chaplain who celebrated in the chapel, was not paid this year, because no one would stay to minister there for the said stipend'. The coastal towns were also heavily hit. The disease was carried along, most probably, by fishing boats, and from the coast it spread up the rivers. The experience of Bodmin seems to be typical of the suffering in Cornwall. The register of the Church of the Friars Minor there estimates that 1,500 people died. The Augustinian priory was almost depopulated. The prior and all but two of the brothers died; and in March 1349 the two survivors wrote to their Bishop pleading to have a superior provided for their house since they 'were left like orphans'.

The disease appeared in London, which was in communication with other ports, in the autumn of 1348; one contemporary account says the pestilence had reached the city by September 29; others say it had a grip on the city no later than November 1. Conditions in London, as in other medieval cities, were such that the disease spread quickly and had a terrible effect. The streets were narrow, crowded and dirty, and houses were poorly ventilated. London tenements had at most one latrine for all occupants and many houses had none at all and were forced to empty their ordure into the yards or directly into the streets. Thousands of privies poured into the Thames, and the air was foul with the odour of slaughtered cattle. After the Black Death officials took action to correct the situation and a number of sanitary ordinances were passed, but even then to little effect. In 1361 the King issued a proclamation to the Mayor and Sheriffs that gives an idea of the conditions in the city:

> Because by the killing of great beasts, from whose putrid blood running down the streets and the bowels cast into the Thames, the air in the city is very much corrupted and infected, whence abominable and most filthy stench proceeds, sickness and many other evils have happened to such as have abode in the said city, or have resorted to it; and great dangers are feared to fall out for the time to come, unless remedy be presently made against it; we, willing to prevent such dangers, ordain, by consent of the present Parliament, that all bulls, oxen, hogs, and other gross creatures be killed at either Stratford or Knightsbridge.

It was not until 1388 that Parliament, prodded by several returns of the plague, passed a Sanitation Act for England which announced:

> For that so much dung and filth of the garbage and entrails, as well of beast killed as of other corruptions, be cast and put in ditches, rivers, and other waters . . . that the air is greatly corrupt and infect and many maladies and other intolerable diseases do daily happen, as well to inhabitants . . . as to others repairing or travelling thither . . . it is accorded and assented, that proclamation be made . . . throughout the realm of England that all they which do cast and lay all such annoyances shall cause them utterly to be removed . . . upon pain to lose and forfeit to our Lord the King.

A hundred and fifty years later Erasmus complained of the condition in English houses where 'almost all the floors are clay and rushes from the marshes, so carelessly renewed that the foundation sometimes remains for twenty years, harbouring there below spittle and vomit and urine of dogs and men, beer that hath been cast forth and remnants of fishes and other filth unnameable'.

The plague raged in London throughout the winter and spring and seems to have been at its height between February and Easter. Parliament, which was to have met at Westminster in January 1349, was prorogued; in the King's words, 'the plague of deadly pestilence had suddenly broken in the said place and the neighbourhood, and daily increased in severity so that grave fears were entertained for the safety of those coming there at that time'. As in other cities, the cemeteries were soon full and new ones were consecrated, the most important of which was in Smithfield where, a contemporary records, every day over 200 bodies were buried, over and above those buried in other churchyards in the city. An historian writing at the end of the 16th century reports that other new cemeteries were consecrated, one on a plot of ground called 'No Man's Land' which had become at the time of his writing a garden retaining the old name of Pardon Churchyard. The same writer says that in 1349 the Bishop of London consecrated an additional thirteen acres and a rood of ground adjoining 'No Man's Land' and he claims to have evidence that 50,000 bodies were buried in this one cemetery. The figure of 50,000 buried in one plot would seem to be a wild exaggeration and Gasquet discounts it. Hecker, however, accepts the figure of 50,000 for the total number of dead in London. Other estimates of the total dead in the city are as high as 100,000, but Dr. Creighton in his *History of Epidemics in Britain* estimates that the total population of London in 1349 was somewhere in the neighbourhood of 45,000. Once again one is confronted with baffling varieties of population figures and death estimates and it would be foolhardy to attempt to fix any figure for the mortality. But if the number of dead is in question, there is not the shadow of a doubt that a large percentage of the population of the city died; the little accurate information that is available makes that abundantly clear. Gasquet cites the increase in the number of wills proved in the 'Court of Hustings'. During the three years preceding the epidemic the average number of wills was twenty-two; in 1349 it jumped to 222. And the wills themselves give clear evidence of the rapidity with which whole families were wiped out; in one instance, a son, appointed executor of his father's will, died before probate could be obtained. Creighton produces evidence from the records of the guilds to show that the eight persons named warders of the Company of Cutlers in 1344 all died in 1349; and similarly in the Hatters' Company all six men appointed warders in 1347 were dead before the summer of 1350.

The episcopal registers for London are lost and there is only fragmentary evidence of the effect of the disease upon the city. From such sketchy bits of information one must try to imagine the suffering and chaos in London. The record is more complete, as we have seen, for many continental cities, and it is unlikely that London escaped the terror, the despair, and the disruption of institutions and moral life that characterized the Black Death in its appearance in other great cities. Defoe describes many scenes from the plague of 1665 that must have also occurred in the earlier epidemic: the rough burial carts rumbling through the streets loaded with sixteen or seventeen bodies, some wrapped in burial clothes, some in rags, some simply piled on naked; the inexpressible grief of a man standing huddled at the burial pit watching as his wife and children are rudely tipped out into a common grave; the horror and despair of a husband who sees the symptoms appear in his young wife, of a mother whose children are stricken. In their despair 'people that were infected and near their end, and delirious also, would run to those pits, wrapt in blankets or rugs, and throw themselves in, and, as they said, bury themselves. . . .'

Other poor despairing creatures who had the distemper upon them, and were grown stupid or melancholy by their misery, as many were, wandered away into the fields and woods, and into secret uncouth places almost anywhere, to creep into a bush or hedge and die. The inhabitants of the villages adjacent would, in pity, carry them food, and set it at a distance, that they might fetch it, if they were able; and sometimes they were not able, and the next time they went they should find the poor wretches lie dead and the food untouched . . . the country people would go and dig a hole at a distance from them, and then with long poles, and hooks at the end of them, drag the bodies into these pits, and then throw the earth in from as far as they could cast it, to cover them, taking notice how the wind blew, and so coming on that side which the seamen call to windward, that the scent of the bodies might blow from them. . . .

He describes the excessive precautions that people took to avoid infection: 'When anyone bought a joint of meat in the market they would not take it off the butcher's hand, but took it off the hooks themselves. On the other hand, the butcher would not touch the money, but have it put into a pot full of vinegar, which he kept for that purpose. The buyer carried always small money to make up any odd sum, that they might take no change.' Men grown weary of death became callous:

They sat generally in a room next the street, and as they always kept late hours, so when the dead-cart came across the street-end to go into Houndsditch, which was in view of the tavern windows, they would frequently open the windows as soon as they heard the bell and look out at them; and as they might often hear sad lamentations of people in the streets or at their windows as the carts went along, they would make their impudent mocks and jeers at them, especially if they heard the poor people call upon God to have mercy upon them. . . .

Westminster, also, was grievously afflicted. Here, as throughout England, the ecclesiastical records are the only complete ones and the effect of the disease upon the clergy most probably gives an indication of the effect upon the population as a whole. In Westminster the monastery was attacked and in May 1349 the abbot and twenty-seven of the monks died and were buried in a common grave in the cloister. The Hospital of St. James was devastated; the guardian and all the brothers and sisters except one died within a short time, and the survivor, William de Weston, was appointed guardian in May 1349. In 1353 the house was still without inmates.

Walsingham in the *Gesta Abbatum* describes the effects of the Black Death at St. Albans, where forty-seven monks died together with the prior and sub-prior. He gives an account of the last days of Abbot Michael Mentmore:

> The pestilence, which carried off well-nigh half of all mankind, coming to St. Albans he was struck by a premature death, being touched by the common misery amongst the first of his monks, who were carried off by the deadly disease. And although on Maundy Thursday he felt the beginning of the ailment, still out of devotion to the feast, and in memory of our Lord's humility, he celebrated solemnly the High Mass, and after that, before dinner, humbly and reverently washed the feet of the poor. Then, after partaking of food, he washed and kissed the feet of all the brethren. And all the offices of that day he performed alone and without assistance. On the morrow, the sickness increasing, he betook himself to bed, and like a true Catholic, having made, with contrite heart, a sincere confession, he received the Sacrament of Extreme Unction. And so in sorrow and sadness he lasted till noon of Easter-Day.

In the nearby counties—Bedfordshire, Buckinghamshire and Berkshire—there is no special record of the epidemic in the chronicles, but other sources of information give evidence of widespread mortality. Certain documents, called *Inquisitiones post mortem*, were filed with the King's Court whenever a landowner died. The whole country belonging, in theory, to the King, inquisitions were made into the value of land when the owner died and dues were levied against the new owner. The number of inquisitions made during the years of the Black Death is considerably higher than the average and in several cases a number of writs are addressed at the same time to the officials to inquire into many deaths in the same place. More interesting than the evidence the inquisitions provide of the death of many landholders is the testimony they give regarding the value of the land after the plague had passed. The chief value of an estate lay in the smaller tenants who paid rent or performed services; where the land was held in common, as was often the case, empty farms meant a decrease in yearly value. The extent of the radical devaluation of land, which may be seen from these documents, indicates the high mortality among the tenants. In Buckinghamshire the condition of the manor of Sladen was inquired into in August 1349, and the jury appointed declared that the mill there was no longer of any value since the miller had died and there were no tenants left in any case to bring corn to be ground. The rents for the land had previously brought in £12 a year, but after the plague there were no tenants at all and the land lay untilled and useless. On the whole manor, prior to the Black Death a prosperous one, there was in the summer of 1349 only one tenant. John Robyns, who occupied a little cottage and cultivated a single strip of land on a service rent worth seven shillings a year. At another place on the same estate only one of the tenants and cottars had survived, and at a third no one was alive at all. In Bedfordshire a cloth mill on the manor of Storington was declared of no value as a result of the plague, and land there, too, is described as uncultivated; even the woods could not be sold because there was no longer anyone to buy. In Berkshire, on the manor of Crokham, which belonged to Catherine, the wife of the Earl of Salisbury, all the free tenants and other holders were dead and the land which previously brought in rents of £13 a year was declared worthless. The same tale is repeated over and over again: no services were performed, no fees paid, no mills used, much of the land lay uncultivated; houses and tenements went unrented or were rented at greatly reduced rates. The drastic reduction in the work-force and in the value of land, occurring in England as it had also occurred on the continent, was to have its effect upon the political and economic situation throughout Europe in the years following the Black Death.

On the other side of London, the diocese of Canterbury, which comprised the south-eastern part of Kent with its long coast stretching from the Medway to the boundaries of Sussex, was very hard hit. Both Dover and Sandwich were chief points of communication with France; and the main road from London to the coast passed through the city of Canterbury. The plague tended usually to follow trade lines, and its situation along such routes made Canterbury especially susceptible. One contemporary estimate holds that less than a third part of the people of the diocese survived. Among the many victims was Thomas Bradwardine, the Archbishop of Canterbury, who had introduced into English several Arabic theorems in trigonometry and whose pupil, Richard Wallingford, Abbot of St. Albans, was one of the leading mathematicians of the 14th century. The diocese of Rochester, which included the western part of Kent, was no less affected. An account of the plague there was left by William Dene, a monk of Rochester and a contemporary of the events he chronicles:

> A plague such as never before had been heard of ravaged England in this year. The Bishop of Rochester out of his small household lost four priests, five gentlemen, ten serving men, seven young clerks, and six pages, so that not a soul remained who might serve him in any office. . . . Alas, for our sorrow! this mortality swept away so vast a multitude of both sexes that none could be found to carry the corpses to the grave. Men and women bore their own offspring on their shoulders to the church and cast them into a common pit. From these there proceeded so great a stench that hardly anyone dared to cross the cemeteries.

The writer goes on to give evidence of the rebelliousness of workers and the defection of the clergy:

> In this pestilence many chaplains and paid clerics refused to serve, except at excessive salaries. The Bishop of Rochester, by a mandate addressed to the Archdeacon of Rochester, on the 27th of June, 1349, orders all these, on pain of suspension to serve such cures. . . . So great was the deficiency of labourers and workmen of every kind in those days that more than a third of the land over the whole kingdom remained uncultivated. The labourers and skilled workmen were imbued with such a spirit of rebellion that neither king, law, nor justice could curb them. . . . And priests, little weighing the sacrifice of a contrite spirit, betook themselves to places where they could get larger stipends than in their own benefices. On which account many benefices remained unserved, whose holders would not be stayed by the rule of their Ordinary. Thus, day by day, the dangers to soul both in clergy and in people multiplied.

To William Dene's account of priests abandoning their parishes for higher salaries elsewhere, may be added the testimony of Stephen Birchington, in his history of the Archbishops of Canterbury, that 'there was such a scarcity and dearth of priests that the parish churches remained almost unserved, the beneficed persons, through fear of death, left the care of the benefices, not knowing where to go'. Although English contemporary accounts of the Black Death do not reveal the lurid details of social and religious demoralization witnessed on the continent, and although England seems to have remained free, for one reason or another, of the most violently hysterical responses to the plague, the subsequent rapid growth of reformist movements and the widespread disaffection from the established clergy provide evidence that the cowardly behaviour of the priests during the epidemic was not an isolated phenomenon.

To the south of London the diocese of Winchester included the counties of Surrey and Hampshire and the Isle of Wight. In October 1348, responding to the news of the plague in other parts of England, Bishop Edynton wrote to his clergy:

A voice in Rama has been heard; much weeping and crying has sounded throughout the various countries of the globe. Nations, deprived of their children in the abyss of an unheard plague, refuse to be consoled because, as is terrible to hear of, cities, towns, castles, and villages, adorned with noble and handsome buildings, and wont up to the present to rejoice in an illustrious people, in their wisdom and counsel, in their strength, and in the beauty of their matrons and virgins; wherein, too, every joy abounded, and whither multitudes of people flocked from afar for relief; all these have already been stripped of their population by the calamity of the said pestilence, more cruel than any two-edged sword. And into these said places now none dare to enter, but fly far from them as from the dens of wild beasts. Every joy has ceased in them; pleasant sounds are hushed, and every note of gladness is banished. They have become abodes of horror, and a very wilderness; fruitful country places, without the tillers, thus carried off, are deserts and abandoned to barrenness. And, news most grave which we report with deepest anxiety, this cruel plague, as we have heard, has already begun to singularly afflict the various coasts of the realm of England. We are struck with the greatest fear lest, which God forbid, the fell disease ravage any part of our city and diocese. And although God, to prove our patience, and justly to punish our sins, often afflicts us, it is not in man's power to judge the Divine counsels. Still, it is much to be feared that man's sensuality, which, propagated by the tendency of the old sin of Adam, from youth inclines all to evil, has now fallen into deeper malice and justly provoked the Divine wrath by a multitude of sins to this chastisement.

Having attributed the plague to Divine wrath, the Bishop proposes

confession, public prayer and processions to be made with bowed
heads and bare feet in towns through the market-places, and in
villages through cemeteries and around the church in the hope that
God 'may cause the severity of the plague to be stayed'. But the
plague was not stayed; by Christmas it had begun and by mid-
January 1349 it had its grip on the diocese. In response to the rising
number of deaths the Bishop, on January 19, granted plenary
indulgence to all who 'should confess their sins with sincere repentance to any priest they might choose'. The indulgence which was
originally to last until Easter was subsequently extended to the feast
of St. Michael.

As the plague ravaged Winchester, the regular cemeteries proved
inadequate to hold the dead. The Bishop ordered that the old ones
be enlarged and new ones consecrated, but these, it would seem, still
proved inadequate. The problem of burial produced a curious
incident which Gasquet cites. In January 1349, a monk of St.
Swithun's, brother Ralph de Staunton, was conducting a funeral in
one of the consecrated cemeteries when he was set upon and severely
beaten by a group of people. Gasquet feels that the incident arose
from a dispute about burial practices: the clergy for obvious reasons
insisting that the dead be buried in consecrated ground, the townspeople saying that ordinary laws and practices had proved inadequate and must, in such an emergency, be set aside. Bishop Edyndon, convinced that the attackers were not citizens of Winchester
but rather 'low class strangers and degenerate sons of the Church',
excommunicated them and ordered sermons to be preached on the
doctrine of the resurrection of the flesh. But the evidence provided
by Gasquet submits of other interpretation, especially in the light
of a further incident which occurred in the next month. The Bishop
filed a charge and the King appointed a commission to investigate
his assertion that the Mayor, bailiffs and citizens of Winchester had
broken down the walls of an enclosure adjoining the cemetery of the
Cathedral Church of St. Swithun's, which the Bishop had recently
consecrated as a burial ground. The citizens, it appears, had
demolished the walls in order to hold markets and a fair. Such
blatant defiance, not only of the Bishop, but of the basic principles
of the Church, would seem to indicate a dissatisfaction with more
than the funeral arrangements in Winchester.

As elsewhere in England, the mortality in the diocese of Winchester seems to have been about fifty per cent. At St. Swithun's
there had been, prior to the plague, some sixty-four monks; after

1349 they were reduced to between thirty-five and forty, and there seem never again to have been more than forty-two until the house was finally dissolved in the reign of Henry VIII. In Hampshire and the Isle of Wight, the average annual appointment to benefices in the years immediately preceding the Black Death was twenty-one, but in 1349 there were 228 institutions registered of which over two hundred beneficed clergy were very probably victims of the plague. At one time or another during the Black Death nearly every living on the Isle of Wight became vacant, and some had to be filled more than once. In Surrey, too, where there were ninety-two institutions in 1349, as against an average of about nine for the preceding years, the mortality among the clergy, and by implication among the people, generally was very high. Further evidence of the extent of the disaster in Surrey is provided by the inquisitions. In March 1349 an inquiry into the condition of the land of William de Hastings reveals that all the tenants but ten were dead and all the other houses, empty for want of tenants, were of no value that year. Elsewhere in the county a watermill was declared valueless because all the tenants who used it were dead, and no one could be found to rent it.

The Church as well as the Manor had its financial troubles. The Abbey of Hyde, as hard hit by plague as St. Swithun's, was forced to surrender its possessions into the hands of Bishop Edyndon to avoid the total destruction of the house. The Benedictine Convent of St. Mary's was reduced to about one half of its previous number and brought to the edge of financial ruin. Once again, the house owed its salvation to Bishop Edyndon. In a letter acknowledging the Bishop as their second founder, the nuns say that 'he counted it a pious and pleasing thing mercifully to come to their assistance when overwhelmed by poverty, and when, in these days, evil doing was on the increase and the world was growing worse, they were brought to the necessity of secret begging'. It appears that Bishop Edyndon and his relatives undertook the support and protection of most of the religious houses of the diocese.

The Bishop's troubles in the diocese were not only financial. In December 1352, he was forced to make an inquiry into the state of the monastery at St. Swithun's which had fallen heavily into debt. In a letter to the prior he says that it has been reported to him 'that in this our church the former fervour of devotion in the divine service and regular observance has grown lukewarm' and that 'guests are not received there so honourably as before; on which account we wonder not a little and are troubled the more because so far you have not informed us'. The same state of affairs existed at Christchurch priory and a similar inquiry was made there. In June 1350, the Bishop complained of Sireborne priory that 'the oblations of sacrifices had ceased, and from very hunger the devotion of priests was grown tepid; the buildings were falling to ruins, and its fruitful fields, now that the labourers were carried off, were barren'. Two months earlier, the Bishop had been forced to issue a general admonition to his clergy. He had received reports, he writes, that some priests 'have most shamefully absented themselves from their churches', so that 'even divine sacrifices had been left off' and the churches themselves 'left to birds and beasts. . . .' He consequently ordered all priests to return to their cures within a month or to find fitting substitutes. And in May, in a joint letter of the Archbishop and Bishops, he ordered priests to serve the churches at their previous stipends, further evidence of the weakening of the bishop's control over the clergy and of the defection of priests from their parishes.

In Winchester itself, the burden of taxation at the pre-plague rates forced many people to leave the city. One document relates that citizens, long resident in the city, 'because of the taxation and other burdens now pressing on them, are leaving the said city with the property they have made in the place, so as not to contribute to the said taxes. And they, betaking themselves to other localities in the county, are leaving the said city desolate and without inhabitants. . . .'

In the rest of England the plague raged with the same ferocity. From Bristol the disease was carried to Gloucester where, the chronicler Galfrid le Baker reports, the people of the town refused to admit men from Bristol in the belief that their breath was infectious. But the attempted isolation was fruitless. The plague seized Gloucester as well and the death toll was as great as in the rest of the country; le Baker estimates it to have been nearly nine-tenths of the population. By the summer of 1349 the disease had appeared in the county of Worcester where nearly half the total number of benefices in the county were at one time or another vacant before the plague abated. Among the dead was the Bishop of Worcester, Wulstan de Braunsford, who died in August 1349. An inquisition into the receipts of the Bishop's estates, from the time of his death until the appointment of his successor in November, reveals a gloomy picture of the state of affairs in the county. The investigator reported that tenants could not be found at any price, the mills were idle, the forges unused, the pigeon houses in ruins and the birds all gone, the harvest was not brought in and even if it had been there was no one left to buy the produce. Of the £140 due in rent £84 was never received. Elsewhere in the county an inquisition into the affairs of the manor of Hartlebury revealed that of seventy-two tenants who had previously paid 106 shillings and 11½ pence a year, nothing at all could be collected 'because all the tenants had died in the mortal sickness before the date of this account'. In the county of Warwick, which, with Gloucestershire and Worcestershire, made up the diocese of Worcester, the results of the plague were the same. Ecclesiastical records show an extraordinary number of livings bestowed; the Mayor of Coventry and the Bishop died. A passage from Smyth's *Lives of the Berkeleys* reveals that in 1349 on the manor of Hame in Gloucestershire 'so great was the plague . . . that so many workfolks as amounted to 1,444 days' work were hired to gather in the corn of that manor alone, as by their deaths fell into the Lord's hands or else were forsaken by them'. Not only is the devastation of the manor apparent but it is interesting to note that in the absence of tenants the landowners were obliged to pay wages to workers to bring in the harvest. The scarcity of workers after the Black Death and the possibility of working for a wage were strong inducements to the surviving peasants to abandon their old landlords and strike out on their own.

In Oxford the suffering was extraordinary even in such a terrible time. In the year of the epidemic the city had no less than three mayors. Those who could fled the city and those that remained were almost totally swept away. The University was particularly affected: school doors were shut, colleges and halls abandoned with hardly anyone left to keep possession of them. The student population seems to have been badly hit, but it is impossible to estimate the total that might have died, and there is even considerable controversy about the number of students in the University in the mid-14th century. Perhaps the best known figure is provided by Archbishop FitzRalph of Armagh, who had been Chancellor of the University before the Black Death. In his *Defensorium Curatorium*, written in 1357, FitzRalph states that while he was Chancellor there were 30,000 students at Oxford, but that at the time of his writing there were not 6,000. The figure of 30,000 is supported by Gascoigne who wrote in the time of Henry VI that there had once been '30,000 scholars at Oxford, as I have seen on the rolls of the ancient Chancellors, when I was Chancellor there'. But even granting

that students came to the University from all over Europe and
that Oxfordshire was, in the mid-14th century, at the height of its
prosperity and the wealthiest county in England, the figure of
30,000 students is quite incredible and another example of the tendency of writers in the Middle Ages to use large numbers to impress
or appal, and to use facts or perhaps even make up 'facts', to add
dressing to argument and rhetoric. In any case, FitzRalph's explanation for the depopulation of the University is not the plague but the
iniquity of the Friars with whom he was engaged in a bitter quarrel.
Coulton dismisses the Archbishop's figure as 'a capital example of
medieval irresponsibility in thought and word, in the face of numbers too great to be checked offhand by rule of thumb' and provides
his own much lower figure of 1,500 students in about 1300, the
University's highest point, and in 1450 probably 1,000 or less. In
discounting FitzRalph's calculations, Coulton offers an additional
insight into the disconcerting lack of accuracy in medieval handling
of numbers. In 1371 the Commons voted a tax on the supposition
that there were 50,000 parishes in England, relying on monastic
chronicles and other records that regularly noted that there were
between 40,000 and 50,000. Had they bothered to refer to the
bishops they would have discovered that in fact there were less then
9,000; but the budget was calculated on the accepted figure and in
consequence there was a deficit of over seventy-five per cent. Perhaps Coulton's figure for the student population in Oxford is too
low, but it seems certain to be closer to the truth than the Archbishop's. In any case, one may assume that the students were no
more fortunate than any other group in avoiding the plague and that
between a third and a half of them were very likely carried off by it.
In 1354 the 'Great Slaughter' at Oxford between Town and Gown
aggravated an already serious situation, and the next year the King
felt compelled to address a letter to the Bishops. He asks them to
help renew the University which had become 'like a worthless fig-
tree without fruit'.

Cambridge suffered as well. In the town, the church of St.
Sepulchre fell vacant in May 1349, and by July several other
churches were without incumbents. A document from 1366 records
the proposal of the Bishop of the diocese to unite two parishes in
Cambridge, the churches of All Saints and St. Giles, since the
parishioners of the former were all dead of the pestilence and those
that remained had gone to the parishes of other churches. The nave
of All Saints was said to be in such ruinous condition that 'the bones

of the dead [are] exposed to beasts'. As in Oxford the University must have suffered with the rest of the town, although here again there are no reliable figures about either the number of students or the number of dead. Coulton, in his discussion of the number of students at Oxford during the period, mentions that in 1450 the average number of degrees conferred there was 91.5 a year while at Cambridge the number of degrees never rose above 50 until the time of Elizabeth, indicating that there were fewer students at Cambridge. Evidence that the University did, in fact, suffer from the plague, is provided by Thorold Rogers who wrote that 'being at Cambridge while the foundations of the new Divinity School were being laid, I saw that the ground was full of skeletons, thrown in without any attempt at order, and I divined that this must have been a Cambridge plague pit'.

Records for the clergy are, once again, more complete and indicate that they suffered terribly. The Bishop of the diocese was abroad when the plague struck and to provide for the continued government of his see he wrote from Rome appointing one John, prior of Barnwell, to dispose of all vacant benefices; then he lists another to take his place in case he should die, and finally, he lists six more to fill the post in the event of widespread deaths. The Bishop obviously had experience of the ravages of the Black Death, and it would seem his precautions were justified. For the three years prior to 1349 the average number of institutions was nine; in 1349 ninety-seven appointments had to be made, and the prior of Barnwell was already dead when the Bishop's letter, commissioning him to fill the vacancies, was delivered.

In the diocese of Norwich which included the counties of Norfolk and Suffolk, the epidemic was at its height during the summer of 1349. In a single year eight hundred parishes lost their priests, eighty-three of them twice, as against a previous yearly average of seventy-seven. The mortality in the religious houses was very heavy. At Heveringland the prior and canons died to a man, and only one survived at Hickling; neither house recovered from the disaster. The Friars of Our Lady, in Norwich, are all reported to have died. Dr. Jessopp in *The Coming of the Friars* says that 2,000 clergy died in the diocese within a few months. Nearby on the manor of Cornard Parva, which had fifty tenants before the disease, some twenty-one families were completely destroyed. Other evidence from the manors indicates that the mortality was as great in Norfolk and Suffolk as elsewhere in England, and with the same

effect: lowered rents, idle land, pastures and mills. Norwich and
Yarmouth were both hard hit. In the former, by 1368 ten parish
churches had disappeared and fourteen more were useless out of a
pre-plague total of sixty. On the authority of an ancient record in the
Guildhall, Blomefield, in his *History of Norfolk*, estimated the population of the city at 70,000 and put down the number of plague-dead
at 57,374. Once again Professor Coulton is on hand to point out the
inaccuracy of medieval records when it comes to figures: although
it is generally accepted that Norwich was one of the most flourishing
cities of England before the Black Death, he says that its population
'pretty certainly never exceeded 17,000, and was in all likelihood
considerably less'. It again seems impossible to arrive at any reasonable figure for the number of dead, but, as in the rest of the country,
it would seem that somewhere in the neighbourhood of half the
inhabitants perished. Yarmouth, too, was a flourishing port. When
London furnished twenty-five ships and 662 sailors for Edward's
attack upon Calais, Yarmouth is reported to have sent forty-three
ships and 1,950 men. Hecker says that 7,052 died there, basing his
figure, it would seem, upon a petition from the people of Yarmouth
to Henry VII in the begininng of the 16th century in which they
assert that the prosperity of the town was destroyed by the plague
during the time of Edward III; 7,052 people, the petition says, were
buried in their churchyard 'by reason whereof the most part of the
dwelling places and inhabitation of the said town stood desolate and
fell into utter ruin and decay, which at this day are gardens and void
grounds. . . .' Gasquet believes that the figure refers to only one
graveyard and disagrees with another estimate which places the
town's population at 10,000 before 1349, noting that it had 220
ships and was preparing to enlarge Yarmouth Church, since presumably, large as it seems today, it was inadequate for the population. The work was never carried out. The unfinished towers of the
church of St. Nicholas at Yarmouth are a continuing reminder of
the Black Death which interrupted the work.

   To the west, the effects of the disease in the county of Leicester
are described by Knighton, the canon of Leicester abbey who
complained about the frivolity of the dress and behaviour of women
at tournaments. He writes:

> In Leicester, in the little parish of St. Leonard, more than 380 died;
> in the parish of Holy Cross, more than 400; in the parish of St. Mar-
> garet in Leicester, more than 700. And so in each parish, they died in
> great numbers. Then the bishop of Lincoln sent through the whole

diocese, and gave the general power to each and every priest, both regular and secular, to hear confessions and to absolve by the full and entire power of the bishop, except only in the case of debt. And they might absolve in that case if satisfaction could be made by the person while he lived, or from his property after his death. . . . During the same year, there was a great mortality of sheep everywhere in the kingdom in one place, and in one pasture, more than 5,000 sheep died and became so putrified that neither beast nor bird wanted to touch them. And the price of everything was cheap, because of the fear of death; there were very few who took any care for their wealth, or for anything else. For a man could buy a horse for half a mark, which before was worth forty shillings; a large fat ox for four shillings, a cow for twelve pence, a heifer for sixpence, a large fat sheep for four pence, a sheep for three pence, a lamb for two pence, a large pig for five pence, a stone of wool for nine pence. And sheep and cattle wandered about through fields and among the crops, and there was no one to go after them or to collect them. They perished in countless numbers everywhere, in secluded ditches and hedges, for lack of watching, since there was such a lack of serfs and servants that no one knew what he should do. For there is no memory of a mortality so severe and so savage from the time of Vortigern, king of the Britons, in whose time, as Bede says, the living did not suffice to bury the dead. In the following autumn, no one could hire a reaper at a lower wage than eight pence with food, or a mower at less than twelve pence with food. Because of this, much grain rotted in the fields for lack of harvesting, but in the year of the plague, as said above, among other things, there was so great an abundance of all kinds of grain that no one seemed to have concerned himself about it.

In addition to providing an account of the ravages of the countryside and the economic chaos occasioned by the plague, the good canon's account reveals something about his own attitudes and, perhaps, about human nature. As we shall see, one of the amazing things about the Black Death is not how much it changed the world and men, but rather how many things it left unchanged. In the midst of an unprecedented disaster, Knighton concerns himself primarily with the price of pigs and takes careful notice of the fact that debtors are not to be included in the Bishop's order of indulgence. At a time when nearly every other human activity seems to have been paralysed, when institutions of all sorts found it necessary to suspend activities, the tax collectors were in action as usual, the inquisitors on hand to evaluate property as soon as the owner died, and peasant and priest alike were off in search of higher wages.

Nearby, in the county of Hereford, the episcopal register of 1352 provides evidence of the effects of the plague there. The Bishop found it necessary in that year to unite the two churches of Great Colington and Little Colington into one parish, and in supporting the Bishop's order the two priests write that 'the sore calamity of pestilence of men lately passed, which ravaged the whole world in every part, has so reduced the number of the people of the said churches, and for that said reason there followed, and still exists, such a paucity of labourers and other inhabitants, such manifest sterility of the lands, and such notorious poverty in the said parishes, that the parishioners and receipts of both churches scarcely suffice to support one priest'. In the diocese of Hereford, which also included part of Shropshire, the average number of institutions to benefices during the years preceding the plague was about thirteen; in 1349 there were 175 institutions and forty-five more the following year. In Derbyshire the effect upon the clergy was the same: out of a total of 108 benefices, fully 104 fell vacant during 1349 and 1350; but of this total, it appears that twenty-two vacancies were the result of resignations.

Further evidence of the immediate economic effects of the Black Death comes from Cheshire and Derbyshire. On the manor of Bucklow in 1350 215 acres of good land were said to be lying waste for want of tenants, some of whom had died and others gone off. It was necessary to remit one-third of the rent on the estate. The remission was not given willingly, however, but under threat of the tenants who 'wished to depart and leave the holdings on the lord's hands, unless they obtained this remission until the world do come better again, and the holdings possess a greater value. . . .' Had the tenants left, they might well have done so to go as paid labourers to bring in the harvest on other manors. They might have found immediate and profitable employment on a not-too-distant estate near Burton-on-Trent where all the tenants are reported to have died, and the harvest was gathered in, not as before by the tenants, but by paid-labour employed at a cost of £22 18s. 10d.

In York Archbishop Zouche was one of the first English prelates to take account of the gravity of the epidemic on the continent, and as early as July 1348 he wrote:

Since man's life on earth is a warfare, those fighting amidst the miseries of this world are troubled by the uncertainty of a future, now propitious, now adverse. For the Lord Almighty sometimes permits those whom he loves to be chastised, since strength, by infusion of spiritual grace, is made perfect in infirmity. It is known to all what a mortal

pestilence and infection of the atmosphere is hanging over various
parts of the world, and especially England, in these days. This indeed,
is caused by the sins of men who, made callous by prosperity, neglect
to remember the benefits of the Supreme Giver.

And he prescribes prayers, processions and litanies; announcing
causes and cures with the same sort of dogmatic assurance that
characterized the utterances of the Paris medical faculty in the early
days of the epidemic.

There is something almost obscene in the Archbishop's bland
assurance that suffering is the punishment for sin and in his sophistry that infirmity perfects strength, in the same way that there is
something nauseating in the patriotic speeches of old men sending
young men off to war and later bestowing their praise and tin medals
upon the crippled survivors. One would think that the Archbishop
might, at least, have read Job. One can maliciously hope that, like
Job's counsellors who showed great courage in enduring the suffering of others and sophistication in justifying it, the Archbishop was
tormented with boils for his presumption; there is no record that
he was. Still, if the Archbishop did not learn the lesson of great
universal suffering, others did, and they came to question some of
the more fatuous pronouncements of great men. One of the lessons
of the Black Death, in the words of Cardinal Gasquet, whose history of the plague in England is the source of so much information,
is that 'it is a well-ascertained fact, strange as it may seem, that men
are not as a rule made better by great and universal visitations of
Divine Providence'. Strange, indeed.

The plague was not turned aside by prayers. The chronicle of
Meaux Abbey reports that Abbot Hugh 'besides himself had in the
convent forty-two monks and seven lay brethren; and the said
Abbot Hugh, after having ruled the monastery nine years, eleven
months and eleven days, died in the great plague which was in the
year 1349, and thirty-two monks and lay brethren also died.' 'This
pestilence so prevailed in our said monastery, as in other places,'
says this observer,

> that in the month of August the abbot himself, twenty-two monks and
> six lay brethren died; and of these, the abbot and five monks were lying
> unburied in one day, and the others died, so that when the plague
> ceased, out of the said fifty monks and lay brethren, only ten monks
> with no lay brethren were left. And from this the rents and possessions
> of the monastery began to diminish, particularly as a greater part of

our tenants in various places died, and the abbot, prior, cellarer, bursar, and other men of years, and officials dying left those, who remained alive after them, unacquainted with the property, possessions, and common goods of the monastery.

The situation of the house deteriorated until, in 1354, in a miserable condition, it was handed over to a royal commission. In York itself there is enduring evidence of the Black Death: the west front and the nave of York Minster were under construction when the Black Death appeared, and as a result a makeshift wood vaulting was added to the nave and the building of the choir was delayed twelve years until 1361; when building resumed the flowing lines of the Decorated style of the west front gave place to the formality of the Perpendicular.

The conditions in the counties on the Scottish border were already bad before the coming of the Black Death. Invasions from the north had rendered much of the land in Cumberland uninhabitable and, added to the usual misery of the population, the plague must have been an intolerable burden. The audit of the accounts of the Vice-Sheriff of the County, Richard de Denton, reveal that still in 1354 the great part of the manor lands attached to the King's castle at Carlisle were uncultivated 'by reason of the mortal pestilence lately raging in those parts'. The report says that for a year and a half after the plague had passed the entire lands had remained 'uncultivated for lack of labourers and divers tenants. Mills, fishing, pastures and meadow lands could not be let during that time for want of tenants willing to take the farms of those who died in the said plague.' From Durham and Northumberland comes evidence that the tenants who remained on the land were in a rebellious mood. An investigation into the conditions of an estate in Durham states that 'there is no one who will pay the fine for any land, which is in the lord's hands through fear of the plague. And so all are in the same way of being proclaimed as defaulters until God shall bring some remedy'. In another record it is reported that 'all refused their fines on account of the pestilence'. On one estate a tenant was 'unwilling to take the land in any other way, since even if he survived the plague, he absolutely refused to pay a fine'.

Nor was Scotland spared. Knighton writes:

The Scots, hearing of the cruel pestilence in England, suspected that this had come upon the English by the avenging hand of God, and when they wished to swear an oath, they swore this one, as the vulgar rumour reached the ears of the English, 'be the foul deth of Engelond.'

And so the Scots believing that the horrible vengeance of God had fallen on the English, came together in the forest of Selkirk to plan an invasion of the whole kingdom of England. But savage mortality supervened, and the sudden and frightful cruelty of death struck the Scots. In a short time, about five thousand died; the rest, indeed, both sick and well, prepared to return home, but the English, pursuing them, caught up with them, and slew a great many of them.

Little is known of the effect of the Black Death upon Wales and Ireland. Galfrid le Baker says simply: 'The following year it devastated Wales as well as England, and then passing over to Ireland it killed the English inhabitants there in great numbers, but the pure-blooded Irish, living in the mountains and high lands, it hardly touched till A.D. 1357, when unexpectedly it destroyed them everywhere.' But some idea of the ravages of the plague in Ireland may be gathered from the account of Friar John Clyn, a Minorite of Kilkenny, who wrote in 1349:

Also this year, and particularly in the months of September and October, bishops, prelates, ecclesiastics, religious, nobles and others, and all of both sexes generally, came from all parts of Ireland in bands and great numbers to the pilgrimage and the passage of the water of That-Molyngis. So much so, that on many days you could see thousands of people flocking there, some through devotion, others (and indeed most) through fear of the pestilence, which then was prevalent. It first commenced near Dublin, at Howth, and at Drogheda. These cities— Dublin and Drogheda—it almost destroyed and emptied of inhabitants, so that, from the beginning of August to the Nativity of our Lord, in Dublin alone, 14,000 people died. . . .
From the beginning of all time it has not been heard that so many have died, in an equal time, from pestilence, famine, or any sickness in the world; for earthquakes, which were felt for long distances, cast down and swallowed up cities, towns, and castles. The plague too almost carried off every inhabitant from towns, cities and castles, so that there was hardly a soul left to dwell there. This pestilence was so contagious that those touching the dead, or those sick of it, were at once infected and died, and both the penitent and the confessor were together borne to the grave. Through fear and horror men hardly dared to perform works of piety and mercy; that is, visiting the sick and burying the dead. . . . This year was wonderful and full of prodigies in many ways; still it was fertile and abundant, although sickly and pro- ductive of great mortality. In the convent of the Minorites of Drogheda 25, and in that of Dublin 23, friars died before Christmas.
The pestilence raged in Kilkenny during Lent, for by the 6th of March eight friars, Preachers had died since Christmas. Hardly ever

did only one die in any house, but commonly husband and wife together, with their children, passed along the same way, namely, the way of death.

And I, brother John Clyn, of the order of Minorites, and the convent of Kilkenny, have written these noteworthy things, which have happened in my time and which I have learnt as worthy of belief. And lest notable acts should perish with time, and pass out of memory of future generations, seeing these many ills, and that the world is placed in the midst of evils, I, as if amongst the dead, waiting till death do come, have put into writing truthfully what I have heard and verified. And that the writing may not perish with the scribe, and the work fail with the labourer, I add parchment to continue it, if by chance anyone may be left in the future and any child of Adam may escape this pestilence and continue the work thus commenced.

To the melancholy account of Friar John may be added that of a monk at Tynemouth who sums up the course of the plague throughout Europe and the British Isles, telling the now depressingly familiar story of death and despair:

In the year of our Lord 1348, and in the month of August, there began the deadly pestilence in England which three years previously had commenced in India, and then had spread through all Asia and Africa, and coming into Europe had depopulated Greece, Italy, Provence, Burgundy, Spain, Aquitaine, Ireland, France, with its subject provinces, and at length England and Wales, so far, at least, as to the general mass of citizens and rustic folk and poor, but not princes and nobles.

So much so that very many country towns and quarters of innumerable cities are left altogether without inhabitants. The churches or cemeteries before consecrated did not suffice for the dead; but new places outside the cities and towns were at that time dedicated to that use by people and bishops. And the said mortality was so infectious in England that hardly one remained alive in any house it entered. Hence flight was regarded as the hope of safety by most, although such fugitives, for the most part, did not escape death in the mortality, although they obtained some delay in the sentence. Rectors and priests, and friars also, confessing the sick, by the hearing of the confessions, were so infected by that contagious disease that they died more quickly even than their penitents: and parents in many places refused intercourse with their children, and husband with wife.

In spite of the monk's assertion that the disease spared the princes and nobles, the Black Death was, as we have seen, no respecter of rank. If the rich were more fortunate than the poor, they were not exempt. Among the dead are numbered two queens of France, two princes of Sweden, the King of Castile and the Queen of Aragon, and Joan, the daughter of Edward III. Nor were the nobles of the Church spared: Cardinal Giovanni Colonna, Petrarch's patron, and the Archbishop of Canterbury were among the dead. Nor yet did natural talent confer any greater immunity than noble birth: Richard Rolle of Hampole, one of the most remarkable poets of the century, and William of Ockham, probably the most influential philosopher of his time, were both victims of the Black Death in England. The catastrophe was world-wide and universal. Perhaps the best summary of its devastation is a brief sentence from an old northern chronicle: 'And in these daies was burying withoute sorrowe and wedding withoute friendschippe and fleying without refute of socoure; for many fled from place to place because of the pestilence; but they were effecte and myghte not skape the dethe.'

Gasquet calculated the population of England before the plague to have been five million and concludes that 2,500,000 died. As we have seen, no estimate of population, and consequently of the mortality, is universally accepted. Gasquet's figure is based upon the Subsidy Roll of 1377 which indicates a population at the end of the reign of Edward III of about 2,350,000; he assumes that several severe outbreaks of plague after the visitation of 1349 would have held the population at a constant level after that time and, given the widely stated estimate that half the population died in that year, he reasons that it must have been double the 1377 figure before the Black Death, hence five million. He supports this figure by arguing that some 25,000 clergy died, a figure that is itself controversial even though more exact rolls for the clergy than for the population in general are available. He then assumes that about one in every hundred people belonged to the clergy, and again arrives at the figure of 2,500,000 for the mortality. It is obvious that the figure cannot be accepted unequivocally. But those who offer a smaller total, and some are as low as two million before the plague, have no surer evidence than the estimate of the amount of cultivated land and the probable number of people it would have supported. It cannot be emphasized too strongly that all figures from the period must be treated with considerable caution.

If the number of men who died of the plague is in doubt, there is no question whatever that the Black Death was an unprecedented catastrophe for which the only parallels are the Biblical story of the Flood and the 20th-century predictions of the effect of an all-out nuclear war. If the population figures for Europe and England during the 14th century are in question, there is widespread agreement with Froissart's estimate that one-third of the people in the world died, and that the population of Europe which had been steadily increasing for three centuries was sharply diminished and remained stagnant until the close of the Middle Ages. But as usual, the statistics, the dates, and the figures, tell only part of the story. Also of interest, perhaps of even greater interest, is what men did and thought about the disaster. It remains to consider the effect of the Black Death upon the attitudes and ideas of men and to investigate the subsequent changes that occurred in the political, economic, religious and cultural life of the Western world. Even if one were to ignore the psychological shock that the Black Death and the continuing plagues of the 14th century produced among the survivors, the sudden and drastic reduction of population alone would warrant a closer investigation of the plague's effects upon the period and upon later history than is normally offered by the general histories of the Middle Ages.

Chapter VII

FEAR, HEDONISM AND MURDER

MEN DO NOT seem to have appreciated the beneficence of the Divine Providence which sent the plague to correct their frivolity and strengthen their virtue. The contemporary chroniclers are agreed about that. The world got worse after the Death: charity grew cold, workers grew arrogant, revenues of Church and State dropped, people everywhere were more self-indulgent and frivolous than ever. Certainly some of the responses to the Black Death reveal the very extremes of human gullibility and cruelty: the frenzied search for preventives and cures, the depravity of the grave-diggers, the fear of poisoners, and, most horribly, the massacre of the Jews. But in considering the excesses of response to the disaster, it is well to keep in mind both the source of the contemporary reports and the general tendency of the age to see everything in extreme terms. The entire era was troubled by a great sense of insecurity and a deep pessimism, a general conviction that impending disaster hung over all and that the world was rapidly going from bad to worse. The obsession with the end of the world which characterizes the Middle Ages colours the response to the Black Death and was reinforced by it. The very name 'Middle Ages' envisions the Apocalypse. Although the term as the Renaissance humanists employed it refers to the ten centuries or so that separated 'ancient' and 'modern' times, it seems first to have been used by Tertullian in the 3rd century who spoke of a *medium aevum*—an age in the middle—to indicate the period between classical times and the day when the Gospel would prevail. The Middle Ages were looking for the end of the world, and to many the Black Death seemed to be it. We cannot ignore this overall pessimistic mood in examining the accounts of the aftermath of plague. In addition, one must bear in mind that the Middle Ages were a time of dramatic contrast characterized by vehement passion and great excitability of soul at all levels of society. It was an age of extremes which could produce both the exquisite art of the cathedrals and the most

145

diabolically sophisticated techniques and instruments of torture. The same extremes characterized the response to the plague. If it brought out the worst in some men, it brought out the best in others. Bad news is invariably more widely reported than good, but in the story of excess and terror that follows, one might keep in mind the surgeons and their youthful apprentices who stayed on to help the sick after the established physicians had fled Venice, or the nuns of the Hôtel-Dieu in Paris who remained at their posts and died comforting their patients.

Nor should one ignore the source for the contemporary reports of the wickedness of the world. One remembers that they were written, for the most part, by clergymen who were deeply committed to the idea of Original Sin and man's essential depravity, and were always on the look-out for evidence to support their convictions. The same writers, with a vested interest in preserving the authority and prosperity of the Church which they saw, and quite rightly saw, challenged by the individualistic religious fervour of groups like the Flagellants and the democratic demands of the peasants, were hardly the ones to appreciate the positive aspects of such movements. The great wickedness that the chroniclers saw sweeping over the world was, in many cases, the natural life force reawakening a numbed and bruised humanity and, in some others, the spirit of revolutionary change which was ultimately to sweep them and many of their privileges away as it created the modern sensibility and made way for the modern world. It is significant that the wickedness the chroniclers complain of is most frequently a slackening of fervour in observation of the forms of worship, the frivolity of dress and habits of common folk, the presumptuous new independence of labourers, and the general lack of respect for the clergy. Few of the chroniclers speak out against the slander of the Jews, and few mention the murders as an example of the evils of the age. The moralists of the 14th century were quick to see that men were wicked for wearing pointed shoes and growing their hair long, but too many of the same moralists gave their silent consent to the massacre of thousands of their fellow men. If the story of hysteria and cruelty that unfolds in the aftermath of the plague reveals the evil in man, it is well to remember that evil is very often more the result of ignorance than of malevolence and that mankind is most probably on the whole more good than bad, at least in its intentions. Besides, the question of whether man is essentially good or bad is, in spite of the chroniclers, almost irrelevant since, although malevolent men surely exist, it is more often than not ignorant good intentions that cause suffering. The 14th-century moralists offer an example. Maniacs and fanatics exist in every age and in every society, but they would be largely powerless without the silent support of ordinary people too careless or timid to oppose them. Surely the most incorrigible vice of mankind must be the ignorance that imagines it knows everything and claims for itself the right to persecute and kill. And the most ironic must be the silence of those who should oppose such ignorance but do not. There can be no virtue or goodness or love without right knowledge and clear thinking. And knowledge and clear thinking as regards the causes and meaning of plague were conspicuously lacking in the 14th century.

In the early days of the epidemic, as we have seen in the serenely detached pronouncement of the Paris medical faculty, it seems that men who were not yet actually afflicted themselves found it hard to conceive of the very credibility of such a disaster. The pronouncement with its firm prescriptions and its unshakeable conviction gives the impression that the doctors still thought everything was possible for them. In essence, by offering sure preventives and cures, they deny the existence of pestilence. Man is free and in control of things, business must go on as usual; but the lesson of plague for the world is that man is not free and business cannot go on as usual as long as such forces exist. Even in the midst of the disaster, many men solipsistically denied the existence of pestilence by conceiving of it as a bad dream, an aberration of the mind, which, could one but cure the mind, would surely pass away as bad dreams pass away. For some, like Boccaccio's young men and women, the cure lay in banishing concern with pleasant company and good talk. They, for the poet's dramatic purposes, succeed in escaping infection, and others, conceiving of the plague in the same way, tried to escape it by the same devices, reinforcing the idea that it was all a miasma and that men, if they set their minds right, could triumph over it. Some in their pride even imagined that having escaped this one epidemic they enjoyed total immunity from all disease. The vagaries of the plague were such that some escaped while their friends and neighbours, whose prior health and outward circumstances had been identical, died. The survivors, quite naturally, attributed their escape to the conscious efforts they had made to escape infection, in the same spirit in which some aged people attribute their longevity to the fact that they do, or do not, smoke or drink. As in the case of one maiden lady who was recently quoted, on the occasion of her one hundredth birthday, as attributing her long life, but not her spinsterhood, to the fact that every day for the previous eighty years she had chewed up a large piece of garlic every morning, the means taken to preserve life reveal more about the tastes of the person than the efficacy of the preservative. By the train of thought that argues *post hoc ergo propter hoc* and sustains superstitions in our own much more scientific age, all sorts of practices came to be accepted as effective plague preventives. The idea that salvation was to be found in positive thinking appears to have been widespread and from many places come tales of the attempts of men to triumph over pestilence by relegating it to the world of dreams and banishing it from the mind. In many places funeral bells and open displays of mourning were officially prohibited. In others it was decreed that burials be made only at night. A number of cities refused to publish the number of the dead. Some men, in the spirit of the Roman *lectisternium*, set about deliberately to cultivate gaiety and the epicurean life, and, for some, dissolute living seemed to offer the best chance of escape.

From time immemorial men have responded to uncertainty and danger by overriding traditional moral codes. Under attack by Sennacherib, Jerusalem turned to pleasure: 'And in that day the Lord God of Hosts called to weeping and to mourning, and to baldness, and to girding with sackcloth: but behold joy and gladness, slaying oxen, and killing sheep, eating flesh and drinking wine: let us eat and drink, for tomorrow we die.' In spite of the admonitions of the moralists, mankind, to its everlasting credit, seems to answer impending disaster with an irresistible burst of joy: the dance beneath the gallows is the wildest dance of all. To some, like the churchmen who lamented the breakdown of morality during and after the plague, and to Defoe to whom the wild living in the midst of death was revolting, such behaviour was worthy only of condemnation; but to others with more direct experience of the plague— one remembers that Defoe was only about six years old in 1665 and that, while his information is accurate, his attitudes towards the epidemic were probably formed more from reports of the plague in Marseilles in 1720 than from that of London and in any case are those of a reporter and historian rather than a witness of disaster— to others like Boccaccio and Pepys, who lived through plague, the gaiety, carefree living, and sexual promiscuity were much more tolerable. Entries from Pepys' diary during the darkest days of 1665 reveal anything but revulsion and despair:

September 30, 1665: So to sleep with a good deal of content, and saving only this night and a day or two about the same business a month or six weeks ago, I do end this month with the greatest content, and may say that these three months, for joy, health, and profit, have been much the greatest that ever I received in all my life, having nothing upon me but the consideration of the sicklinesse of the season during this great plague to mortify me. For all which the Lord God be praised!

December 31, 1665: I have never lived so merrily (besides that I never got so much) as I have done this plague time . . . and great store of dancings we have had at my cost (which I am willing to indulge myself and wife) at my lodgings. The great evil of this year, and the only one indeed, is the fall of my Lord of Sandwich, whose mistake about the prizes hath undone him.

Another forthright autobiographer, Benvenuto Cellini, experienced the plague in Rome in 1523 and, in some apprehension about the state of his health, set about enjoying himself in a conscious effort to promote the cheerfulness of mind which he felt was the best preventive. The activities that seem to have pleased him most were shooting pigeons among the ancient monuments and amorous sporting among the city's serving girls. The first, he feels, preserved his health and kept away the plague to which many of his friends succumbed. The latter seems to have finally brought him the infection, for after spending the night with a servant girl he developed the symptoms of plague. He recorded his initial reaction:

I rose upon the hour of breaking fast, and felt tired, for I had travelled many miles that night, and was wanting to take food, when a crushing headache seized me: several boils appeared upon my left arm, together with a carbuncle which showed itself just beyond the palm of the left hand, where it joins the wrist. Everybody in the house was in panic: my friend, the cow [a prostitute] and the calf [the serving girl] all fled. Left alone there with my poor little prentice, who refused to abandon me, I felt stifled at the heart and made up my mind for certain I was a dead man.

Cellini sought amusement as a cure as well as a preventive, and while the bubo was still open, went out riding on a little wild pony. After his recovery, he and other survivors held a joyous reunion which led to the formation of a club of all the leading painters, sculptors and goldsmiths of Rome, a club which seems to have been devoted much more to merrymaking than to artistic discussion.

Machiavelli may have been another who found in plague an excuse for amorous adventures. A document, *Descrizione della Peste di Firenze dell' anno 1527*, attributed to Machiavelli but whose authenticity is doubted by some, including Macaulay, catalogues the activities of licentious monks and the sexual exploits of the writer with all the frankness of Pepys and Cellini. Plague, like other ill winds, blows good for some, and one's naïveté would be considerable if one were surprised to discover that there are some men who find positive value in such a disaster. One such was the poet Francesco Berni, a contemporary of Machiavelli, who wrote:

The pestilence time is good—a fig for other times. . . . First, it carries off the rabble, it destroys them, makes holes among them and thins them out—like a housewife among the geese at Allhallowtide! In the churches there are none to press upon you. Besides, none keep any record of buying or borrowing. Yea, buy and make debts, for there will be no creditors to trouble you. And if a creditor should come, tell him that your head aches, and your arm pricks, he straight will go away, and will not turn him round! If you go out, no one will cross your path: rather is place yielded to you, and honour done you, especially if you are clothed in rags. You are lord of yourself and lord of others. You can watch the folk's strange antics and laugh at others' fear. Life has then new laws: every pleasure is allowed. . . . Above all, there need be no work done. It is a choice life, serene, and large: time passes very gaily from dinner time to supper.

Before we condemn such responses out of hand as irresponsible hedonism, it is best to remember that the duty of men under dire threat is not to despair but to survive. There is time for repentance after the world has recovered. Boccaccio in his later years repudiated the vernacular and his former life and work to retire in about 1360 to prayer and repentance. But immediately after the Black Death he composed the ribald tales of *The Decameron*, an assault upon traditional sexual morality so strenuous that, even in these days of licence, lurid advertisements for the book still appear occasionally in the back pages of cheap men's magazines offering to ship the volume in plain brown wrapper to any who are desperate, repressed or ignorant enough to send in two guineas.

It is impossible to determine whether the promiscuous behaviour described in *The Decameron*, in the romances of courtly love, and in the *fabliaux* of the 14th century was simply a literary convention or whether it was actually practised. The Middle Ages have not provided us with a satisfactory contemporary social history, and it may

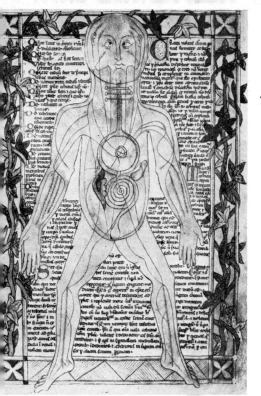

THE BLOOD-SYSTEM

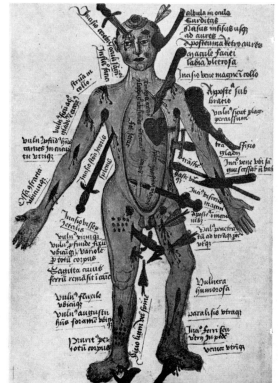

A MEDIEVAL SURGEON'S
CHART OF A MAN WITH
MULTIPLE WOUNDS

A DOCTOR FEELS THE PLAGUE PATIENT'S PULSE, PROTECTING HIMSELF BY HOLDING AN IMPREGNATED SPONGE TO HIS NOSE. THE SERVANTS ARE BURNING AROMATICS

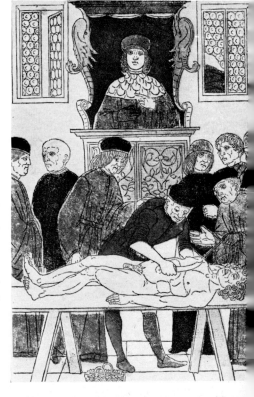

AN ANATOMY LESSON IN 15TH-CENTURY PADUA. THE LECTURER IS HELPED BY A DISSECTOR AND A DEMONSTRATOR

be as dangerous to assume that the literary conventions of the age were also social conventions as it would be to conclude that lurid 20th-century popular novels accurately reflect the social customs of our day. *The Decameron* may be as far removed from ordinary life as *Peyton Place, City of Night, Couples,* and *The Housewife's Guide to Promiscuity.* Even so, there is some evidence that small plague societies actually existed and that groups of young nobles did, in fact, imitate Boccaccio's company and retire to castles to spend their days with stories, games and the sport of love until the plague had passed. The evidence comes mostly from the condemnation of chroniclers who take evident satisfaction in noting that the plague mocked at the moats and walls and destroyed the sinners together with more conventional folk. Although the Paris doctors warned against sexual intercourse during the plague, ordinary men seem to have referred more frequently to a natural increase in sexual energy which, during wars and pestilence, provides for the replenishment of population. The disease itself, which often produced delirium, may have provided extraordinary stimulus and opportunity for sexual adventures. There are frequent reports of stricken women running naked through the streets and of their abandonment of traditional modesty before doctors, nurses and plague attendants. During an earlier plague in Paris, Geoffroy de Paris wrote:

La nuit, gisoient toutes nues
Les bonnes Genz par les rues.

The dramatic circumstances and the near certainty of death also tended to increase passion and inspire otherwise cautious men to seize the day, as in the case of the 16th-century painter Giorgione who, as Vasari reports, fell deeply in love with a plague victim, shared her infection, and died with her. The contemporary chroniclers, at least, seem to have felt that sexual morality, traditional modesty, and the institution of marriage were corrupted by the plague; and the more personal accounts of witnesses to later epidemics support the contention that there were some to whom plague brought sexual emancipation and some to whom it brought the opportunity for quick wealth through hasty, and cynical marriage.

Others, like the young revellers of Chaucer's Pardoner's Tale who spent their days swearing, dicing and drinking, found in the plague the excuse to abandon other restraints. Even if, like Chaucer's characters who set out drunkenly to kill Death and died in their folly, particular men failed to preserve themselves by the dissolute life, there were always some who did. And their example served as an excuse for others. In any case, the widespread failure of a popular remedy does not always bring it into disrepute, because its adherents can always say that it was not applied with sufficient vigour or that, bad as they are, things would have been very much worse without the application of their wisdom. But flight and careful and solicitous care for one's person, if not the indulgence of one's more basic appetites, did actually work in some cases, particularly well for one group of 14th-century men, the bishops, who were, Gasquet says, 'strangely spared, although it is certain that they did not shrink from their duty, but according to positive evidence remained at their posts'. But their duties involved primarily the issuing of letters of institution from their country manors where they avoided personal contact as much as possible and enjoyed, no doubt, a quite comfortable life. Perhaps for this reason, the mortality among them was considerably lower than among the clergy in general.

The reports of the abandonment of sexual morality gain credence from the nature of marriage conventions which, in the Middle Ages, were such as to encourage promiscuity and cynical materialism. The *mariage de convenance* was the normal arrangement for all classes from nobles to peasants. The principal consideration was a favourable settlement of property, and the suitability of the couple, much less their own wishes, was little considered. In the time of Henry III it was possible to ratify a marriage between four- and five-year-old children; there are frequent instances of seven-year-olds being betrothed by parents and guardians, and even the Church said no more than that babies in the cradle should not be given in marriage except under pressure of some urgent need, such as the desire for peace. As late as 1526 Erasmus wrote that 'it is no uncommon case, especially in France, for a girl of scarce ten years to be married and a mother next year. . . . It seems portentous, and yet we sometimes see it, especially in Britain and in Italy, that a tender child is married to a septuagenarian. . . .' Not surprisingly, when the marriage arrangements were primarily contracted to insure the exchange of property, people themselves were bought and sold like cattle. Coulton repeats the sad tale of Grace, daughter of Sir Thomas of Saleby, who, in about 1200 on the death of her father, became a great heiress and was given in ward to Adam Neville by the King. When Grace was four years old Adam proposed to marry her.

Although the Bishop forbad the marriage, it was none the less solemnized by a priest. Later, presumably after the death of Adam, King John sold the girl to his chamberlain for two hundred marks; when he died, Grace was sold again, this time for three hundred marks to a third husband. Coulton has also preserved the report of Bishop Stapledon, the founder of Exeter College, Oxford, who was sent by Edward II to inspect Philippa of Hainault to see if she would make a suitable wife for the future Edward III. The Bishop titled his report *Inspection and Description of the Daughter of the Count of Hainault, Philippa by name*, and he wrote:

> The lady whom we saw had not uncomely hair, betwixt blue-black and brown. Her head is clean-shaped; her forehead high and broad, and standing somewhat forward. Her face narrows between the eyes, and the lower part of her face is still more narrow and slender than the forehead. Her eyes are blackish-brown and deep. Her nose is fairly smooth and even, save it is somewhat broad at the tip and also flattened, yet it is no snub-nose. Her nostrils are also broad, her mouth fairly wide. Her lips somewhat full, and especially the lower lip. Her teeth which have fallen and grown again are white enough, but the rest are not so white. The lower teeth project a little beyond the upper; yet this is but little seen. Her ears and chin are comely enough. Her neck, shoulders, and all her body and lower limbs are reasonably well shapen; all her limbs are well set and unmaimed; and nought is amiss so far as a man may see. Moreover, she is brown of skin all over, and much like her father; and in all things she is pleasant enough, as it seems to us. And the damsel will be of the age of nine years on St John's day next to come, as her mother saith. . . .

When the Queen of Henry VII died in 1503, he sent three men to Spain to inspect the young Queen of Naples, widow of Ferdinand II, giving them very business-like instructions 'to note the clearness of her skin . . . to mark whether there appear any hair about her lips or not . . . to approach as near to her mouth as they honestly may, to the intent that they may feel the condition of her breath . . . to mark her breasts and paps, whether they be big or small.' Froissart comments on the subject that 'it is the usage in France that any lady, daughter to any great lord, if the king should marry her, first she should be seen and viewed all naked by certain ladies thereto admitted, to know if she were proper and meet to bring forth children'.

Marriages could be made and broken much more easily than might be supposed. Although it was claimed as a Sacrament from the time of Peter Lombard in the 12th century, the present orthodox doctrine was not made a question of faith until the Council of Trent at the end of the 16th century; and matrimonial litigation was among the most frequent and most confused of the Middle Ages. Although marriage was extolled as a Sacrament, the Church was not indispensable: the only necessary parties were the couple themselves, and the exchange of a verbal pledge and cohabitation constituted a valid marriage. Such marriages were termed 'irregular' and the couple was liable to punishment if the Church chose to proceed against them; but there was no question of the validity of the marriage. A marriage of this nature without witness or priest could be proved only if the parties involved testified on oath to its existence, and it could just as easily be denied. And, since boys of fourteen and girls of twelve could take such a step, some of them very likely were dissolved or denied later. But even the most carefully arranged marriages might be invalidated on a number of grounds, the most frequent of which was consanguinity. Until the Lateran Council in 1215, if the parties were related within the seventh degree the marriage was void; and later, if the couple were related within the fourth degree—that is if the husband and wife had a common great-great-grandparent—the marriage was void unless a papal dispensation could be procured. In the average village, where there were perhaps about seventy families, the chances of finding a legal husband or wife would have been small. It was among the nobility, rather than among the villagers, that the most frequent litigation for the dissolution of unsatisfactory, or unprofitable, marriages took place; and in these cases not only blood-relationship, but relationship through godparents, was adequate grounds for declaring a marriage null and void. Considering the inadequacy of records, and the complete absence of baptismal registers in the case of godchildren, a husband who wearied of a wife could easily enough discover that they were related. St. Anselm, Archbishop of Canterbury from 1093 to 1109, charged that marriages in Ireland 'are dissolved and changed without any reason. . . . It is said that men exchange their wives for those of other men as freely and publicly as any one changes one horse for another.' The accusation is echoed over and over again in the 14th century. Langland in *Piers Plowman* says that men may get rid of their wives simply by giving a judge a fur cloak and that Church lawyers 'make and unmake matrimony for money'. And a satire from the time of Edward II asserts:

If a man have a wyf,
And he love her nowt,
Bring hyr to the constery [consistory court]
Ther trewth schuld be wrowt.
Bring twei fals wytnes with hym,
And hymself the thrydde,
And he schal be deperted
As fair as he wold bydde,
   Fom his wyf;
He shal be mayntend fulle wel
   To lede a sory lyf.

When he is deperted
From his trew spowse,
Take his neyghëborës wyf
And bryng her to house. . . .

The marriage celebration itself was hardly a fit introduction to a life of moderation and fidelity. Erasmus complained that Christian marriage preliminaries, which were current when he wrote and had been customary for hundreds of years, were almost more indecent than those of the heathen, and that even after a proper Church ceremony, the couple returned home

> to a public and tumultous feast. They rise from table to join in wanton dances until supper, where the tender girl cannot refuse any man, but the house is open to the whole city. Then the unhappy maiden is compelled to join hands with the drunken, the scabby, and sometimes with criminals who are come more intent upon theft than upon dancing: In Britain she must even kiss with them. After an uproarious supper, dancing again, then fresh drinking; scarce can the wearied pair go to bed even after midnight. After a scanty interval, all revel with mad tumult at the chamber door, burst into the room, with obscene words, and return to the madness of yestereen. For, in some regions, this Corybantic fury is prolonged for three days. . . .

If Erasmus's distress seems a bit fastidious, it was certainly shared by people of his time: not only were monks forbidden to attend weddings, but the Rule of the Third Order of St. Francis even prohibited pious laymen from going.

Nor was the clergy as committed as it might have been to the sanctity of marriage. Concubinage was common among priests in the Middle Ages, and, if people learn by example, the example of the local clergy, in some places, would not have strengthened their

chastity. In 1248, when Archbishop Odo of Rigaud made a visit to
rural churches in Normandy, he found an extraordinary number of
priests to be 'ill-famed with women'. Typical of his discoveries was
that

> the priest of Ruiville was ill-famed with the wife of a certain stone-
> carver, and by her is said to have a child; also he is said to have many
> other children; he does not stay in his church, he plays ball, he does
> not stay in his church, he rides around in a short coat. . . . Also the
> priest of Gonnetot is ill-famed with two women, and went to the pope
> on this account, and after he came back he is said to have relapsed.
> . . . Also, the priest of Wanestanville, with a certain one of his parish-
> ioners whose husband on this account went beyond the sea, and he
> kept her for eight years, and she is pregnant; also he plays dice and
> drinks too much, he frequents taverns, he does not stay in his church. . .

Also, many more. The great stories of love in the Middle Ages are
frequently tales of adultery, for example, that of Tristan and Iseult;
and they must have represented the dreams, if not the practice, of a
great many unfortunates bound to an unloved mate in a marriage
of convenience and surrounded by blatant promiscuity even among
the clergy. The Black Death would seem not so much to have corrupted sexual morality as to have broken down some of the hypocrisy that surrounded sexual and marital life. Thucydides wrote of
the plague in Athens that 'men now coolly ventured on what they
had formerly done in a corner'. The 14th-century moralists would
seem to have preferred the common folk to have their sin in a
corner. They have much more to say about the open immorality
than about the inhuman and cynical marriage conventions that
made such behaviour inevitable. They have the same cloudy vision
in other areas. When the peasants brought their suffering out of the
corner and became openly rebellious, the moralists were quick to
condemn the rebellion but were almost silent about the system that
caused the suffering. Ours is not the only century that has been
plagued with fatuous guardians of good taste and morality whose
principal concern is that we should hide our energy and our despair
behind a façade of decorous commonplaceness. But people in the
14th century were coming out of their corners to suffer and have fun
openly. Chaucer's wife of Bath is a good example. She is so forthright that she still shocks tender readers with her naturalistic argument for sexual enjoyment. Her attitude and her marital experience
—her first three marriages were to rich old men, at the funeral of
her fourth husband she was interrupted in her mourning by her

interest in the comely legs of the man who was to be her fifth husband, and her trip to Canterbury is in part a search for a sixth— may not have been typical but they were certainly not unique. The Black Death made many rich widows and widowers and it is hardly surprising that in a society that saw marriage as a quite proper avenue to wealth there were many hasty marriages. Nohl has found evidence of one woman in Nimeguen who was married three times in the space of six weeks.

Other more exotic instincts seem also to have been liberated by the plague. Nohl reports a number of strange cases. In Corsica in 1355, one party introduced the common sharing of goods and women. He quotes a 'Munich manuscript' not otherwise identified, which describes the activities of another heretical sect: 'When they go to confession and come together and he preaches to them, he takes the one who is the most beautiful among them all and does to her according to his will, and they extinguish the light and fall one upon the other, a man upon a man, and a woman upon a woman, as it just comes about. Everyone must see with his own eyes how his wife or daughter is abused by others, for they assert that no one can commit sin below his girdle.' In his investigations, Nohl has discovered that a fresco in the cathedral of Albi depicts sodomites at work. He quotes also from the confession of Johannes and Albert Brünn of the Brothers of the Free Mind during the trials of the Beguines and the Beghards in the 14th century: 'And if one brother desires to commit sodomy with a male, he should do so without let or hindrance and without any feeling of sin, as otherwise he would not be a Brother of the Free Mind.' The Beghards accepted a life of poverty and Hay says the English 'beggar' derives from the name of the sect; one wonders, if Nohl's information is correct, if it might not also be the source of a common mild obscenity. 'Other curious doctrines,' Nohl continues, 'such as that incest is permissible, even when practised on the altar, that no one has the right to refuse consent, that Christ risen from the dead had intercourse with Magdalena, etc., all indicate the deterioration and confusion of moral ideas caused by the great plagues, particularly by that of 1348.'

Widespread deaths and the consequent sudden and unexpected transfer of wealth led to excesses far more deplorable than multiple marriages and sexual experimentation. During the Black Death and in later plagues, the helplessness of those stricken with the disease, the general breakdown of morality and the absence of effective law enforcement, led to a pervading fear of servants and even of wives, husbands, and children whose loyalty was too often more the result of economic advantage than of affection. Ignorance of the causes of the disease led many to suspect that it was the work of poisoners, and men who were frequently the victims of the intrigues of rivals in the best of times grew suspicious of anyone who stood to gain by their deaths. Ripamonti, the historian of the plague of Milan in 1630 quoted by Manzoni, wrote:

> And while the corpses always strewn about and lying in heaps before our eyes and underfoot made the entire city seem like an immense charnel-house, there was something even more ghastly, even more appalling in that mutual frenzy, that unbridled orgy of suspicion . . . not only was a neighbour, a friend, or a guest distrusted; even those names that are the bonds of human love, husband and wife, father and son, brother and brother, became words of terror; and (horrible and infamous to tell!) the family board and the nuptial bed were feared as hiding-places for the lurking poisoner.

Popular literature of the 14th century frequently found humour in a young wife's deceiving an old rich husband—one remembers Chaucer's Miller's Tale and his Merchant's Tale—and although the literary convention is hardly proof that such deception was common, the popularity of the subject insures that many a 'riche old gnof' wedded to a 'fair yonge wyf' would have, even in a normal time, 'demed hymself been lik a cokewold', and, in time of plague, harboured even more dire suspicions.

In the disordered conditions of a plague-ridden city, robbery was common and murder was not unknown. Defoe cites stories of murder from London in 1665, stories of a nurse 'that laid a wet cloth upon the face of a dying patient whom she tended, and so put an end to his life, who was just expiring before; and another that smothered a young woman she was looking to when she was in a fainting fit, and would have come to herself; some that killed them by giving them one thing, some another, and some starved them by giving them nothing at all.' To be sure he discounts most of these reports, but the truth or falsity of a rumour has little to do with its effect upon those who hear it in a moment of crisis; and fear and suspicion seem to have been the attendants upon plague in nearly every age and place where it appeared. Manzoni tells a story of such terror and treachery during the Milan epidemic of 1630 when the dread of being carried off to the hideous *lazzaretto* was as great, or perhaps even greater, than the fear of death itself. The *monatti* were men employed to remove the corpses from the houses, streets, and *lazzaretto*, carting them to the pits and burying them; in Milan, as in earlier and later plagues, they were recruited from the dregs of society and numbered among them convicts freed upon a promise to serve in that ghastly and dangerous capacity. They wore bells at their ankles to announce their coming and warn people away.

One night, towards the end of August, just at the very height of the plague, Don Rodrigo was on his way home in Milan, accompanied by the faithful Griso, one of the three or four who had remained alive out of his whole household. He was on his way back from a gathering of friends who were in the habit of carousing together to banish the gloom of the times; and on every occasion there were new faces present and old ones missing. That day Don Rodrigo had been one of the merriest; and, among other things, had made the whole company laugh by a sort of funeral oration on Count Attilio, who had been carried off by the plague two days before.

As he walked along, however, he felt a sort of uneasiness, a heaviness, a weakness of the legs, a difficulty in breathing, a burning feeling inside him which he would have liked to attribute to the wine, the late hour, or the season of the year. He never opened his mouth the whole way; and his first words on reaching home were to order Griso to light him to his room. When they got there, Griso noticed his master's face —distorted, inflamed, with his eyes starting out and shining brilliantly. And he kept his distance, for in those circumstances every ragamuffin had had to acquire what is called the doctor's eye. . . .

Griso took the lamp, and wishing his master good night, hurried away, while the latter got under the covers.

But the covers seemed like a mountain. He threw them off, drew up his knees and tried to rest; for he was, in fact, very sleepy. But scarcely had he shut his eyes than he woke up with a start, as if someone had come and shaken him out of spite; and he felt the heat getting more oppressive, the frenzy increasing. He fell back again on the thought of August, the white wine, the excitement; and he longed to put all the blame on them; but these ideas invariably gave way to the one which was then associated with every thought, which entered, as it were, in every sense, which had infiltrated even into the talk during the carouse, as it was easier to turn it into a joke than to pass it over in silence—the plague.

After a fitful night, troubled by violent dreams, Don Rodrigo woke to feel 'a violent throbbing of the heart, a buzzing of the ears, a continuous whistling, a fire raging within him, a heaviness in all his

limbs worse than when he had gone to bed. He hesitated some time
before looking at the place where he felt the pain. Finally he un-
covered it and gave a fearful glance'. Under his left arm he discovered a hideous tumour of a livid purple hue.

He realized he was lost. The terror of death seized him, and with
it perhaps even more strongly the terror of falling a prey to the *monatti*,
of being carried off and flung into the *lazzaretto*. And as he was casting about for some way of avoiding this horrible fate, he felt his
thought going dark and confused, and realized the moment was
approaching when he would be conscious of nothing but despair. He
seized the bell and shook it violently. Griso, who was on the alert,
appeared at once. He stopped a certain distance from the bed, looked
at his master attentively, and became certain of what he had suspected
the night before.

'Griso!' said Don Rodrigo, raising himself up with a great effort,
'you've always been my trusty one.'

'Yes, your lordship.'

'I've always done well by you.'

'Of your kindness.'

'I can count on you. . . .'

'Of course!'

'I'm ill, Griso.'

'I'd noticed it.'

'If I recover, I'll do even more for you than I've ever done in the
past.'

Griso made no reply, and stood waiting to hear where all these
preambles were leading.

'I wouldn't trust myself to anyone but you,' went on Don Rodrigo.
'Do me a favour, Griso.'

'At your service,' said the latter, using his usual formula in reply to
the other's unusual one.

'D'you know where Chiodo the surgeon lives?'

'Very well.'

'He's a decent fellow, and keeps his patients secret if he's paid well.
Go and call him: tell him I'll give him four, no six *scudi* a visit—more
if he asks for it. But he's to come at once: and do it all so that no one
notices.'

'Good idea,' said Griso; 'I'll go and be back at once.'

'Listen, Griso; give me a little water first. I feel such a thirst I can't
stand it any longer.'

'No, my lord,' replied Griso. 'Nothing without the doctor's advice.
These ills are treacherous: there's no time to lose. Keep calm, now,
and in three shakes I'll be back with Chiodo.'

So saying, he went out, leaving the door half shut.

Don Rodrigo, back under the covers, accompanied him in the imagination to Chiodo's house, counting his steps and calculating the time. Every now and again he would look at his tumour again, but quickly turn his head away with a shudder. After some time he began to strain his ears for the sound of the surgeon arriving; and this effort of attention numbed the pain and kept him in his senses. All of a sudden he heard the faint tinkling of a bell, which seemed, however, to come not from the street, but from inside the house. He listened intently. He heard it get louder, more regular, and with it a shuffling of feet. A horrible suspicion crossed his mind. He sat up and listened still more intently. He heard a muffled sound in the next room, as if some weight was being carefully put down; then flung his legs out of bed, as if to get up, looked at the door, saw it opening, and at it appear and advance toward him two filthy red uniforms, two diabolical faces—in a word, two *monatti*. He saw half of Griso's face, hiding behind the half-closed door, and stopping there to look on.

'Ah, you foul traitor! . . . Get out, you scum! Biodino! Carlotto! Help! Murder!' shouted Don Rodrigo; and thrust his hand under the pillow to find a pistol: he seized it, pulled it out. The quickest was on him before he could do anything, and had wrenched the pistol from his hand, flung it away, pushed him down on his back, and held him there, shouting, with a grimace of mingled rage and contempt: 'Ah, you villain! Attack the *monatti*! Attack the servants of the Tribunal! Attack those who're doing the work of Mercy!'

'Hold him fast, till we take 'im away,' said his companion, going toward a chest.

And at that in came Griso, and proceeded to force the lock with him.

'Scoundrel!' shrieked Don Rodrigo, glaring at him from under the man who was holding him, and writhing in his sinewy arms. 'Just let me kill that swine,' he said to the *monatti*, 'and then do what you like with me.' Then he began shouting again for his other servants with what voice he had left; but in vain, for the abominable Griso had sent them all out some way away, with false orders from their master, before going to the *monatti* and suggesting their coming on this job and dividing the spoils.

'Be good, now, be good,' his jailer kept on saying to the wretched Don Rodrigo as he held him pinioned on the bed. Then, turning toward the pair who were looting, he shouted, 'Do it like gentlemen, now.'

'You! you!' Don Rodrigo was bellowing towards Griso, whom he saw busy breaking things open, pulling out money and valuables and dividing them up. 'You! After . . . ! Ah, you devil in hell! I may still recover! I may recover!'

Griso did not breathe a word, or even turn, if he could avoid it, in the direction from which the words were coming.

'Hold him tight,' said the other *monatti*. 'He's raving.'

And this was true by now. After a loud scream, after a last and more violent effort to release himself, he suddenly fell back in an exhausted swoon; his eyes were still staring, however, as if he were in a trance, and every now and again he would give a start or a moan.

The *monatti* took hold of him, one by the feet and the other by the shoulders, and proceeded to lay him on a stretcher they had left in the next room. One of them came back to fetch the loot; then, taking up their miserable load, they carried it off.*

One must try to imagine the chaos and horror of a plague-stricken city in which such treachery and degeneration could become commonplace, The last great plague to ravish Europe occurred in Marseilles in 1720. Although one cannot argue with certainty that the frightful conditions of that city in the early 18th century were identical with those of cities in the 14th, still it seems reasonable to assume that the medieval cities were no better prepared to deal with such widespread death. Reports from Constantinople, from Florence, from Paris during the Black Death are not as detailed as the much more recent reports from Marseilles, but they are clear in their assertion of the appalling conditions. The horror in Marseilles is probably a repetition of many scenes in many cities during the Black Death. From the very first the mortality in Marseilles was such that it was nearly impossible to bury the dead. The Assembly resolved that carts should be used to carry the bodies to huge pits where they were buried in lime. At first beggars were recruited to carry the dead, but soon the bodies began to accumulate in houses and in the streets and convicts were requisitioned on the promise that they would be freed: a promise that was never kept. The burial crews proved ignorant of the management of horses and carts and their idleness and lust for robbery were such that sheriffs on horseback were compelled to follow them to superintend the work. Soon, in the older parts of the city, where streets were too narrow for the carts to go, bodies piled up in the streets. An order was issued that the vaults of churches in the upper town should be used for burial in quick-lime and, when full, sealed up with cement. Soon the streets were strewn with bodies, some in an advanced state of decomposition, mingled with countless cats and dogs that had been killed and bedding thrown down from the houses. The docks were covered with bodies brought to shore from ships to which, as in

* Alessandro Manzoni, *The Betrothed*, trans. Archibald Colquhoun (London, 1952), pp. 447–52.

London 1665, whole families had retreated in the belief that plague could not reach them on the water. More than two thousand bodies lay unburied in the streets. On the esplanade of La Tourette a thousand dead had lain rotting for weeks in the sun, too putrid even to be lifted into carts and too foul to be carried to the pits. Officials, perhaps remembering Procopius, conceived the idea of throwing bodies into two huge vaults in the old ramparts close to the esplanade after breaking in the roofs. One hundred galley-slaves were recruited for the task and, with handkerchiefs dipped in vinegar tied over their faces, they set about their work. At the same time fishermen netted ten thousand dead dogs floating in the port and towed them out to sea.

The horror, fascination and revulsion which such scenes inspired in many who were forced to witness them is apparent in a passage from Abraham à Santa-Clara who left an account of a plague in Vienna in 1679:

Come with me to several places in Vienna, where huge trenches have been filled with corpses; just contemplate what you have adored, to what you have paid so many compliments, given more flattery than was lavished on Egyptian cats, with what you drove to the pleasure gardens, there in the cool grottoes by the clear water sullied your own conscience, what frequently you clothed in red robes and dresses and in return deprived of the white of innocence; look at what robbed you of sheep and sleep, of peace and plenty, of science and conscience: come here, and gaze into the graves in which so many thousands lie. There she lies who charmed you with her crinkly curls—now they are but lousy mats and no longer powdered with musk, but stuck together with matter and dirt like a dried-up varnish-brush; behold there she who with her magnetic eyes attracted your heart, the clearness of whose eyes you valued more than diamonds—now they lie sunken in her head and are but hollows made for worms to nest in; look, take away that handkerchief from your nose, so that you may the better see there the roses of her whose cheeks often converted you into a golden butterfly. Follow me still further: there is another trench and in it lie many thousand persons like pickled game in a barrel, solely with the difference that instead of salt quick-lime is used. Behold there her whose ruddy lips were sweeter to you than sugar-candy—now the quick-lime has consumed these delicacies, that now the teeth grin out like those of a snarling dog on its chain.

Under such conditions it is understandable, if not excusable, that some of the revulsion would be projected upon the wretched men who undertook the job of removing and burying the corpses. Since many were, indeed, criminals and others undertook the task only for the quick monetary reward it offered, a terrified populace, ignorant of the true causes of the epidemic, began to suspect that the buriers themselves had spread the disease for their own profit. And since there are always some who, in the spirit of Francesco Berni, find profit in the distress of others, not all the accusations were false. In 17th-century Milan, some criminals wore the costume of the *monatti* to confer immunity upon themselves as they went about robbing and looting. The horror the grave-diggers and buriers inspired led to charges that they deliberately threw infective matter from the carts; and the plague was not very old in 14th-century Europe before the old suspicion of poisoners was once again prevalent. Hecker reports that in Leipzig, Magdeburg, Brieg and Frankenstein, at least, the grave-diggers were accused of poisoning wells.

The ineffectiveness of medical treatment and the cruelly painful surgical techniques that doctors sometimes employed led to a quickening of the ancient and enduring suspicion of doctors. Some accused them of enriching themselves by the misfortune of others, and some suspected that the doctors in collusion with the grave-diggers were actually the source of the disease. After a 15th-century epidemic of plague in Parma, the physicians were arrested and imprisoned, arraigned of all kinds of murders, and the money they had made during the visitation was confiscated. Chaucer repeats the common accusation in his description of the Doctour of Phisik in the General Prologue to *The Canterbury Tales*:

> In sangwyn and in pers he clad was al,
> Lyned with taffata and with sendal;
> And yet he was but esy of dispence;
> He kepte that he wan in pestilence.
> For gold in phisik is a cordial,
> Therefore he lovede gold in special.

The suspicion that the disease was caused by poisoners fell into the fertile soil of ignorance and terror and was nourished by ancient precedent and contemporary malevolence. It has been noted how in the Biblical plagues of Pharaoh the proximate cause was Aaron or Moses stretching out his hand or tossing dust in the air, and how in the literature of Greece and Rome the idea that epidemics were the result of acts of individual men was repeated and sometimes acted upon. As always unwilling to accept that they were victims of chance, men sought a cause: the more credulous believed that demons and witches brought the disease; but those who rejected superstitions and accepted the idea of contagion may, ironically, have contributed still more to the hysteria that produced the hunt for poisoners. Even Defoe, who rejects supernatural causation and discounts the wilder rumours, notes that because of its infectious nature, the disease may be spread by apparently healthy people who harbour the disease but have not yet exhibited the symptoms. Such a person was in fact a poisoner, 'a walking destroyer perhaps for a week or a fortnight' before his death, who might have 'ruined those that he would have hazarded his life to save . . . breathing death upon them, even perhaps his tender kissing and embracings of his own children'. There seem to have been others who in their delusion or wickedness deliberately went abroad when they knew they had the plague, either in the hope that the disease would pass from them if they infected another or simply out of malice and despair. Defoe reports that physicians had debated the causes of this desire to infect others; some held that it was in the nature of the disease 'that it impresses every one that is seized upon by it with a kind of rage and hatred against their own kind—as if there was a malignity not only in the distemper to communicate itself, but in the very nature of man, prompting him with evil will or an evil eye, that, as they say in the case of a mad dog, who though the gentlest creature before of any of its kind, yet then will fly upon and bite any one that comes next him, and those as soon as any who had been most observed by him before.' In such an atmosphere of ignorance, doubt and fear, rumours of poisoners were sure to take firm hold. If there were in fact no real poisoners, there were certainly many real spreaders of rumour. In some places criminals are said to have induced people to abandon their houses by telling them that the place had been poisoned. But it is not to the evidence that there were actual poisoners among the grave-diggers, or actual murders committed by doctors and nurses, or deliberate rumours spread by unscrupulous men, that one turns for an explanation of the massacre of supposed poisoners, but rather to the predisposition of men to try to reduce disaster to controllable proportions. The doctors of Paris prescribed sure cures, others put the plague first in their minds and then out of them with good living and positive thinking. Still others required a human scapegoat into which they could project all the anger and fear the disaster inspired: someone to receive real blows and bleed real blood to make up for all the days of resignation, despair, and shaking of fists at the sun. In the midst of death men sought a cure for death in killing.

One of the essential traits of an acceptable scapegoat is that it be helpless, since, in the words of a song once popular among Afro-Americans, 'hunting wouldn't be so much fun if the rabbit had a gun'. Although we have seen in the report of Guy de Chauliac that the nobles as well as the Jews were suspected of poisoning the world, it was the Jews who were killed. It was not, of course, the first instance of persecution of the Jews in Europe. They had been subject to prejudice from the earliest days of the Church. As the religion of the State and with the power of the Empire at its back, the early Church moved against Jews, Manichees, pagans and heretics with all the ferocity that had previously characterized the anti-Christian massacres of Rome. There were pogroms and forced conversions of Jews in 7th-century Spain, but the tradition of the fanatically brutal persecutions of the Middle Ages may be traced to Emico, Count of Leiningen, whose religious zeal during the first Crusade led him no farther than the Rhineland and into no more dangerous adventures than the plunder and massacre of the Jews there. In England in the reign of Richard I Jews had been murdered in Lincoln and York by defaulting debtors, and in 1290 Edward I expelled them altogether. In France Philip IV the Fair had driven out the Jews in 1306, and they had been massacred in southern France and Spain during earlier epidemics of 1320 and 1333. Although misplaced religious zeal and racial animosity was clearly a factor in these persecutions, the massacres and expulsions of Jews in the Middle Ages were frequently motivated by economic interest.

With the growth of trade and industry and the increasing importance of cities and the merchant class, the need to borrow money to finance long-term and long-distance operations became a very important reality of medieval life. The Church traditionally considered profit-taking ignoble and constantly thundered against those who lent out money at interest. The early guilds had done everything in their power to ensure equal opportunity for all members and to discourage competition among them. No man could keep longer hours than a fellow member of his guild, members of the same craft frequently congregated in the same quarter, and no one was allowed to advertise or recommend his wares. Shop-owners were not permitted to attract a customer's attention in any way, and even a cough or a sneeze, if it were suspected of calling a buyer's

notice to a shop, could be punished by the guild. The realities of
economic life had forced a modification of the Church's position on
profits, and in the 13th century Thomas Aquinas elaborated the
concept of the 'just price', by which a seller was allowed enough
profit to keep himself and his family in reasonable comfort. But if
the Church came to accept some capitalistic practices, it still continued to condemn money-lending. Usury, in its modern sense,
denotes the lending of money at exorbitant interest, but in the
Middle Ages the term was applied to the lending of money for any
interest whatever, although in general practice interest rates were
indeed often exorbitant. Not only merchants but nobles and even
the Church had recourse to usurers, to the extent that in 1208 Pope
Innocent III admitted that, if all money-lenders were banned in
accordance with the opinion that usury was a mortal sin and as
required by canon law, every single church might well have to be
closed. Money traffic thrived in the late Middle Ages in spite of
the Church's prohibition and partly as a result of the Church's
recourse to money-lenders. From the simple beginning in the early
Middle Ages when travelling money-changers exchanged currencies
for merchants at fairs, conducting their business on a simple bench,
or *banc*, the bank had flourished and the great banking families
emerged and wielded enormous influence everywhere on the Continent. There were a number of devices by which money could be
lent and a fee collected without violating the laws against usury:
Pope Innocent IV in the mid-13th century sanctioned a system by
which money was lent for nothing, but 'damages' charged for any
delay in repayment. Although many Christians by such devices
were able to lend money, the trade was in many places in the hands
of Jews. Since they were not regarded as bound by Church pre-
cepts regarding usury and since they were barred from guild membership and thus the opportunity to make a living in most crafts
and trades, Jews found themselves practically restricted to the trade
in money. They were particularly liable to suffer if a debtor chose
to default, since as lenders to kings and bishops they were at the
mercy of those who borrowed from them. Although many persecutions of Jews were justified with pious or fanatical religious arguments, the real cause was often economic: Philip's order of expul-
sion, for instance, extended to his Italian bankers as well as to the
Jews. In some places the taxes had been farmed out to Jews and
this practice could only have contributed to the zeal with which
many people lent their support to the persecutions.

Prohibited from participation in the crafts and in trade, many Jews turned their talents to the professions, especially to medicine, to such an extent that the profession was, at least in southern Europe, very largely in the hands of Jewish physicians. Jewish doctors played a particularly important role at Montpellier and Avignon. By a cruel irony, the fact that many Jews were doctors, and it would seem often good and conscientious ones, increased suspicion and animosity against them. As physicians they seem to have recognized that water supplies were often unclean and the source of all sorts of infections. Consequently they avoided wells and springs and warned others against them, a quite practical precaution which nonetheless fed the suspicions of their detractors, who very early accused the Jews of a plot to exterminate Christians by systematically poisoning wells. According to accounts widely circulated throughout Europe, this secret operation was directed from Toledo from which a concoction of poisons brewed up with parts of spiders, owls and other supposedly venomous animals was distributed to individual Jews who then poisoned the water supplies in their towns. The first massacre occurred in Provence in May 1348, and the purge spread quickly to Narbonne and Carcassone. By summer the situation was so serious that the Pope issued a bull in July forbidding the plundering and slaughtering of Jews on pain of excommunication. In September, Clement issued a second bull to the same purpose and with the same effect: the persecutions were under way and they were not to be stopped by letters from Avignon.

The 14th century was no less ingenious than our own in finding irrefutable evidence for its fantasies and in developing legal processes to institutionalize and make respectable its most despicable crimes. As early as September 1348, the persecution had passed from the hands of fanatical and frightened mobs to those of sober and learned judges. On September 15, 1348, at Chillon on the Lake of Geneva, investigators obtained confessions from ten Jews, confessions that not only supported the charges of well-poisoning brought against them as individuals but also implicated the entire Jewish community. Copies of the confessions were duly sent from the Castellan of Chillon to Strasbourg and Berne, and from Berne solemn exhortations to prosecute Jews as poisoners were sent on to Basle, Freiburg and Breisgau. The documents from Chillon, which Hecker has preserved, with their cold legality, infuriating paternalism, and contrived display of justice are almost more

terrible than the stories of the massacres. They demonstrate not
only that torture can produce the most detailed confession to the
most improbable crimes but that in the face of torture and overwhelming accusation the human spirit can be made to shrivel and
die. They remind us too that there is always someone evil, or
conscientious, enough to ensure that where evidence is supposed to
be found it will be found. There is hardly any crime so despicable or
improbable that, if it is passionately and widely believed in, someone will not come along who believes he has committed it himself.
And others will be found to ensure that the proof of their guilt is
discovered. The documents also reveal the extreme risk run by
Christians who tried to protect their Jewish friends, and explain, in
part, the failure of right-minded men to stop the insanity. Charges
of guilt by association are as ancient as they are dangerous.

The Castellan of Chillon, after announcing his greetings to the
mayor, senate and citizens of Strasbourg, informs them that 'many
Jews were put to the question, others being excused from it,
because they confessed, and were brought to trial and burned.
Several Christians, also, who had poison given them by the Jews,
for the purpose of destroying the Christians, were put on the wheel
and tortured. The burning of the Jews and torturing of the said
Christians took place in many parts of the county of Savoy.' He then
appends a document entitled 'The Confession made on the 15th
day of September, in the year of our Lord 1348, in the Castle of
Chillon, by the Jews arrested in Neustadt, on the Charge of Poisoning the Wells, Springs and other places; also Food, etc. with the
design of destroying and extirpating all Christians.' There follows
the report of the confessions of ten men, the first of whom is
Balavignus:

Balavignus, a Jewish physician, inhabitant of Thonon, was arrested
at Chillon in consequence of being found in the neighbourhood. He
was put for a short time to the rack, and being taken down, confessed,
after much hesitation, that, about ten weeks before, the Rabbi Jacob of
Toledo, who, because of a citation, had resided at Ahamberi since
Easter, sent him, by a Jewish boy, some poison in the mummy of an
egg: it was a powder sewed up in a thin leathern pouch accompanied
by a letter, commanding him, on penalty of excommunication, and by
his required obedience to the law, to throw this poison into the larger
and more frequented wells of the town of Thonon, to poison those who
drew water there. He was further enjoined not to communicate the
circumstances to any person whatever, under the same penalty. In
conformity with this command of the Jewish rabbis and doctors of the

law, he, Balavignus, distributed the poison in several places, and acknowledged having one evening placed a certain portion under a stone in a spring on the shore at Thonon. He further confessed that the said boy brought various letters of a similar import, addressed to others of his nation; and particularly specified some directed severally to Mossoiet, Banditon, and Samoleto of Neustadt; to Musseo Abramo and Aquetus of Montreantz, Jews residing at Thurn in Vivey; to Benetonus and his son at St. Moritz; to Vivianus Jacobus, Aquetus and Sonetus, Jews at Aquani. Several letters of a like nature were sent to Abram and Musset, Jews at Moncheoli; and the boy told him that he had taken many others to different and distant places, but he did not recollect to whom they were addressed. Balavignus further confessed that, after having put the poison in the spring at Thonon, he had positively forbidden his wife and children to drink the water, but had not thought fit to assign a reason. He avowed the truth of this statement, and, in the presence of several credible witnesses, swore by his Law, and the Five Books of Moses, to every item of his deposition.

On the day following, Balavignus, voluntarily and without torture, ratified the above confession verbatim before many persons of character, and, of his own accord, acknowledged that, on returning one day from Tour near Vivey, he had thrown into a well below Mustruez, namely that of La Conerayde, a quantity of the poison tied up in a rag, given to him for the purpose by Aquetus of Montreantz, an inhabitant of the said Tour: that he had acquainted Manssiono, and his son Delosaz, residents of Neustadt, with the circumstance of his having done so, and advertised them not to drink of the water. He described the colour of the poison as being red and black.

On the nineteenth day of September, the above-named Balavignus confessed, without torture, that about three weeks after Whitsuntide, a Jew named Mussus told him that he had thrown poison into the well, in the custom-house of that place, the property of the Borneller family; and that he no longer drank the water of this well, but that of the lake. He further deposed that Mussus informed him that he had also laid some of the poison under the stones of the custom-house in Chillon. Search was accordingly made in this well, and the poison found: some of it was given to a Jew by way of trial, and he died in consequence. He also stated that the rabbis had ordered him and other Jews to refrain from drinking of the water for nine days after the poison was infused into it; and immediately on having poisoned the waters, he communicated the circumstance to other Jews. He, Balavignus, confessed that about two months previously, being at Evian, he had some conversation on the subject with a Jew called Jacob, and, among other things, asked him whether he had also received writings and poison, and was answered in the affirmative; he then questioned him whether he had obeyed the command, and Jacob replied that he had not, but had given the poison to Savetus, a Jew, who had thrown it into the Well de Morer in Evian. Jacob also desired him, Balavignus, to execute the command imposed on him with due caution. He confessed that Aquetus of Montreantz had informed him that he had thrown some of the poison into the well above Tour, the water of which he sometimes drank. He confessed that Samolet had told him that he had laid the poison which he had received, in a well, which, however, he refused to name to him. Balavignus, as a physician, further deposed that a person infected by such a poison coming in contact with another while in a state of perspiration, infection would be the almost inevitable result; as might also happen from the breath of the infected person. This fact he believed to be correct, and was confirmed in his opinion by the attestation of many experienced physicians. He also declared that none of his community could exculpate themselves from this accusation, as the plot was communicated to all; and that all were guilty of the above charges. Balavignus was conveyed over the lake from Chillon to Clarens, to point out the well into which he confessed having thrown the powder. On landing, he was conducted to the spot; and, having seen the well, acknowledged that to be the place, saying, 'This is the well into which I put the poison.' The well was examined in his presence, and the linen cloth in which the poison had been wrapped was found in the water-pipe of a notary-public named Heinrich Gerhard, in the presence of many persons, and was shown to the said Jew. He acknowledged this to be the linen which had contained the poison, which he described as being of two colours, red and black, but said that he had thrown it into the open well. The linen cloth was taken away and is preserved.

Balavignus, in conclusion, attests the truth of all and everything as above related. He believes this poison to contain a portion of the basilisk, because he had heard and felt assured, that the above poison could not be prepared without it.

The other men implicated by Balavignus were also questioned and confessed. In concluding his report the Castellan writes:

The above-named Jews, prior to their execution, solemnly swore by their Law to the truth of their several depositions, and declared that all Jews whatsoever, from seven years old and upward, could not be exempted from the charge of guilt, as all of them were acquainted with the plot, and more or less participators in the crime. . . . I must add, that all the Jews of Neustadt were burnt according to the just sentence of the law. At Augst, I was present when three Christians were flayed on account of being accessory to the plot of poisoning. Very many Christians were arrested for this crime in various places in this country . . . who at last and in their dying moments were brought to confess and acknowledge that they had received poison from the Jews. Of these

Christians some have been quartered; others flayed and afterwards hanged. Certain commissioners have been appointed by the magistrates to enforce judgment against all the Jews and I believe that none will escape.

From such beginnings the fear, the accusations and the massacre of Jews swept through Germany, Italy, France and Spain. It is a sad and sorry story. Nobles, the bourgeoisie, peasants, in some instances priests, and in at least one city a bishop, bound themselves by an oath to destroy the Jews by fire and sword. The summons sent from Chillon to Berne was passed on to other cities. The city council of Zofingen forwarded little bags of poison, which they claimed to have found in the town cisterns, to authorities of other towns on the upper Rhine. In Basle the Burgomaster and the Senators resisted the demands of the townspeople that the Jews be killed, but later under threat from the guilds they took the oath to burn the Jews and to prohibit for two hundred years the entry of any Jew into the city. Purely on the urging of a terrified and inflamed populace, without even the semblance of legal sanction, the Jews of Basle were herded together in a large wooden building set up on an island in the Rhine, which was then set on fire and in which they died. The people of Freiburg murdered the Jews of their city in the same manner. At Strasbourg as at Basle the deputies of the city at first defended the Jews and resisted the persecution since no criminal charges had been proved; but the populace demanded blood and, at the urging of their bishop, they raised such an outcry against the deputies that they finally passed a resolution condemning the Jews. A wooden scaffold was erected in the Jewish burial ground at Strasbourg and two thousand men, women and children were burned to death upon it. A few Jews who consented to be baptized were spared as were several women who excited the pity, or perhaps the lust, of the crowd; but those who escaped forcibly from the flames were run down and murdered in the streets. The senate of Strasbourg revealed the real cause of much of the fanatical desire to destroy the Jews when it ordered that all pledges and bonds held by them be returned to the debtors and that all money and property they possessed be divided among the citizens of the town. In an orgy of greed, the crowds stripped the clothes from men being led to their death and tore them apart to find the coins that their frenzy convinced them were sewn there. Those who felt some reluctance to receive the money and property of the men they had murdered were encouraged by their confessors to donate it to the monasteries which seem to have been willing enough to accept it. The bricks from the destroyed houses of the Jews and the stones from their destroyed graveyard were used for the repair of churches and for the building of new belfries.

At Mainz contemporary accounts say that 12,000 Jews were burned, although once again one must be cautious of the figure. It is also reported that the execution fires there were so huge that the lead in the window-panes and the bells of St. Quirius' Church melted in the heat. The persecutions in Mainz appear to have been sparked off by the Flagellants who had entered the city in August and precipitated bloody quarrels with the Jews. It seems to have been frequently the case that the religious frenzy inspired by the Flagellants inflamed the suspicions and fears of the people into whose cities their processions came. At Mainz, and later at Speyer and Eslingen, to escape murder at the hands of fanatical crowds the Jews burned themselves to death in their own houses. At Eslingen, according to the Limburg Chronicle, the entire Jewish community gathered together in the synagogue, then set it on fire and perished together. Guillaume de Nangis says that mothers often threw their children on to the pile to prevent their being baptised, and then threw themselves into the flames. At Speyer, where the Jews had burned themselves in their houses, their bodies were collected, put into empty wine casks and rolled into the Rhine, lest they infect the air of the city; but the senate did not neglect to search the burned houses for treasure.

The massacres continued. At Frankfort and Oppenheim the Jews who did not burn themselves were burned by mobs. At Nuremberg all the Jews are said to have died, and in many towns in Thuringia they were slaughtered to the last man. In northern Germany and the Hansa towns there were few Jews, but the persecutions moved against them nonetheless and they were burned and, in some cases, buried alive. Throughout all Germany they were hunted down and killed. Those who escaped from the persecutions in the cities were frequently murdered in the countryside by the peasants. There were very few places where the unfortunate Jews were not regarded as outlaws to be tracked down and burned. But there were a few: Schaffhausen protected its Jewish community and Erfurt tried to, although in the end the mobs prevailed and over two hundred were burned. Individual Christians who endeavoured to save their Jewish friends were tortured and killed with them, as they had been in Chillon. Far too often, those who, by their education and position of authority, had an opportunity to raise the voice of reason remained silent or actually led on the mobs to murder and plunder.

The wholesale slaughter spread to Austria, Italy and Spain as well. In Austria the chief persecutions were in Krems, Stein and Mautern. Duke Albert offered protection to the Jews, sent a company of men-at-arms against the mobs, and arrested and hanged the leaders; but even so he was unable to save the Jews even in his own palace at Kyberg where hundreds were burned. The Emperor Charles IV attempted to check the outrages committed by the nobles of Bohemia, who saw in the persecutions an opportunity to relieve themselves of their creditors; but again with little effect, since he refused to use force against them. Other lesser princes proffered assistance to the Jews, but far more often moved to action by bribes than by a sense of justice. The only real refuge for the hounded Jews was in the East. As early as 1264 Jews had been granted freedom of conscience in Poland, and Casimir III, the Great, practised religious tolerance and gave his protection to many Jews who fled from Germany.

The importance of the Jews in the economic life of many cities, which had been a prime factor in the persecutions, was soon acknowledged in another way: no sooner had the murders ended than kings, lords and municipalities rushed to invite them back to provide the money necessary for their enterprises and to pay the large taxes to which they were subject. The Golden Bull of Charles IV permitted princes to 'keep' Jews, and thus the rest of Europe avoided the economic catastrophe that the massacre of Jews wrecked upon Castile in 1391 and later upon all Spain under the 'Catholic Kings'.

But the accusations against the Jews served to revive other ancient slanders: that they coined base money, that they defiled the host, that they murdered Christian children and nailed them to crosses to mock the Passion. At Zurich in 1349, a little boy, said to have been tortured and murdered by Jews, was interred in the cathedral and worshipped as a saint. In England Chaucer revived the slander in the Prioress's Tale and reminded his readers of Hugh of Lincoln, a boy alleged to have been murdered in 1255 by 'cursed Jewes'. If Chaucer felt any revulsion at the torture and massacre of Jews he recounts so eloquently in the Prioress's Tale, he conceals it well. And among the conventional moralists of the time, who almost universally lament the worsening of the world during and after the Black Death and catalogue the sins of man, one waits, usually in vain, for a clear condemnation of the murder of the Jews. The self-professed guardians of morality in the Middle Ages, as in our own time, seemed to find it easier to condemn the vices that have no victims—sexual promiscuity, fastidiousness of dress, excessive enjoyment of food and drink, swearing and gambling—than to speak out against murder.

In the search for an explanation of their misery and a cure for rampaging death, some men turned to a life of pleasure and others turned to massacre. Both courses were the product of self-delusion, but if a choice among delusions must be made, one can hardly avoid expressing a preference for those of the hedonist. It may be argued that the two are not mutually exclusive and that, like some concentration camp guards, men may have returned from the murders to a glass of good wine, a well-roasted joint of meat, and the company of jolly friends. But the fact remains that in that sorry time, one of the few voices to speak out clearly for religious tolerance is that of Boccaccio, who is also one of the frankest in telling, with obvious sympathy, the ribald tales of the enjoyment of natural life. *The Decameron* begins with two stories that present portraits of Jews drawn without prejudice or condescension. And one of them, the story of the three rings, asserts that the three Laws—the Jewish, the Saracen and the Christian—given by God to men, were 'so like unto one another that the true might not be known', and that while 'each people deemeth itself to have his inheritance, His true Law and His commandments . . . the question (of which in very deed hath them) yet pendeth'.

Chapter VIII

THE CHURCH AND THE MANOR

THERE ARE times when it almost appears that the principal accomplishment of the Church has been to inoculate the mass of Western men with small doses of the outward forms of Christianity so as to make them forever immune to its spirit. The shameful massacre of Jews by supposedly Christian men with the assent, in many cases, of the bureaucracy of Christian society and sometimes even of the clergy is only the most dramatic of many well-known abuses of the spirit of Christianity to have occurred in the Middle Ages. The corruption in the Church at all levels was a matter of common knowledge. It was even the source of much of the popular humour of the time, like all humour of disappointed expectations, often bitter, pessimistic and cynical. In the hands of a master like Chaucer or Boccaccio the theme of corruption offers more than just a chance to ridicule the follies and vices of those who would present themselves as the servants of man and God: in Chaucer's portraits of the Monk and the Prioress, people of importance in the hierarchy, as well as those of the more lowly Friar, Pardoner and Summoner, one senses all the bitterness of a man betrayed by the hypocrisy of those he should be able to trust. In Boccaccio's tale of the good Jew Abraham we find an even more direct condemnation of the dereliction of the churchmen; and Boccaccio, unlike Chaucer, levels his accusations at the highest levels of the hierarchy.

Abraham is a merchant in Paris, a wise and honest man, and a friend of a Christian, Jehannot de Chevigné, who tries on every possible occasion to convert him to Christianity. Abraham has no intention of changing his faith, but in deference to his friend he finally announces that he will go himself to Rome to see God's Vicar on earth and his Cardinals and, if what he sees convinces him that Christianity is the better faith, he will convert. This is not at all what Jehannot had in mind and he does everything he can to dissuade his friend 'for that, an he go to the court of Rome and see the lewd and wicked life of the clergy, not only will he never become a Christian, but, were he already a Christian, he would infallibly turn Jew again'. But Abraham will not be put off and goes to Rome where he discovers that the clergy 'from the highest to the lowest most shamefully [were] given to the sin of lust, and that not only in the way of nature, but after the Sodomitical fashion, without restraint or remorse or shamefastness, insomuch that the interest of courtezans and catamites was of no small avail there in obtaining any considerable thing'; and 'moreover, he manifestly perceived them to be universally gluttons, winebibbers, drunkards and slaves to their bellies, brute-beast fashion, more than to aught else after lust. And looking farther, he saw them all covetous and greedy after money, insomuch that human, nay, Christian blood, no less than things sacred, whatsoever they might be, whether pertaining to the sacrifices of the altar or to the benefices of the church, they sold and bought indifferently for a price, making a greater traffic and having more brokers thereof than folk at Paris of silks and stuffs or what not else.' All this 'was supremely displeasing to the Jew, who was a sober and modest man', and he returns quickly to Paris. When Jehannot asks him, rather cautiously, how he found things in Rome, Abraham answers that, as far as he can judge, 'your chief pastor and consequently all the others endeavour with all diligence and all their wit and every art to bring to nought and banish from the world the Christian religion'. But then, to the amazement and joy of his friend, Abraham announces that after what he has seen nothing in the world could keep him from becoming a Christian, since, in spite of everything the clergy does to destroy the faith, it continues to increase 'and waxeth still brighter and more glorious': clear evidence that 'the Holy Spirit is verily the foundation and support thereof, as of that which is true and holy over any other'.

The *fabliaux*, popular ribald tales of the time, of which Chaucer's Miller's and Reeve's Tales are the best-known examples in English, find such humour in the vices of monks, friars and ecclesiastical students that they frequently figure as the comic seducers of the stories. The corruption of the medieval Church is so well-documented and so widely acknowledged that in this case, at least, there is no question that the literary convention accurately reflects the fact. The sale of indulgences was so common that, it is reported, they were sometimes offered as prizes in lotteries. Ecclesiastical offices were won or lost at dice. Although all secular clergy above the grade of sub-deacon, as well as all regular clergy, professed celibacy many priests had mistresses and some openly married. Concubinage and marriage were very common during the 10th and 11th centuries in Germany and Italy, and the clergy often founded families and son followed father as priest, just as privilege was passed on in the noble fiefs of the knightly class. In the Breton dioceses of Quimper and Nantes the bishoprics themselves were transmitted from father to son. Since high ecclesiastical office brought power and opportunity for wealth, some men sought office with only wealth and power in mind. One such, an 11th-century Archbishop of Rheims, complained that his office would have been 'enjoyable if it had not been incumbent on its holder to say masses'. Various reform movements sprang up from time to time, but the Church was far from having acquitted itself from the charges of simony, lust, greed and general corruption. There seems to have been hardly any enterprise that profit-hungry churchmen considered unworthy of their support. In London many of the houses of prostitution were under the jurisdiction of the Bishop of Winchester, and in 1321 an English Cardinal purchased a brothel in London as an investment for sacerdotal funds. The reproaches for such corruption came from inside as well as outside the Church. In 1348 Friar Johannes of Winterthur and the Dominican Heinrich of Herford wrote:

> How contemptible the Church has grown, especially in its most important representatives, who lead a bad life and have sunk even deeper than the others. For the shepherds of the Church feed themselves instead of their flocks, these they shear or rather fleece; their conduct is not that of the shepherd but of the wolf! All beauty has vanished from the Church of God; from head to toe there is not a sound spot in it. Simony has become so prevalent among the clergy that all secular and regular clerics, whether of high, middle or low rank, shamelessly buy and sell ecclesiastic livings without blame from anyone and much less with punishment. It looks as if our Lord had not driven the buyers and sellers from the Temple, but had rather invited them to remain there. Prebends, livings, dignities, rectorships, curacies, and altars are all for sale for money, or can be given in exchange for mistresses and concubines. They are staked at dice, lost and won. Even abbeys, priories, guardianships, professorships and readerships, and other posts, however insignificant they may be, are bought by ignorant, young, inexperienced, and stupid people, if only they possess money which they may have acquired by theft or in any other way.

For all the bitterness of such complaints they were most often directed against individuals who through their vices had corrupted

an institution universally acknowledged to be good. The point is
an important one. One might easily assume that such bitter denunciation of members of the hierarchy was an attack upon the institution that supported them, but that does not seem to have been the
case at all. In fact, the very opposite seems to have been true: the
most bitter attacks upon the vices of the clergy came from those who
were most firmly convinced that the Church was a God-given
institution. It seems to have been generally acknowledged that God's
Truth had been placed in imperfect vessels, for after all no man after
the Fall is free of imperfection. One could point out and deplore the
cracks in the vessels without implying any criticism whatever of
either the truth or of God's having placed it in such vessels, for
after all what man or human institution is worthy of receiving the
perfect Truth? Certainly neither Boccaccio or Chaucer question
God's Truth or the legitimacy of the Church's claim to contain it.
Among educated men the criticism of the abuses of the Church was
not a criticism of Christianity but of Christendom. As is apparent
from the tale of Abraham, Boccaccio makes a clear distinction
between the two and can even arrange it so that the corruption of the
visible Church becomes proof of the purity and strength of the
Faith. This is an argument that one seldom hears today except in
the pronouncements of those whose job it is to rationalize decadent
or totalitarian economic and political systems; but in the Middle
Ages such a hypothesis was not cynical sophistry but a statement of
the truth as seen by nearly all educated men. Institutions were
things in themselves, not just the sum of the acts of the people who
make them up; and the idea of institutional criticism was not yet
born. Men of learning could criticize the activities of the organized
Church in the severest terms without implying any attack on the
faith the Church was supposed to embody and existed to propagate.
The blatant vices of the Pardoner moved Chaucer to acute criticism
of individual men who were vile enough to use their authority to
further their own ends but never to a condemnation, or even to a
serious questioning, of the whole complex of institutions and doctrines that the Pardoner represented and which made him possible.
Less sophisticated men, unfamiliar with the subtle abstractions of
Scholasticism, seem, however, to have tried the Church by the
simple Scriptural injunction that by their fruits ye shall know them.
And they found it wanting in some inexcusable ways. Bede wrote
that during a 7th-century pestilence men turned to the old gods
again when they found that the cross was ineffective as a talisman

against plague; and there is much evidence from Rome that in times of epidemic men went in search of new gods. The suddenness and the universality of such a disaster inspired men with both scepticism and an intense desire for authentic religious experience. In the 14th century the search for such experience led many to look outside the organized Church and down strange paths.

Among the many popular religious movements of the time, one especially seems to have received its principal impetus from the Black Death. As early as the spring of 1349 the Flagellants had begun to march. A popular tradition held that the movement had begun in Hungary where 'gigantic women', marching and singing curious songs, divested themselves of their clothes and scourged themselves publicly with rods and whips. By Lent 1349, when the first clearly authenticated account reports their appearance in Dresden, the Flagellants seem to have been well organized. Calling themselves the Brotherhood of Flagellants or the Brethren of the Cross, they had accepted leaders and a strict code of behaviour. It was their intention to take upon themselves the repentance of the people for the sins they had committed, and through prayer, supplication, and a personal imitation of the suffering of Christ, to avert the plague. They conceived of themselves as being divinely appointed to their task, and chroniclers report that they frequently referred to a letter which they believed to have been written by Jesus Himself and which had supposedly fallen from the sky. The letter, which probably originated in the first part of the 13th century during the earlier, similar demonstrations of the *Devoti*, described the plague as a punishment for not keeping the Sabbath and asserted that the anger of Christ could only be appeased by a flagellant pilgrimage of thirty-three and a half days, the number of days being the same as the years in Christ's life. Those who would join the Brotherhood were required to stay in for the full thirty-four days and were required to have a small sum of money at their disposal, since they were strictly forbidden to receive alms, seek free quarters, or enter a house uninvited: prohibitions that no doubt added to the enthusiasm with which the Brethren were frequently received in towns and villages. If a man were married, he needed his wife's consent to join; and he was asked to give assurance that he was reconciled to all men. During the course of the pilgrimage the penitent promised not to converse with women. Neither could he bathe, wash his head or shave. Pilgrims were required to avoid all luxury and comfort. Any who broke the rules were obliged to confess to the

Master who sentenced them to several lashes of the scourge as penance. The leaders of the movement were not, however, ecclesiastics; indeed, according to the original law of the Brotherhood, priests could not become masters or take part in the secret councils. Hecker says that the bands were usually under control of men of learning and he feels that 'the leaders must have been intimately united, and have exercised the power of secret association', although he offers no proof of such an association beyond the similarity of the regulations and rituals of the various groups of Flagellants. The bands themselves seem to have been made up initially of people of the lower class, some drawn to the movement by sincere contrition and others by the opportunity for idleness and excitement. But soon they were joined by people of all classes: nobles, ecclesiastics, women and children, and even nuns.

The processions appear in most places to have been well organized and orderly. The Brethren marched through the cities in pairs, singing psalms and new hymns which were composed especially for the Cross-bearers and which they sang in the vernacular. They went with their heads covered as far as their eyes and their look fixed on the ground, and exhibited the deepest contrition and mourning. Generally they wore sombre clothes with red crosses stitched to the breast and back, and carried scourges. A contemporary chronicler says the scourge 'was a kind of stick from which three tails with large knots hung down. Right through the knots iron spikes as sharp as needles were thrust which penetrated about the length of a grain of wheat or a little more beyond the knots. With such scourges they beat themselves on their naked bodies so that they became swollen and blue, the blood ran down to the ground and bespattered the walls of the churches in which they scourged themselves. Occasionally they drove the spikes so deep into the flesh that they could only be pulled out by a second wrench'. The place of scourging was sometimes a church, sometimes an open square, where the Brethren in the midst of their candles, torches and banners of velvet and brocade would strip to the wasit and perform the ritual whipping. Lying in a circle, the penitents would accept a blow from the Master and then rise to follow him as he scourged the others until the procession had again been formed; then each would strike himself on the breast and back while making the sign of the cross, chanting hymns, and praying for the averting of the plague. The ceremony ended with the reading of Jesus' letter which seems invariably to have caused great commotion among the people who had gathered

to watch. An eye-witness quoted by Hecker says that 'the lamentation was piteous. . . . Many were hence induced to search into their
own hearts, to turn to God, and to abandon their wicked courses:
parents warned their children, and instructed them how to pray,
and to submit to the ways of Providence: neighbours mutually
admonished each other. . . . Many persons, and even young children,
were seen bidding farewell to the world: some with prayers, others
with praises on their lips.'

The movement spread quickly throughout Hungary, Germany,
Bohemia, Silesia, Poland and Flanders. The processions were
greeted in many places with veneration and enthusiasm: bells were
rung and people flocked from all quarters to hear the hymns and to
witness the penance. The hymns especially seem to have excited the
enthusiasms of the crowds; the new songs were memorized and
passed on to the extent that at the time of Hecker's writing in 1832
one of the hymns of the Flagellants was still extant in Germany in a
variety of dialects. Perhaps for the first time hymns were sung by
the laity in their own language at a public worship. Nor was this the
only evidence of the attempt of people disillusioned with the Church
to appeal directly to God without intervention of clergy. The
Masters of the movement, almost always laymen, ignored the
Church's claim to the exclusive power of binding and releasing and
assumed for themselves not only the right to preach but also the
right to grant absolution. Based emphatically upon the laity, the
Flagellant movement assumed the right of men to commune directly
with God. Nohl quotes a contemporary account: 'When the Flagellants were asked, "Why do ye preach having received no mission,
and teach what ye do not understand, as ye are not read in the Scrip-
tures", they replied, turning the tables, "Who then gave you a
mission, and how do ye know that ye consecrate the body of Christ
or that what ye preach is the true Gospel?" If they were told that
the Church could not err as it was guided by the Holy Ghost, then
they replied that they received their instruction and mission most
directly from the Lord and the Spirit of the Lord.' The direct appeal
to God found many excited adherents, and the number of Flagellants was soon considerable. At Erfurt they are said to have numbered three thousand; at Günstadt some six thousand marched. At
Aix-la-Chapelle so many gathered that the Emperor, Charles IV,
was unable to pass through the city and was forced to wait at Bonn
until the procession moved on. In the summer of 1349 at Constance
the Brotherhood claimed to have assembled forty-two thousand men.

THE BURIAL OF PLAGUE
VICTIMS AT TOURNAI

A FLAGELLANT

THE TRIUMPH OF DEATH

The popular reception of the Flagellants was not everywhere so cordial. In Berne they were mocked and their hymns parodied, and when some sixty Brothers crossed from Holland to parade in the streets of London they were quickly ejected as undesirable aliens. Among those whose enthusiasm for the Flagellants was cool were the clergy, who found their churches invaded and their influence over the people superseded. Although the intentions of the Flagellants were probably pure enough—a sincere desire to imitate the suffering of Christ and to cure the body of excessive appetites—they soon began to make extravagant claims for themselves. They advertised their power to cast out evil spirits and on at least one occasion attempted to perform miracles: in Strasbourg they tried, and failed, to revive a dead child. Then, too, it was frequently the appearance of the processions of Flagellants that precipitated the persecution of the Jews. Finally, the motley processions undoubtedly spread the plague as they tramped from town to town to fulfil their mission of averting it. At Paris the Sorbonne applied to the Holy See for assistance against the heretical excesses of the Brothers, which seemed to them to be destroying the authority of the clergy everywhere; and soon secular authorities grew alarmed that the Brotherhood, well-organized and under bold anti-authoritarian leaders, might exert its influence in the affairs of state. Charles IV and Philip VI of France supported the judgement of the Sorbonne, and Philip forbade their reception in France. Manfred, King of Sicily, threatened the Flagellants with death. In response to a petition from Charles IV and in accordance with the opinion of the Sorbonne, the Pope issued a bull against them in October 1349, alleging that they had killed Jews and Christians and stolen property from both laity and clergy, as well as having arrogated to themselves the authority of their superiors. The bull, which required the laity as well as the secular and monastic clergy never again to enter into relations with any member of the sect, did not in fact prohibit self-scourging—from then on everyone was advised to practise it in his own home and under the control of the Church—and it seems clear that it was not flagellation to which the Church objected but the power and influence of the Brotherhood with its new and radical ideas of personal religion.

In some places public opinion was so strongly in support of the Flagellants that the authorities did not dare to issue the bull: the Archbishop of Treves entrusted its reading to the sheriff, fearing for the lives of his parish priests if they should publish it. But elsewhere the authorities moved quickly and ruthlessly against the Brotherhood. In Breslaw one of the masters was condemned and publicly burned. Throughout Germany public opinion turned against the Flagellants as quickly as a few months before it had supported them, and the Brothers were turned away from the towns and finally pursued as if they had been the cause of every misfortune. The processions were soon abandoned altogether, but the spirit that inspired them lived on. The fanatical aspect of the Flagellants inspired several later pilgrimages in the 14th century, most importantly those of the *Bianchi* or *Abati* in Italy in 1399; in Germany in the 15th century it was deemed necessary in several places to destroy Flagellants with fire and sword; and as late as 1710 processions of Cross-bearers were still seen in Italy. But much more important than the desire for self-torture, which the Flagellants liberated, was the concept of a direct and personal approach to God without the intercession of clergy which lived on in the more respectable and serious reform movement of the late Middle Ages and culminated in the Reformation.

Neither the corruption in the Church nor the conception of flagellation originated with the Black Death, of course; as early as the 11th century there is clear evidence that there was need for reform in the Church, and the idea of mortifying the flesh by scourging is of ancient origin. At least as early as the 11th century brotherhoods were devoted to ritual flagellation, and processions of flagellants probably originated in the 13th century: St. Anthony organized such a movement in 1231 and there is evidence of a brotherhood calling themselves Flagellants having appeared during a plague in Vienna in 1261. But as in so many other areas, the trauma of the Black Death revived old antagonisms, and, by creating situations in which the authority of the traditional hierarchies was tested and found wanting, aroused latent individualism. Deprived temporarily of the guidance of Church and State, people turned to themselves, their own devices, and their own leaders, in an attempt to create some sort of order to supplant the discredited and paralysed old rule. For a time at least, until the Church and other formal institutions could reassert their control, it was a truly revolutionary situation. The revolution was doomed from the start. The Church was neither so weak, nor its attackers so well-organized, that it could hope to succeed. If Hecker is correct that the leaders of the Flagellants were in secret communication, consciously promoting a 'fearful opposition to the Church', they were premature. The Church had not yet undergone the humiliation of the Schism and

the rebellion had not yet found its Luther. Like so many revolution-
aries, the Flagellants were long on activism, discontent, and personal
enthusiasm but short on constructive ideas and positive programmes.
The Flagellants constituted an active reaction against the Church,
but they could only react; and in this sense the movement was, in
fact, reactionary. In opposition to the weakness and corruption of
the Church, it exaggerated the worst vices of the Church, much as
naïve activists today combat the violence and hypocrisy in their
societies with violence excused by sophistries even more naïve than
those employed by the authorities they oppose. If revolutions begin
with the urge to break with moribund traditions and institutions,
then a revolution had begun, and in this sense the enthusiasm of the
Flagellants was liberating and progressive. But it is one thing to
perceive error and quite another to find truth. The revolutionary
fervour of the late 14th century, anti-authoritarian, protestant and
democratic in spirit, had yet to find positive, constructive programmes to offer in place of those it attacked. And lacking such
programmes, it failed to enlist the support of enough sophisticated
men to succeed. Instead, it polarized attitudes and stiffened the
opposition of those in authority. The early reform movements
demonstrated and increased the repressive nature of authority. If
the final result of the individualistic religious fervour inspired by
the Black Death was the Reformation, the immediate result was the
Inquisition.

The Black Death did not create the corruption in the Church but
it most certainly had an immediate and profound effect upon the
Church's effectiveness. The most obvious and best-documented of
these effects was the large number of deaths among the clergy and
the subsequent lowering of standards in replenishing the ranks.
From every quarter of Europe contemporary accounts record that
when the disease entered a house it frequently carried off every
occupant. The experience of Petrarch's brother, who found himself
the only survivor of the monastery at Monrieux, was certainly not
unique. The reports are everywhere the same. Hecker says that
30,000 Minorites died in Italy; at Montpellier only seven out of 140
Dominicans survived; at Avignon over 350 Dominicans died; in
Marseilles, the Bishop with the entire chapter of the cathedral and
nearly all the friars, preachers and Minorites perished; in Germany,
by Hecker's estimate, nearly 125,000 Franciscans died. One of the
immediate effects of the widespread mortality was a decline of
fervour and discipline in the monastic orders. The Dominicans

suffered so severely that they were driven to receive postulants of little education, in fact in Majorca they were obliged to recruit children; and that order, which had constituted the intellectual élite of Christendom, went into serious decline. A comment on the decline of discipline among Franciscans is provided by Waddington, an annalist of the Order, who writes of the Black Death:

> This evil wrought great destruction to the holy houses of religion, carrying off the masters of regular discipline and the seniors of experience. From this time the monastic orders, and in particular the mendicants, began to grow tepid and negligent, both in that piety and that learning in which they had up to this time flourished. Then, our illustrious members being carried off, the rigours of discipline relaxed by these calamities, could not be renewed by the youths received without the necessary training, rather to fill the empty house than to restore lost discipline.

Chaucer says of the Monk among the Canterbury pilgrims, whose principal passions are for hunting and eating:

> Ther as this lord was kepere of the celle,
> The reule of seint Maure or of seint Beneit,
> By cause that it was old and somdel streit
> This like Monk leet olde thynges pace,
> And heeld after the newe world the space.
> He yaf nat of that text a pulled hen,
> That seith that hunters ben nat hooly men,
> Ne that a monk, whan he is recchelees,
> Is likned til a fissh that is waterless,—
> This is to seyn, a monk out of his cloystre.
> But thilke text heeld he not worth an oystre;
> . . . . .
> What sholde he studie and make hymselven wood,
> Upon a book in cloystre alwey to poure,
> Or swynken with his handes, and laboure,
> As Austyn bit? How shal the world be served?
> Lat Austyn have his swynk to hym reserved!

And of the Friar:

> In alle the ordres foure is noon that kan
> So muchel of daliaunce and fair langage.

He hadde maad ful many a mariage
Of yonge wommen at his owene cost.

. . . . .

He knew the tavernes well in every toun
And everich hostiler and tappestere
Bet than a lazar or a beggestere;
For unto swich a worthy man as he
Acorded nat, as by his facultee,
To have with sike lazars aqueyntaunce.
It is nat honest, it may nat avaunce,
For to deelen with no swich poraille,
But all with riche and selleres of vitaille.

Among the rest of the clerical body the mortality was nearly as great and the effects just as severe. The religious living together in a community were especially liable to infection, but the parish priests also ran special risks. Although these lived under less unsanitary and less crowded conditions than the average artisan and peasant, such advantages were counterbalanced by their contact with the sick. Unlike the more privileged members of the hierarchy, a priest could not often afford to hire a substitute or retreat to a more isolated and healthy place. He was required to sing his daily mass and to shrive the sick, and if he chose to protect himself he could only do so by cynically repudiating his sacred responsibilities. The record of the mortality among priests in England has already been cited, and although records from other countries are not so complete, it appears that the clergy throughout Europe suffered greatly. It is also clear that many, in England and elsewhere, deserted their parishes out of fear of the disease and refused to return except on the promise of a considerably increased stipend. To the accounts from Canterbury, Bath and Wells, and Rochester may be added that of Knighton:

At this same time there was so great a lack of priests everywhere that many widowed churches had no divine services, no masses, matins, vespers, sacraments, and sacramentals. One could hardly hire a chaplain to minister to any church for less than ten pounds or ten marks, and whereas, before the pestilence, when there were plenty of priests, one could hire a chaplain for five or four marks or for two marks, with board, there was scarcely anyone at this time who wanted to accept a position for twenty pounds or twenty marks. But within a short time a very great multitude whose wives had died of the plague rushed into holy orders. Of these many were illiterate, and it seemed, simply lay-men who knew nothing except how to read to some extent.

By the direction of King and Parliament, the Archbishops and Bishops tried to prevent the clergy from making such demands for higher wages. In a letter to his Bishops, Archbishop Islip, the founder of Canterbury College, Oxford, complained of 'the un-bridled cupidity of the human race' which is so great that unless it is checked 'charity is to be driven out of the world'. He takes note of the fact that the priests who survived the plague, 'not considering that they are preserved by the Divine will from the dangers of the late pestilence', have abandoned their curates for more profitable offices for which they are demanding an increase on what they were paid before. The Archbishop warns that if the practice is not stopped, 'many, and indeed most of the churches, prebends, and chapels of our and your diocese, and indeed of our whole Province, will remain absolutely without priests'; and he urges people not to employ such chaplains and compels the clergy under ecclesiastical censures to serve the ordinary cures at the usual salaries. The dearth of priests was so great after the plague that the Dominicans, in England and elsewhere, adopted the policy of farming out pre-scribed districts (limits) for preaching and confession. The 'limitor' had exclusive rights and made of them what he could. Chaucer's Friar is a limitor and if he is an example of the type, the practice can only have worsened an already unhappy situation. Langland complains of the cupidity of priests in *Piers Plowman*:

> Parsons and parish priests pleyned them to the bishop,
> That their parishes were poor with the pestilence-time,
> To have a licence and a leave at London for to dwell,
> And singen there for simony; for silver is sweet.

And Chaucer's praise of the good Parson implies that his willingness to serve his parish at a modest salary is quite an extraordinary virtue:

> He sette nat his benefice to hyre
> And leet his sheep encombered in the myre
> And ran to Londoun into Sainte Poules
> To seken hym a chaunterie for soules,
>
> . . . . .
>
> He was a shepherde and noght a mercenarie.

Although English ecclesiastical records are the most complete of any country, those of the Continental chroniclers are just as clear, if not as numerically certain. Nearly every one who touches on the subject of the behaviour of the clergy during the Black Death comments upon the frequency of desertions through fear of infection or the desire to find higher wages elsewhere. The testimony of the chroniclers, nearly all of whom are clerics themselves, is almost unanimous in its agreement that the clergy did not distinguish itself with any special self-sacrifice during the plague. Of these reports Coulton writes:

> Briefly, we have the judgment of 22 chroniclers, English and foreign, upon the behaviour of the clergy during the pestilence. Of the eight least favourable, one only is entirely favourable; but he speaks only for his own neighbourhood (Catania). The next two best, while praising the friars or the nurses, contrast these with the negligent behaviour of the parish priests. The remainder are frankly, and sometimes violently unfavourable. It would be difficult to find any historical question, involving so directly and so deeply the reputation of an enormously numerous and influential body, with exceptional facilities for self-defence and self-advertisement, in which the evidence is so overwhelming against them. Even though all these chroniclers had been mistaken as to the facts (though ... the official documents go far to support them), there would still remain the plain consideration that, whatever the priests had actually done, public opinion did judge them to have fallen, as a body, far below the height of their sacred office.*

And what people think is often just as important as the truth. The truth is, of course, that the clergy was no worse than any other class of men: the doctors and the bureaucrats fled as well. But for people who had accepted the almost superhuman pretensions of the priesthood and their enormous privileges, it was not enough that the clergy were no worse than other men, nor was it even enough that they were, as they certainly were in many cases, better. They were proved by the plague to be not sufficiently superior. The priests, who as a class had been almost deified, showed themselves to be only human, and a disillusioned populace concluded, echoing the words of St. Bernard, that 'the priests are worse than the people'. This attitude is deeply ingrained in the remainder of medieval history. The anti-clerical attitudes of the period are apparent everywhere, in legend and literature and among clergymen themselves. A popular belief in Germany after 1348 held that the Emperor Frederick II was not dead but would return to persecute the clergy. Jean Gerson, chancellor of Paris University, urged his sister not to

* G. G. Coulton, *Medieval Panorama* (London, 1961), II, 136.

enter a nunnery and risk contamination. And Ambrogio Traversari, early in the next century, urged St. Bernardine of Siena not to accept a bishopric for fear of compromising himself.

The very nature of the Church's authority made it particularly susceptible to such anti-clerical sentiments. The fiercely logical system constructed by the Schoolmen was very nearly unassailable, and it was almost universally accepted. Much like authoritarian political systems, it explained everything and allowed for no debate of essential issues. One can escape such a system only by denying the validity of the logic upon which it is based and retreating into a private world of mysticism. But those, of a more pragmatic nature than the mystics, who accepted the same logical basis of thought as the Church, were trapped by that system into reaching the same conclusions as the Schoolmen. The fact that the basic tenets of Scholasticism—the 'belief in a barbarian's hell, and in the in-errancy of a written book, and in the infallibility of the Church', as Coulton puts it—were never tested by scientific inquiry was much less important to an age that had not yet developed the scientific method of inquiry than the overwhelming logic of its presentation. Had the teachers of the system only shown their faith by their works, they would probably have had no more serious threats to deal with than those presented by occasional mystics who denied the validity of their logic, witches who accepted the logic but aligned themselves with the forces of Evil, and heretics who quar-relled with individual points of doctrine within the system. But the manifest failure of the clergy to exemplify the ideals of the system in their lives made the logical arguments irrelevant. It was especially upon simple men that the failure of the clergy to exemplify the ideals of the Faith was to have its most profound effect, for it was they who were most likely to judge the Church by its fruits, being least educated in the logic of the Schoolmen and thus least able to ration-alize the failure. As Erasmus wrote: 'If the people see a man to be a true priest and bishop, his exhortation will not be without fruit. But if his publicly irreligious life, his impure morals, his gross ignorance, his insatiable greed, and his barbarous savageness have utterly alienated people's minds, how shall they profit by his pre-cepts?' Or as Chaucer put it more simply:

> . . . if gold ruste, what shal iren do?
> For if a preest be foul, on whom we truste,
> No wonder is a lewed man to ruste;

> And shame it is, if a prest take keep,
> A shiten shepherde and a clene sheep.

The corruption of the clergy in the higher levels of the hierarchy had been common knowledge for centuries; but the activities of great men in distant places do not have the same sort of immediate emotional effect upon people who are remote from the centres of power and receive their news by word of mouth months or years after the event, as they do upon societies that receive their news instantly, see their leaders, and hear their voices. The great modern scandals which have destroyed the careers of statesmen and brought down governments are pathetically mild little sins compared to the debauchery of officials of the Church hierarchy in the Middle Ages. But just as rather common and innocuous indiscretions—the intemperance of Cabinet ministers or the greed of Presidential aids, for instance—can have a pronounced effect upon the faith a people puts in the whole structure of government, when they are revealed dramatically and have a personal impact, as nearly all news does that comes into one's house over the television; so the revelation that the parish priest was not quite as good as he was supposed to be—not necessarily that he was evil, but just that he was human—had a far greater effect upon ordinary folk than any number of tales of debauchery from Rome or Avignon. And it was at this level that the Black Death most profoundly affected the Church. There is an old Army joke that the military is a system designed by geniuses for execution by idiots, and the continued existence of armies proves that almost any system can be made to work. But the secret of the continued existence of the military may be that the great majority of those who administer the system conscientiously embody its values. When the sergeants and corporals stop shaving and shining their shoes; when the company officers desert in the face of the enemy, even that most anachronistic of systems will be in danger. Chaucer's Pardoner asserts that 'For though myself be a ful vicious man, / A moral tale yet you telle kan'. Chaucer and a great many less perceptive men had come to be disgusted by vicious men preaching morality. And when the vicious men held them in such contempt that they openly displayed their vices, people reacted in the spirit, if not with the rudeness, of the Host, who shouts at the Pardoner:

> Thou woldest make me kisse thyn olde breech,
> And swere it were a relyk of a seint,

Though it were with thy fundement depeint!
But, by the croys which that Seint Eleyne fond,
I wolde I hadde they coillons in myn hond
In stide of relikes or of seintuarie.
Lat kutte hem of, I wol thee helpe hem carie;
They shul be shryned in an hogges toord!

No logic in the world can prevail against such revulsion. And even those who were still willing to agree that a vicious man might embody God's truth had their faith shaken when, during the plague, even the vicious fled and there was, for a while, no one at all to tell the tale. The desertion of the priests and the Church's continued failure to improve itself turned emotional anti-clericalism into organized movements for reform.

In England reformist sentiment crystallized around John Wyclif and the Lollards. Wyclif's principal idea was that men are directly responsible to God and that human mediators and traditional forms are more or less irrelevant. Although many of his doctrines were offensive to orthodoxy—the assertion that masses for the dead and papal indulgences were a delusion, that penance and confession were good only if voluntary but unchristian if compulsory, and his denial of Transubstantiation—it was his theory of dominion and his arguments for clerical disendowment that earned him the enmity of Church and State and a wide following among the people. Dominion is possession justified by right, it involves both privilege and obligation. Since God holds dominion over all the earth, those who possess temporal power do so as a grant from Him. But since only the righteous have just dominion, evil men can have rightful possession of nothing. Earlier writers had propounded such arguments. In the 13th century the Franciscans introduced anti-authoritarian ideas. Robert Grosseteste founded a school at Oxford which counted among its members Adam Marsh and Roger Bacon and championed independence of judgement and first-hand knowledge rather than dependence upon authority. Duns Scotus demonstrated the weakness of Aquinas' system, and Ockham went even farther, bringing philosophy down from its speculative heights to the level of common sense, observation and induction. And, as we have seen, both Ockham and Marsilius of Padua had championed the supremacy of secular authority. But the practice of medieval theorists like Marsilius and Ockham was to write in terms of the abstract and the ideal. Wyclif not only went farther than they but, in addition, made his appeal directly to the people and spoke of contemporary situations. He defined righteousness not as obedience to the visible Church but rather as obedience to God: what really mattered was not membership in the Church but membership in God's elect. Rightful possession of power and property in the eyes of God is granted only to the righteous; and since the hierarchy of the Church, judged by the rigid standards that such a doctrine required, was sinful and perverted by greed, it followed that the Church was rightful possessor of nothing, neither its power nor its property. Such an assertion of theoretical communism was a direct challenge to all those who possessed privilege, and Wyclif's doctrines obviously threatened political as well as religious authority: Parliament complained in 1382 that Lollard preachers were creating 'discord and dissensions among the different estates of the realm'. But they were also calculated to make a direct appeal to the people, an appeal that was so great that Knighton wrote in 1382 of the Lollards that 'they multiplied exceedingly like budding plants, and filled the whole realm everywhere, and became as familiar as though all had come forth on the same day. For this sect was held in the greatest honour at the time; and it multiplied so greatly that you could scarce meet two men on the road but that one of them was a disciple of Wyclif'. Public enthusiasm was increased, no doubt, by Wyclif's exaltation of the Bible as the infallible rule of human actions and by his fathering the scheme to have it translated into English. After Wyclif's death in 1382, his influence grew, but so did the persecutions of the Lollards until in 1414 they attempted a revolt. This was put down mercilessly and the sect driven underground. But its spirit remained strong. Some forty years after his death, the Council of Constance decreed that Wyclif's body be exhumed and burned. Thomas Fuller's *Church History* describes the execution of the decree: 'In obedience thereunto, Richard Fleming, bishop of Lincoln . . . sent his officers . . . to ungrave him accordingly. To Lutterworth they come, Sumner, Commissary, Official, Chancellor, Proctors, Doctors, and the servants . . . take what was left out of the grave, and burn them to ashes, and cast them into Swift, a neighbouring brook running hard by. Thus this brook hath conveyed his ashes into Avon, Avon in Severn, Severn into the narrow seas, they into the main ocean. And thus the ashes of Wickcliffe are the emblem of his doctrine, which now is dispersed all the world over.'

In eastern Europe Wyclif's ideas caught fire among the Hussites.

John Hus, born about 1370 at Husinec (from which his name is abbreviated), was an influential figure at Prague University. His early tolerance of Wyclif's doctrines grew until at the opening of the Council of Constance he had accepted many of them as his own. He denounced indulgences, declared that men were justified in disobeying unrighteous papal commands, that the true Church consisted of the elect and that the existing Church order was abusive and unwarranted by Scripture. Invited to attend the Council under safe-conduct, Hus went to Constance but was imprisoned as a heretic and tried. Before the Council he admitted to having taught the doctrines he was accused of teaching but refused to recant unless he could be convinced to do so by Scripture. Such a declaration in defiance of the authority and infallibility of the General Council sealed his fate, and he was burned at the stake in July 1415. But the burning of Hus was no more effective in arresting the spread of the belief in the liberty of the individual conscience than was the burning of Wyclif's body. Like Wyclif, Hus had appealed to the nationalistic as well as the religious feelings of men—it is to him that the Czech nation owed the development of a literature in the vernacular —and the religious-nationalist revival begun by the Hussites was to have wide consequences in the time of the Great Schism.

The Great Schism, which began in 1378, increased popular disillusionment with the Church. After three-quarters of a century of papal residence in Avignon, Pope Gregory XI returned to Rome and died there. Most of the cardinals who met to elect a successor were French, but the Romans demanded an Italian Pope. As a compromise the cardinals elected Urban VI, a Neapolitan prelate who was thought to be acceptable to the French interest. But when Urban demonstrated himself to be a bitter critic of the cardinals, a number of them withdrew from Rome, disowned Urban and elected Clement VII, a Frenchman. Meanwhile Urban had nominated new cardinals and Christendom found itself divided into two obediences: Rome and Avignon. The Schism had a profound effect upon Wyclif, Hus, and many other thinking men. For centuries the Popes had claimed to judge practically every aspect of political, social and even domestic life on the plea that their authority descended directly from God through Peter to whom God had given the Keys of Heaven. Even the harshest critics of the corruption of the papal court had previously been able to maintain their faith with the argument that the true Faith could, by God's will, be propagated by even the most fallible of men; but with the Schism no one

could avoid the question of which fallible man embodied the Faith.
St. Catherine maintained that Urban was the true son of Peter and
Clement the son of Judas, but St. Vincent held exactly the opposite
view. The logical conclusion of the Schism was that half of Christendom was in mortal sin, but no one could say with absolute cer-
certainty which half. A popular belief in the last quarter of the 14th
century held that no one had entered Paradise from the beginning
of the Schism. As if this confusion were not enough to shake the
faith of the most pious, in 1409 the cardinals of both obediences met
at the Council of Pisa and elected a Pope who, although he was
accepted by most of Christendom, failed to command the allegiance
of all the supporters of the pontiffs of Avignon and Rome. There
was thus for a time a third Pope. And one of the claimants, Peter
of Luna, Benedict XIII, was known in France as '*le Pape de la
Lune*': one can only imagine what simple men thought of that.

The Schism endured for nearly forty years until it was ended by
the Council of Constance, and its effects were widespread and disastrous. The uncertainty and confusion of the question of the papal
succession and inspiration were serious enough, but the Schism
increased the incidence of corruption at all levels. Discipline declined throughout the entire hierarchy: pluralism, the holding of
more than one benefice by a single individual, was common; the
lower clergy were heavily taxed, and only illiterate and boorish
clerks could be found to perform parish work; income from endow-
ments declined so drastically as a result of the heavy taxes and the
loss of value of land after the Black Death that many convents fell
into such a ruinous state that ultimately monks and nuns were
allowed to hold private property and lead private lives. Far from
repairing the damage the Black Death had wrought, the Church
wallowed in confusion for half a century; and when it finally came
to attempt to reform itself in the 15th century, the measures taken
were too little and too late. The democratic, individualistic, anti-
clerical sentiments inspired in a primitive form in the Brotherhood
of Flagellants by the Black Death grew in sophistication and popularity until they undermined the whole structure of the Church.

That other great medieval institution, the Manor, came under
attack nearly as much as the Church. As has already been noted, the
lot of the serf had been gradually improving during the 13th century. Services performed by the peasant population had been
reduced; in place of services, money changed hands and the serfs
became, in many places, rent-paying tenants. The members of the

knightly class, possessed of capital rather than only goods and services, embarked on a new way of life; and, although the lot of all
improved, the lord's lot improved faster and more dramatically
than the peasant's. Castles grew larger and more richly furnished,
the nobility treated themselves to fine clothes and dainty food. The
difference between peasant and lord became increasingly apparent.
There were already signs of peasant hostility and unrest early in the
14th century, and all that was needed was economic regression to
throw the entire feudal economic machinery out of gear. And severe
economic repression was one of the immediate consequences of the
Black Death. As we have seen, contemporary accounts from England
make clear that the plague had a profound effect upon prices, wages
and land values. Immediately following the epidemic, land values
dropped throughout the country by as much as half, while prices of
commodities doubled. Iron, salt and clothing, in particular, doubled
in price, and some prices rose even higher. Fish, a staple of the diet
of the age, was so expensive that during Lent, William Dene writes,
even those 'who had been wont to live well, had to content themselves with bread and potage'. The economic disruption appeared
not only in England but wherever the plague struck. John of Parma
reported in 1348 that 'labourers could not be got, and the harvest
remained on the fields, since there was none to gather it in'. The
same story is told everywhere: in Provence, in Germany, in Flanders, in Scandinavia, in Ireland; wherever the chroniclers have
commented on the condition of the countryside.

The immediate result of the scarcity of labour was that peasants
refused to rent the land at the old rates and landowners were
required to hire temporary workers to bring in the harvest. The
situation was so serious that in many places the highest authorities
found it necessary to command the peasants to return to the land;
such legislation, of course, was inspired by the drastic reduction in
tax revenues that resulted from land devaluation. The Emperor
Charles IV ordered workers back to the fields and threatened landowners if they did not pay taxes at the pre-plague rates. In England
the King and Council attempted by legislation to prohibit the
tenants from leaving the land and the owners from hiring new
tenants and labourers at elevated wages. But the legislation proved
unworkable. The fines levied against the landowners and servants
could not be collected. The landowners pleaded as excuse the fact
that what wealth they possessed had gone to pay the excessive wages
they were being fined for having granted. Servants and labourers

simply disregarded the regulations. Finally the king was compelled to order the imprisonment of any who were guilty of demanding excessive wages; but the order was obviously self-defeating: the imprisonment of workers only increased their scarcity. In addition, the legislation aggravated the peasant's already rebellious attitude towards the nobility. The chronicler Knighton reports on the situation:

Meanwhile the king ordered that in every county of the kingdom, reapers and other labourers should not receive more than they were accustomed to receive under the penalty provided in the statute, and he renewed the statute from this time. The labourers, however, were so arrogant and hostile that they did not heed the king's command, but if anyone wished to hire them, he had to pay them what they wanted, and either lose his fruit and crops or satisfy the arrogant and guilty desire of the labourers as they wished. When it was made known to the king that they did not obey his mandate, and had paid higher wages to the labourers, he imposed heavy fines on the abbots, the priors, the great lords and the lesser ones, and on others both greater and lesser in the kingdom. . . . Then the king had many labourers arrested, and put them in prison. Many hid themselves and ran away to the forests and woods for a while, and those who were captured were heavily fined. And the greater number swore that they would not take daily wages above those set by ancient custom, and so they were freed from prison. It was done in like manner concerning other artisans in towns and villages.

William Dene wrote at the same time: 'So great was the want of labourers and workmen of every art and craft, that a third part and more of the land throughout the entire kingdom remained uncultivated. Labourers and skilled workmen became so rebellious that neither the King nor the law, nor the justices, the guardians of the law, were able to punish them.' The Lincolnshire Assize Roll of 1353 records the rebelliousness of one William de Caburn, of Lymbergh, a ploughman who would 'not work except as a day-labourer or a monthly labourer. And he will not eat salt meat, but only fresh meat; and for this cause he hath departed from the township; for no man dared to hire him in this fashion contrary to the statute of our lord the King'. Langland, too, records the new spirit of rebellion among labourers:

Labourers, that have no land to live on but their hands,
Deigned not to dine to-day on yesterday's cabbage,
May no penny-ale please them, nor no piece of bacon,

But if it be fresh flesh or fish, fried or baked,
And that hot and hotter still, to keep the chill from their maw
And, but if he be highly hired, else will he chide
And wail the time that ever he was workman born.
And then curseth he the King, and all his council with him. . .

The feudal lords were as incapable of recognizing and adapting to
a new reality as were the authorities of the Church; like them they
responded with repressive measures and intensification of old
programmes. Unable to collect sufficient revenue from taxation,
they turned to foreign adventures and civil war, which only intensified the damage caused to agriculture and the peasantry by the
Black Death. The response of the peasantry was to organize and
press their demands. They formed co-operative societies and
threatened to strike; and when such measures failed to improve their
status sufficiently, they broke into open revolt. The preamble to an
Act passed in 1377 in England states that villeins and land tenants
everywhere 'gather themselves in great routs, and argue by such a
confederacy that everyone shall resist their lords by force'. The
revolt of the peasantry in the 14th century constituted nothing less
than an attempt at widespread social revolution. The first of these
uprisings occurred in Flanders in 1323–28, even before the Black
Death. Early in the century the craftsmen of Flanders were in the
same situation in which many other workers found themselves after
the plague: the towns were under the control of the merchants, and
the workers of the cloth and metal industries were their mere employees. Unlike the typical medieval system of craft-guilds of
'small masters', they were under an early régime of capitalism, and
the 'patricians', as the merchant-manufacturers called themselves,
kept their employees, the despised 'blue-nails', under tight control
and did all they could to keep wages low. Resentment among the
'blue-nails', who in Ghent made up sixty per cent of the population,
smouldered until 1323 when it broke into open revolt. The craftsmen were joined by the coastland peasants and battled against the
nobles in a brutal civil war that was not ended until Philip VI,
coming to the aid of the Count of Flanders, crushed the Flemings in
the battle of Mount Cassel in 1328.

Obviously social unrest did not originate with the Black Death,
nor is the plague the sole cause of the economic regression that
intensified rebellious feeling in the second half of the century. The
steady expansion of population which characterized the 13th cen-

tury had already slowed and in some places had stopped before the mid-14th century. From the end of the 13th century there is evidence in some places of a drop in agricultural productivity, a decrease in the export and import of staple commodities like wine and wool, and a shrinking of the occupied area within the walls of some cities and towns. The over-exploitation of land and the erosion that resulted from indiscriminate felling of forests may have contributed to the slowing of population growth before the plague; and the widespread reports of famine in the first half of the 14th century would seem to suggest that this was the case. The terrible effects of the Black Death may, themselves, be in some part the result of the weakening of the populace by the famines. One cannot easily generalize about economic phenomena; and it is safer to assume that the Black Death, and the epidemics which recurred for the next two centuries to inhibit population growth, aggravated an existing situation, than to suppose it was the cause of social unrest. But there is no question that social unrest became more widespread and more violent in the second half of the century. There were serious revolts in France in 1358, in Florence and in the Low Countries in 1379, and in England, Tuscany, Flanders and France around 1380.

The French peasantry rose in revolt in May 1358 against the nobles who exploited them and failed to protect them from wandering bands of mercenaries. The Jacquerie, as it was called from the *jacque*, a peasant's jerkin, spread quickly; and before the rebellion was put down in the summer, castles had been burned and the gentry ferociously attacked. The revolt in Florence was fomented by workmen, most of them underlings of the Art of Wool, as the earlier riots in Flanders had been. As is often the case with the politics of medieval Florence, the causes of the rebellion are murky and confusing, but one might note that unrest here rose among the artisans and that the war between the Florentines and the Papacy a few years earlier had been an aggravating factor. A wave of rioting spread over Europe around 1380. Peasants and workmen rose up in France in opposition to heavy taxes, which the government quickly repealed. When the local Estates were required to replace the revenues, the rioting spread to the towns. In Paris people threw open the prisons and stormed about the streets armed with lead mallets. The government answered with executions, and the rebellion was decisively ended at Roosebeke in November 1382, when the French chivalry trampled down the Flemish pikemen. In England, as elsewhere, the rebellion was fierce but localized; and, like the attempts to revolt against Church authority, characterized more by discontent and anti-authoritarian fervour than by positive programmes of reform. There, as in France, the immediate grievance was the unjust and oppressive taxation which had been resorted to in order to replenish the treasury depleted by the devaluation of land and scarcity of labour that persisted after the plague. The revolt was mainly confined to the home counties and East Anglia where, perhaps ironically, the peasants were most prosperous. With their prosperity, however, came class consciousness which was fed by agitators like John Ball, a mutinous priest preaching doctrines of equality much like those of Wyclif, and demanding the abolition of villeinage, the disendowment of the Church, and the punishment of those responsible for the unfair taxation. The movement found its leader in Wat Tyler, and outbreaks, which began in Essex in May 1381, spread over Kent and soon reached London. Workers within the city also rose up, and joined the peasants in plundering London. Wat Tyler broke into the Tower and murdered the Chancellor and the Treasurer of the royal Council, while anarchy and murder reigned in the city. The next day King Richard met the rebels at Smithfield. It was a violent and confused confrontation in which Walworth, the Mayor of London, wounded Tyler and Richard dramatically rushed forward to declare himself the new leader of the rebels and to grant them charters abolishing villeinage. By this time the citizens of London were enraged by the anarchy of the mobs and armed themselves against them. Without their leader and confronted by the armed citizenry, the rebels dispersed. Mayor Walworth went looking for Tyler and found him in the hospital for the poor by St. Bartholomew's where he had been carried by friends. The Mayor had him dragged back to Smithfield and beheaded. The King's charters were quickly revoked and the remaining rebels harshly suppressed. The Bishop of Norwich put down the revolt in East Anglia by armed force in a campaign that could only have increased the anti-clerical sentiments of the peasantry. The remaining rebels were hunted down and many were hanged. When the fire had gone out of the movement, the King granted pardon to all who remained alive on condition that they should never rise again.

There do not seem to have been any very impressive results from the peasant rebellions that shook Europe after the Black Death. The long, slow and halting change away from serfdom and towards money-rents continued; but it may, in fact, have been set back by the anger of the landowners who hardened their attitude towards the peasantry after the riots. In Germany, although the diet in 1356 granted them the right to prosecute their lords in the royal courts, the condition of the peasants deteriorated. The struggles over wages and the open rebellions in Germany brought an actual recrudescence of serfdom. Even in England and France, where the rebellions are most frequently thought to have hastened the end of serfdom, the greatest effect was probably upon thought and literature. As in the case of the early, bold attempts to reform the Church, the feudal system was too strong, too firmly entrenched, and the rebels too poorly organized and too lacking in constructive programmes of change, for the rebellion to have succeeded in drastically changing existing institutions. The attack upon the landowners may have weakened the petty nobility, but the decline of the local nobles strengthened the power of the monarchy. The great political movement throughout Europe in the late 14th and the 15th centuries was the triumph of the monarchy and the consolidation of power. It is in this period that the concept of the divine right of kings was advanced. Even the continuing process that changed the serf into a free peasant brought him a freedom which was often more legal than real. No longer possessing the right to his land, the peasant was economically weaker and at the mercy of landlords who sensed the capitalistic spirit already established in the towns and began to develop their lands as economic units, by enclosure and by the cultivation of a staple crop. Like Wat Tyler's rebels, who forced the King to grant charters abolishing villeinage only to see them quickly annulled, the peasant learned that his freedom, lacking a foundation in economic power, was illusory. But brave lost causes are only temporarily lost if their spirit endures; and the spirit of democratic equality, the resentment of the rich, and the distrust of the corrupt hierarchy of the Church lived on in the literature of the late Middle Ages and in the hearts of men.

This democratic spirit is clearly apparent in the literature of England in the second half of the 14th century. Piers Plowman, the labouring peasant, became the type of Christian holiness, not the priest. Chaucer's good Parson, himself a poor and simple man, is accompanied on the pilgrimage by his brother, the Plowman, who is a model of secular virtue:

> A trewe swynkere and a good was he,
> Lyvynge in pees and parfit charitee.

God loved he best with al his hoole herte
At alle tymes, thogh him gamed or smerte,
And thanne his neighebor right as hymselve.

The portrait is all the more interesting if one remembers that the
peasant is most often pictured in earlier medieval literature as a
dullard and a buffoon, the butt of jokes and the object of ridicule.
Chaucer's praise of the working man is coupled with intense criticism of the privileged clergy and gentle satire on the nobility—one
remembers that Chaucer depended for his livelihood upon the good
graces of the Court. The Knight is a 'verray, parfit gentil knyght', to
be sure, but his son, the Squire, is a frivolous dandy. In the contrast
between the two, one has a picture of the actual condition of the
nobility. Knighthood and the code of chivalry were in decline. The
chivalric ideals of courage, loyalty, courtesy, generosity, protection
of the weak, defence of Christendom, and the passion for adventure
and devotion to a lady, had, in any case, been embodied in only a few
real men. Although both are extreme examples, Sir John Falstaff is
probably closer to the type one would most frequently encounter
during the late Middle Ages than Chaucer's Knight. The ideals
lived on more in the courts than on the battlefield. In the tournament knights could still meet in single combat, but the tournament
became more and more divorced from the actualities of warfare. One
of the most important events of the century was the routing of the
magnificent army of French knights by simple Flemish pikemen at
Courtrai in 1302. Bad generalship on the part of the French ob-
scured the lesson that plebeian infantry was quite the match for
armoured chivalry; but the victory of the English archers at Crécy
and Agincourt made the lesson clear: the noble with his armour and
his code was an anachronism. From now on wars were to be fought
more and more by mercenaries who often had small regard for
chivalric conventions. Wars fought by poor foot soldiers led by
violent and greedy mercenaries are hard to glamourize. With the
decline of the military nobility came a decline in respect for the
ideals of chivalry. A new *noblesse de cour* was taking its place and still
preserved something of the former ideals, but more as a literary
convention than as a guide to behaviour. As the contrast between the
Knight and the Squire makes clear, the mystique of the courtier is
considerably less impressive than that of the warrior. Chivalry moved
from the battlefield to the court and from the court into literature
where it became, as often as not, the object of satire and ridicule.

The nature of warfare was also changing in such a way as to diminish the glamour that had previously been attached to the military virtues. The long bow and artillery, which was also developing in the 14th century, are area weapons; they are aimed at groups of men, not at individuals. The new weapons emphasized the equality of all and the increasing irrelevance of individual courage. The bravest of men and the basest of cowards, the foot soldier too poor to value his life above a few shillings and the richest noble, died together in the same storm of arrows and shot without ever having so much as seen the faces of the men who struck the blow. The plague had taught that all men were equal before death, and the new methods of warfare emphasized that egalitarian lesson. Another lesson of the Black Death, that virtue and courage are as often the attributes of simple men as of men of privilege, led people at all levels of society to question the nature of nobility. A clear indication of the spirit of the age can be seen in the tale of the Wife of Bath in which Chaucer introduces a discussion of *gentillesse*, or true nobility, and demolishes the traditional basis for it:

> But, for ye speken of swich gentilesse
> As is descended out of old richesse
> That therfore sholden ye be gentil men,
> Swich arrogance is not worth an hen.

As if it were not enough just to deny hereditary wealth as the basis of nobility, Chaucer puts the argument into the mouth of a simple old woman speaking to a young knight whose greatest adventure has been to rape a defenceless girl. The pretensions of the chivalric class could indeed no longer be voiced with complete confidence.

Everywhere in Europe in the generations following the Black Death there arose a powerful anti-clerical, egalitarian, democratic spirit. Everywhere there was growing discontent with the old systems and the hope of new beginnings. Real democratic change would only come later when the population began again to increase and when the people began to develop a solid economic base for their demands. But if the struggles of the serfs to emancipate themselves, and the struggles of the religious reformers to assert their freedom of conscience, did not produce an authentic revolution, they kept alive and gave stimulus to a revolutionary spirit. The authorities of the medieval Church and of feudalism stiffened their resistance and increased their repression. But then, as now and always, those who were elegantly descending the stair in their velvet slippers might have heard, had they dared to listen, the sound of hobnailed boots coming up from below.

Chapter IX

AND AFTER

THE BLACK DEATH did not bring the Middle Ages to an end; it did not cause the decline of chivalry and feudalism; it did not hasten in the Renaissance; nor did it cause the rise of nationalistic spirit, humanism, science, the passion for exploration, realism in literature, national languages, or the democratization and secularization of society which we associate with the period that followed it. The Black Death did not bring about these developments in precisely the same way that no other single event caused them. Great revolutions in institutions, values and culture are invariably the product of long and complex processes of change, and it is simplistic to assign to any one event, no matter how momentous, the full responsibility for such change. Assigning causes to historical events is such a dangerous undertaking that one might do well to abandon the practice altogether and concern oneself with historical coincidence within broad patterns of change. It is certainly so with the Black Death. Even the decline in population during the 14th century, which it would seem absolutely safe to declare to be an effect of the plague, had, in fact, begun earlier in the century and may have been a natural response to the rapid rise in population during the 13th century. It is even possible to consider the Black Death to be one of the consequences of demographic change rather than the cause of it. Or perhaps it was both. Pascal reduced the argument for historical causality to the absurd with the proposition that if Cleopatra's nose had been a bit shorter the history of the world would have been different; as indeed it would have been, if the fate of the Roman Empire had an affect upon history, and if Antony's passion for Cleopatra had an effect upon the Empire, and if Cleopatra's beauty had an effect upon Antony, and if the size of a woman's nose has an effect upon her beauty.

It is hazardous to assign causes for political and economic movements, it is even more dangerous to trace the sources of ideas and attitudes. Ideas are in the air; they are the property of all men. The

difference between the educated and the simple man is not that one
has ideas and the other does not, but that the educated man knows
the source of his ideas and possesses the capacity to rationalize his
prejudices, whereas the simple man just acts upon his. The world is
full of men who strike Byronic poses, never having read Byron; and
many semi-literate men who take their families to the woods for a
picnic respond to nature as if they were students of Wordsworth,
never having heard his name. To imagine that one can find the
exact source of such ideas is to engage in deliberate self-delusion.
Yet so many of the attitudes of the late Middle Ages and the
Renaissance seem to have been formed at least partially by the
plague, that some attempt, no matter how tentative, must be made
to review them in the light of that catastrophe. Historical ages are
marked off *ex post facto* by scholars to make life easier, or perhaps
more difficult, for students, but the choice of which event brought the
Middle Ages to a close—the Black Death, the fall of Constantinople,
the explorations of the 15th century—is largely a matter of personal
preference and predisposition. Those who require schematic cate-
gories into which to fit their thoughts may take their choice. It is to
make no special plea for the Black Death as a *deus ex machina* to
point out that whether one assigns primary importance to political
and economic events, or to demographic change, or to subtle evolu-
tions in ideas and attitudes, the Black Death is involved in the
process of change that culminated in the Renaissance. These processes did not originate in the Black Death, but they cannot be
discussed for long without some reference to it.

In some areas of the arts, the plague had an unquestionable effect.
It has already been mentioned, for instance, that the Black Death
permanently interrupted the building of the Duomo at Siena and
of St. Nicholas in Yarmouth. But there is no such general certainty about its effect upon the art of building. The Cathedral of
Milan, one of the most glorious of all the Gothic churches, was
begun shortly after the plague. The building of St. Stephen's
Chapel in Westminster and the completion of the Abbey cloisters
seem to have proceeded without interruption and with no change
of style. In England it is possible that the change from the Decorated
to the Perpendicular style of architecture was in some part due to the
lack of builders after the plague. Masons, who were in short supply,
moved from one district to another and were taken away from the
conditions of local stone favourable to their best work. The inevitable result was that the architectural style that was most easily

expressed in all types of stone prevailed, and that style was the Perpendicular. Examples of the change can be seen in the nave and cloisters of Canterbury Cathedral and in the west front of Winchester Cathedral. There is also evidence of a decline in the figure-sculpture and traceries of the period. Such sculpture, which had previously been an integral part of the church and was executed by the builders on the site, became in the late Middle Ages mere furniture of the church. The constructing masons left niches for statues which were made in shops in the city and could be added to the building at any time. Thus statues and reliefs, which ceased in the 15th century to be carved by the mason upon the building, had a less intimate relation to it. Gasquet maintains that there was a similar breach of continuity in the manufacture of stained glass and a noticeable change in style after the Black Death.

In the graphic arts one can find clear evidence of the influence of the plague upon the subject matter chosen by painters and hints of a possible influence upon style. Plague was epidemic throughout Europe for more than two centuries after the Black Death and occasioned a large number of plague banners, votive and commemorative paintings, and actual reproductions of plague scenes. Plague banners, or *gonfaloni*, are a characteristic product of the Umbrian school of painting, especially the Perugian branch. The banners were intended to be carried in the processions of repentance and expiation, and they most frequently depict Christ or the Madonna or one of the popular plague saints. The *gonfaloni* produced for the devotional activities of large groups of people had their counterpart in the more humble *Pestblätter*, which were mostly rough wood-cuts and engravings intended for private devotional purposes. The *Pestblätter* were widely circulated in the 15th and 16th centuries in Flanders, the Netherlands, Italy and France, as well as in Germany. A number of paintings of plague scenes also exist from the 16th and 17th centuries; the earliest of these is Raphael's drawing of 'Plague' in the Uffizi Gallery at Florence.

More interesting than the banners or scenes of plague are the many pictures of the Dance of Death and the Triumph of Death. One of the most impressive of the many Triumphs of Death is that of Peter Brueghel the elder, now in the Prado. A typical example, it depicts an army of skeletons ravaging a city and indiscriminately murdering nobles, merchants, clergy and common folk. To reinforce the idea that Death mocks worldly power and piety, the death's heads are all fixed in a gruesome grin. One of the earliest such scenes appears in the Campo Santo at Pisa and was attributed by Vasari to Andrew Orcagna who worked at the time of the Black Death. The fresco shows three young men, hunting on horseback, who have been brought up short by three open coffins in which there are a skeleton and two dead bodies, reminding them of the transitory nature of human pleasure. The Dance of Death was a variation of this theme; and typical examples show skeletons dancing about an open grave, leading children by the hand, kissing women before an open coffin, or leading a procession of the living in a formal dance, sometimes to the music of drums and violins. Dancing has been associated with death from the earliest times and figured in the funeral celebrations of Greeks, Romans and Etruscans. Virgil included in the *Aeneid* a description of the dance in the land of the dead; and representations of funeral dances have been found in Greek and Etruscan tombs. Christianity, in conceiving of death as the punishment for sin, was bound to take a gloomy view of it; and it is hard to think of anything farther removed from the Christian conception of death than the gay and erotic sculpture of the Etruscan tombs. But in the aftermath of the Black Death artists turned frequently to similar scenes of gaiety and eroticism, perhaps as part of the process by which man generally found himself forced back upon elemental reactions and basic assertions of the life force. Perhaps, too, the impulse that led men to conceive of death, at least partly, in pagan terms derived from the broader anti-authoritarian attitudes that developed during the 14th and 15th centuries when men in all areas of art and learning began to find inspiration in pagan literature. The growing egalitarian spirit of the age had its effect upon the style of painting. The abstract speculation of the Middle Ages was giving way in many areas to a concern with this world, just as Aristotelian logic was giving way to observation and inductive analysis. In accord with this spirit, the painting of the late Middle Ages became much more naturalistic in its presentation of things seen.

One of the most important things to happen in the 14th and 15th centuries was the emergence of a national language in England, France and Italy. The development of English, at least, was due in part to the effects of the Black Death. After the Norman Conquest French had gradually become the dominant language in England until ultimately nearly everyone who wrote, framed public policy, or expressed public thought, did so in French, and many could think and talk in no other language. English continued to be spoken in a variety of dialects in the villages, and many townspeople were bilingual, but the upper classes used French almost exclusively. Most of the education was in the hands of the clergy, and since many Frenchmen had been put in charge of monasteries and of parochial cures, French spread generally throughout the educated of the nation. Inevitably the languages became fused. English took to itself French words and syntax, and French, especially after the loss of Normandy, began to be changed for lack of any standard of purity to limit corruption. In such a situation, English, which as the native tongue was continually being purified while French became more corrupted, would ultimately have triumphed as the national language. But the change was accelerated by the Black Death. The plague had carried off many of the monks and nuns who had done the teaching, and their replacements were often poorly trained and almost always of native stock. The result was that English grammar began to be taught more and more widely, and French, as it was spoken in England, became even more quickly perverted. In about 1387 Thomas Usk, in his *Testament of Love*, alludes to the utter corruption of the imported French; and the Prioress of *The Canterbury Tales*, who spoke French 'ful faire and fetisly',

> After the scole of Stratford atte Bowe,
> For Frenssh of Parys was to hire unknowe.

About the middle of the 14th century Higden wrote in his *Polychronicon* that French was the language almost universally taught in schools, but in 1385 Trevisa, Higden's translator, commented that:

> This maner was myche yused tofore the first moreyn [before the Black Death], and is siththe som dele ychaungide. For John Cornwaile,
> . a maister of gramer, chaungide the lore in gramer scole and construction of Frensch into Englisch, and Richard Pencriche lerned that maner teching of him, and other men of Pencriche. So that now, the yere of owre Lord a thousand thre hundred foure score and fyve, of the secunde King Rychard after the Conquest nyne, in alle the gramer scoles of England children leveth Frensch, and construeth an Englisch.

Even as early as 1362 English had taken the place of French to the extent that Parliament was opened in that year with a speech in English. The growth of egalitarian sentiment after the plague may also have had its influence upon the growing use of the popular language. Even today English contains some clear evidence of the class distinctions that existed during the period of its growth: in the words 'pig' and 'pork', 'cow' and 'beef', and 'sheep' and 'mutton' one may notice that the animal on the hoof, as it was known by the peasant, has a name of Anglo-Saxon derivation, but as food, as it was most frequently seen by the privileged, it has a French name.

The triumph of the vernacular in England produced important changes in literature and paved the way for Chaucer and Langland. But one should not forget that England has a rich literature in Old and Middle English dating from long before the Black Death and that, if there was a revolution in literature in the second half of the 14th century, it was almost as inconclusive as that of the peasants: there is no writer until Spenser who can compare with Chaucer and Langland. In Italy, as well, the 14th century saw a flowering of vernacular literature. *The Decameron*, one of the great monuments of Italian literature, was written between 1348 and 1353 and there is no question of the influence of the Black Death upon that work; but *The Divine Comedy* had been completed a quarter of a century before the plague. In fact, the vernacular literature of Italy went into sharp decline after the Black Death. Petrarch abandoned Italian to write epistles and dissertations in Latin, and his influence led Boccaccio to forsake the vernacular as well. It was not until the 15th and 16th centuries that Italian literature again regained its strength with the work of Tasso and Ariosto. In France the schools suffered as they had in England, and Guillaume de Nangis wrote that after the plague 'few were found who could or would teach children the rudiments of grammar in houses, cities, or villages'. The growth of the vernacular in France is indicated by the fact that the King, Charles V, had translations of classical works prepared for himself and his kinsmen.

In its themes, the literature of Europe, following the Black Death and the continuing succession of plagues, reflects attitudes of people forced to live with such an enemy always at the gates. Petrarch wrote a *Triumph of Death*; Chaucer's Pardoner's Tale is set in plague-time and the Prioress's Tale has as its theme the slander of the Jews; Langland makes frequent reference to the pestilence. Many of the conventional literary themes of the late Middle Ages and early Renaissance reflect attitudes that became widespread during the Black Death, most notably the Renaissance conception of Death the Leveller and the much-repeated reminder of the necessity to 'seize the day. Folk literature of the period is full of parables of death and resurrection that may have derived some of their inspiration from the plague; one remembers, for instance, that Sleeping

Beauty falls into a deathlike sleep after having been pricked with a needle and that, in a common figure of speech, the plague was spoken of as having pricked or stung its victims.

Dramatic literature may have received some impetus from the Black Death. It has been noted that plays were brought to ancient Rome as a plague-preventive; and during the Middle Ages mystery and miracle plays may have been presented together with the processions and other public manifestations of repentance to appease the anger of God. There is no clear evidence that they were, but the plays were current from as early as the 12th century and the first complete miracle play was produced in the presence of Charles IV in 1380. By the 16th century, they were definitely performed to avert the plague. During an epidemic of 1565, people of the district of Maurienne, in southern France, vowed to present a miracle play of their patron, St. Martin, if the town were spared; and a vast production involving no less than seventy-four actors, all men of the working class, was ultimately presented. Another town, Villard-le-Lans, staged a play about St. Sebastian. According to local legend, the Oberammergau Passion Play had its origin in a vow made by people of the town in 1633 to produce a play every ten years if the plague ceased, which it immediately did. The literature of the late 14th and 15th centuries reflects the ideas that were gaining strength; the new curiosity about man and the visible world is reflected in an increasing realism, the democratic spirit is reflected in the increasing interest in the lives and thoughts of common folk. And, of course, literature crystallized thought and disseminated it, aided vastly by the invention of printing from moveable type which brought the word to many who would otherwise have remained illiterate, extended the boundaries of education, and broadened the range of knowledge everywhere.

The efforts of the human spirit to escape from the thraldom of religious and feudal despotism, which produced an inquiring spirit and a new realism in art and literature, brought also new interest in the natural sciences. In medicine, the attempt to break with the theoretical practice of the past in favour of observation and experiment was particularly apparent. Doctors and laymen alike were profoundly impressed by the failure of the ancient theories to help prevent or cure the plague. While the plague still raged at Avignon, the Pope gave his permission for bodies to be dissected in an attempt to discover the cause of the infection. Guy de Chauliac arranged to have the dissection of bodies established as a regular practice. The result of such beginnings was the publication in 1543 of Vesalius's *Fabrica Corporis Humani* which asserted that it was necessary to challenge every past authority and be guided solely by observed facts. But between the time of the Black Death and the establishment of modern medicine, progress was slow; those who perceived the errors of the ancient authorities were not always able to correct them and sometimes fell into greater error themselves. In the single area of plague preventives and cures one may see the kind of stumbling progress and crashing reversal that characterized the efforts of all the sciences to put themselves on an experimental basis. One of those who turned away from ancient theory to his own observation was the 16th-century Swiss physician Paracelsus. Having initially undertaken the study of medicine at Wurzburg, he grew disgusted with the academy and set out wandering about Europe to discover the truth of nature by observing nature. He is said to have proclaimed: 'Whence have I all my secrets, out of what writers and authors? Ask rather how the beasts have learned their arts. If nature can instruct irrational animals, can it not much more men?' His detractors said of him that he lived like a pig, looked like a coachman, kept company with the loosest and lowest of men, wrote as if he were eternally drunk, and died in a tavern brawl. But he also abandoned the humoral theory of Galen, assembled his students at the bedside of the patient, rather than in the classroom, and used the vernacular for the first time in medical writing. His careful observation led him to devise more effective treatments for wounds and fractures than those of the academic physicians of his day, but they also led him to adapt and publish theories that put his followers on the wrong course for generations. One of those theories held that certain magnetic forces could stimulate the vital spirit of human beings and also attract diseases. The Paracelsists came to feel that blood and excrement possessed such magnetic properties, and prescribed them as plague cures and preventives. Beyond the fact that the doses of urine and menstrual fluid, which some of the followers of Paracelsus recommended, were unpalatable as well as useless, reliance upon such therapy inhibited the investigation of the contagious nature of infectious disease. But, in spite of such setbacks, the science of medicine progressed, and Paracelsus, who broke with the academic tradition to learn from nature, was one of the pioneers.

The spirit of empiricism was everywhere, and it would be hard to find a more prophetic voice in the 14th century than that of the Wife of Bath who announces:

Experience, though noon auctoritee
Were in this world, is right ynogh for me. . . .

In all areas of science and learning men wanted to find out for themselves and preferred their own errors to the untested 'truth' of authority. In the area of scholarship, Petrarch, who has been called the Father of Humanism and 'the first modern man', was the first scholar to entirely desert medieval learning. He advocated the study of Greek and Roman literature and greatly influenced the movement to recover lost and forgotten works of ancient writers. Under the influence of the Humanists, university curricula were revised to make the classics the basis of a liberal education. The Italian Humanists, at least, were in revolt against Scholasticism; they often attacked the teachings of the Church and ridiculed the idea that one's task in this life is to prepare for the next. During the Black Death many men feared that the end of the world was upon them. When the plague was over, many acted as if the old world had, in fact, ended. In all the arts and sciences men struck out for new worlds. And some actually set out in boats to find them. One of the most important developments of the 15th century was the development of new navigational techniques, the exploration of new trade routes to the East, and the discovery in actual fact of a new world. One wonders if somewhere in the impulse to find new frontiers was not buried the recollection that the old trade routes had been avenues by which the plague came into the old world. Whatever the causes, the result is clear: everywhere men began to insist that this world was interesting and good, worthy of study, appreciation and unashamed enjoyment. The old authoritative moulds of thought were being broken and the old boundaries transcended.

Joy in life and interest in this world were apparent not only in the scientists, scholars and artists who survived the Black Death. Less well documented but just as real and influential was the release of life force in simple men. The Wife of Bath with her elaborate clothes, her empirical philosophy, and her unabashed sensuality, is as good a symbol of the mood of the time as one could hope to find. The dour moralists of the age were right: men did not learn to be modest and contrite from the agony they had suffered; they learned to be joyful and defiant. Death had done its worst but it hadn't quite killed all of them and those who were left were going on. As might be expected, local authorities report an extraordinary number of marriages immediately following plague; stranger is the apparent increased fecundity of women. Hecker has found evidence of many double and triple births following the Black Death. Men began to rebuild their personal lives and their families; cities and towns began to reorganize. It seems possible that the population would soon have reached pre-plague levels if the disease had not returned in practically every generation for the next century and a half. Certainly everyone seems to have done his best. With the new vigour and life came humour and frivolity. Nearly every plague has produced stories that mock at death. A plague in Vienna has given the world the story of the street-singer Augustin. Having lost all his customers to the plague, he is said to have sat one night drinking heavily in a tavern and composing the song which one still hears in Viennese *Weinstuben*, '*O du lieber Augustin*'. Later, on his way home, he fell into a drunken sleep in the street and was picked up by the burial teams who mistook him for a corpse. He was dumped into a plague pit where he slept the night. Waking in the morning to find himself among the dead but unable to climb back out of the deep pit, he shouted and swore and tramped about on the corpses until the astonished grave-diggers pulled him out. He seems to have been no worse for his adventure, and survived for another quarter of a century before he died, reportedly drunk and probably singing, in a tavern. And from London in 1605 comes the story of a piper, who, drunk and asleep, like Augustin, in the street, was taken up into the death-carts and nearly buried among the corpses that were piled on top of him. As Defoe tells it:

> At length the cart came to the place where the bodies were to be thrown into the ground . . . and as the cart usually stopped some time before they were ready to shoot out the melancholy load they had in it, as soon as the cart stopped the fellow awaked and struggled a little to get his head out from among the dead bodies, when, raising himself up in the cart, he called out, 'Hey! where am I?' This frighted the fellow that attended the work; but after some pause John Hayward [one of the buriers] said, 'Lord, bless us! There's somebody in the cart not quite dead!' so another called to him and said, 'Who are you?' The fellow answered, 'I am the poor piper. Where am I?' 'Where are you?' says Hayward. 'Why, you are in the dead-cart, and we are going to bury you.' 'But I an't dead though, am I?' says the piper, which made him laugh a little— . . .

The poor piper's question resounds through history. And others, who were surprised to find themselves alive, laughed a little too.

One of the strangest phenomena to follow the Black Death was a

passion for dancing that began in Italy in 1374 and swept over
Europe. It reached such proportions and was attended by such
violent ecstasy that it has been labelled the Dancing Mania and
treated as an example of mass psychosis by modern medical writers.
Contemporaries report that people would suddenly, without warning or preparation, appear in the streets, join hands and dance with
such frenzy, for hours and in some places for days, that they lost all
control of themselves. The only thing that seemed to calm the
dancers was music; and some community authorities found it necessary to hire musicians to play as the only means of keeping a semblance of public order. A less dramatic but more widespread reaction to the dismal time of plague was a greatly increased interest
in clothes. There was an extravagant love of dress after the mid-
14th century and, as might be expected, an equally extravagant
denunciation of it. To the dismay of the pious and humble, people
of all classes began to sport clothes of exotic cut and brilliant colour.
Sacchetti, writing from Italy, is obviously disgusted by such
displays:

> How many fashions have been altered in my time by the changeable-
> ness of those persons now living, and especially in mine own city!
> Formerly the women wore their bodices cut so open that they were
> uncovered to beneath their armpits! Then with one jump, they wore
> their collars right up to their ears. And these are all outrageous fashions
> ... nowadays it seemeth to me that the whole world is united in having
> but little firmness of mind. . . . The young maidens, who used to dress
> with so much modesty, now have raised the hanging ends of their
> hoods and have twisted them into caps, and they go attired like com-
> mon women, wearing caps, and collars and strings round their necks,
> with divers kinds of beasts hung upon their breasts. . . . The young
> men for the most part go without cloaks and wear their hair long; they
> need but divest themselves of their breeches and they will then have
> left off everything they can, and truly these are so small that they
> could easily do without them. . . . For whoever liveth but one day in
> this world changeth his fashions a thousand times; each one seeketh
> liberty and yet depriveth himself of it. The Lord created our feet free,
> yet many persons are unable to walk on account of the long points of
> their shoes. . . . Truly there would be no end to describing the women's
> attire . . . and how every day they are up on the roofs, some curling
> their hair, some smoothing it, and some bleaching it, so that often they
> die of the colds they catch!

Clothing and hair-styles are the most obvious marks of one's per-
sonality, of one's social and economic status, and even of one's

political sympathies; and they are also the easiest to change. After
the Black Death, as in so many other periods of great danger and
anxiety, the new fashions, as an understandable, and perhaps a
necessary, part of the reawakening of life, had an irresistible appeal.
The Limburg Chronicle states quite simply: *'Darnach, da das
Sterben, die Geiselfarth, Römerfarth, Judenschlacht, als vorgeschrieben
stehet, ein End hatte, da hub die Welt wieder an zu leben und fröhlich
zu seyn, und machten die Männer neue Kleidung.'* When the Death,
the processions of Flagellants, the pilgrimages to Rome and the
slaughter of the Jews were at an end, the world began to live again,
and to be joyful, and people put on new clothes.

The world revived and joy revived and people put on new clothes
and some things changed and some things remained the same and
the Black Death passed into the memories and then into the history
of men. But what exactly is one to make of it as an event in history?
After the death and the suffering, the social, political, economic and
spiritual disruption of those few years, what lasting effects did the
Black Death have upon the course of human history? Even the
most superficial attempt to put the Black Death into historical
perspective requires more than a study of history, it demands a
questioning of the whole theory and concept of history. The story
of the Black Death is usually accorded only a few pages in the
general text-books on the period, and one might assume from the
lack of stress laid upon it that it is an unimportant event. There are
some good reasons for this lack of emphasis. One is that 20th-cen-
tury historians are anxious to correct the view of some earlier writers
who saw in the Black Death the essential cause of the break-up of
medieval institutions, who, in fact, used it to explain all sorts of
economic and political changes that ended the Middle Ages. The
modern historian has seen that this earlier view of economic and
political change is simplistic and that the Black Death is only one of
a number of causes of such change. In any case it does not lend itself
easily to analysis in economic and political terms; there were no
great battles and no important dates, no kings, popes, or generals who
distinguished themselves in any remarkable way. No great institutions collapsed as a result of the Black Death; no national boundaries
changed; after a brief interruption, economic, political, religious
and even cultural life went on very much as before. The trouble
with such a view is not that it is wrong—for surely it is right—but
that it is beside the point. The Black Death was not principally an
economic, political or cultural event. It was not primarily a tragedy

of the rich, the powerful, the talented or the privileged. Neither was it characterized by great acts of courage or even by unique debauchery, and consequently it does not lend itself to analysis by those who view history as the succession of acts and decisions of powerful men. The Black Death was none of these things; yet anyone who can dismiss as relatively unimportant a catastrophe that in the space of two years reduced the population of the Western world by as much as a third and the population of some countries by a half is surely suffering from some sort of mental blindness.

The Black Death was not primarily a disaster endured by great men or institutions. It was a tragedy of ordinary men. As such, the story of the Black Death is not a story of economic and political events. It is only partially a story of change. As a tragedy of the poor, the under-privileged, the unpretentious, the weak, it is a story, not of change, but rather of endurance. It is the story of the suffering, confusion, endurance and rebirth of men whose names we shall never know. It is the story of the preservation of institutions, more than of their destruction, of the reassertion of values after temporary demoralization. It is the story of the persistence of ordinary life in the face of universal disaster: a story of the harvest brought in and the children borne, reared, and loved in spite of everything. In a very real sense this is the true history of the world; not the history of the generals, kings and popes—that history is a record of insanity as often as not—but of the poor, the workers, and the unpretentious whose endurance and fortitude provide the basis of power for the great whose acts are recorded as history. To see only the great men, or to see only the economic and political ripples of history, is to watch the waves and ignore the ocean. The Black Death was a tragedy of simple men; it is the story of endurance; it is not a story of death but of life. Mankind survived this most deadly catastrophe of recorded history, and survived very much intact.

The story of the Black Death carries a message of hope, but also a warning. It is encouraging that mankind often responds to great disaster with a burst of joy and vigour, and a new freedom of spirit. But freeing the individual spirit is a dangerous business. The same force that liberates the poet and the philosopher from inhibiting forms of thought also frees the maniac from traditional sanctions against violence. It seems inevitable that such movements be attended by atrocities. Following the Black Death men indulged in excesses of all sorts, from harmless self-indulgence to ideological fanaticism, blind violence, and the passion to murder their fellow-men. If

history is to be anything more than a pleasant pastime for the anti-
quarian, it should lead the student not just to deplore the excesses of
the past but to try to modify the excesses of the present. Perhaps the
excesses of troubled times are truly inevitable, but anyone who takes
comfort in that idea and gives up the struggle against seeming
inevitability must be complacent to the point of madness.

No analogies are so inexact or misleading as historical ones. If one
reads history to find insight into present problems, it is best to
remember the axiom that history teaches us nothing so surely as that
history can teach us nothing for sure. Even so, with the greatest
caution, one can perhaps consider the similarities between the 14th
century and our own. The frightening spectre of a nuclear holo-
caust, and the sure and progressive starvation of ever-larger numbers of people as population begins inexorably to increase beyond
the capacity of men to feed themselves, confront the second half of
the 20th century, for the first time in six hundred years, with the
possibility of a catastrophe of the proportions of the Black Death. In
some ways the anticipation of disaster has as profound an influence
upon the thought and institutions of men as does the disaster itself:
men distinguish themselves from other creatures not in that they
die but in that they are aware of the coming of death. The anticipation of such a disaster, like the disaster itself, calls forth great energy
and great expectation. The revolutionary fervour throughout the
world today is not unlike that which followed the Black Death. The
extravagant hopes and expectations of people everywhere seem
influenced by the conviction that everything must be accomplished
now. Nations that cannot grow enough wheat and rice to feed their
people divert their resources to build dams and steel mills; nations
that produce so much food that it must be systematically destroyed
and farmers paid to keep land out of production, that produce so
much steel that the disposal of old cars becomes a national problem,
divert their resources to bold, but pathetic, schemes to shoot men
at the moon. And everywhere in the world children suffer from
hunger. Like Wat Tyler's rebels we would do everything now, today,
or at the latest next year. The word on the buttons worn by many
American civil rights activists in the early 1960's might almost be
the motto of all the world: NOW. But in the 14th century, at least,
revolutionary fervour did not produce a revolution. It was not
enough that the hopes of the age were fervently held, it was not even
enough that they were for the most part noble; without organization, discipline, and a constructive and realistic programme of

action they failed. Southern red-neck sheriffs wore buttons that said: NEVER. But change comes anyway and many of these sheriffs are out of work. Still, not all change is progress; in the 14th century some petty tyrants were deposed only to be replaced by greater tyrants. We ought to be on guard against demagogues who tell us we must demand everything now or that we must relinquish nothing ever, who would turn our legitimate hopes into chaos and self-destructive violence by preaching over-simplifications. It is not to deplore the revolutionary spirit or to exalt the *status quo* that one urges caution upon the extremists. It is not even to argue for evolution and gradual change. It is rather to point out the apparent lesson of the 14th century: that demagogues who promise radical change do not always produce it and in some cases actually inhibit it. Change will come whether we desire it or not, and thoughtful men have a duty to resist the excesses of both those who seek it and those who oppose it, so that it may come more quickly and without atrocities. Demagogues thrive in times like these. Everywhere one hears of the efficacy of violence: nations employ it to bring order to international affairs, those who recognize that transparent hypocrisy employ violent means to make their protest. All political power grows out of the barrel of a gun, they cry. But many are not statesmen, only shooters. You cannot make an omelette without breaking eggs. But not all those who are breaking eggs know how to make an omelette, and it doesn't speed the cooking if the kitchen is full of idiots breaking eggs all over the place.

We have little control over the individual acts of violence committed by the madmen in our midst, but we still have the chance of urging restraint upon our leaders whose power derives from our support. The most tragic and ironic atrocities are those committed or assented to by men of good will who have let themselves be persuaded that murders committed in the name of justice are justified. If that condemnation of violence sounds like all the other windy preachments of the bourgeois moralists, one might consider that apart from some questionable therapeutic value that violence has for those who have been long oppressed, it has produced very ambiguous results in political and economic life. Students in the streets of Paris and Berlin, Black Power advocates in Harlem and Watts, national liberation guerillas in Viet Nam have all learned, as the peasant rebels and the popular religious reformers of the 14th century learned, that those in power, hollow as they may be, are not quite paper tigers. If the just and legitimate hopes of the oppressed are not to be crushed, they must be fought with more subtlety and to more purpose than Wat Tyler and his men, or Hus and his, fought for theirs. The repressive force of the 14th century's paper tigers was great enough to drive the rebellion of simple men underground and into literature for generations. Unless the leaders of the activists hope to be only martyrs or characters in future novels, they might listen to the voices from the past. They might recall that after the Black Death the legitimate religious frustration of men and their legitimate anger at economic oppression turned them against the Jews. That was not an isolated case. The power of the privileged often is such that initial acts of revolutionary violence direct themselves against defenceless scapegoats in such a way as really to strengthen those in power. In such an instance, the supposed therapeutic value of violence actually defeats the revolutionary goals. After an orgy of pointless destruction, men return to their former lives, their energy spent and their passion cooled and chastened, more powerless than before to organize against the real oppressors. Angry men find simple solutions to complex problems, but the legitimacy of their anger does not confer validity upon their programmes. One must pause and try to see clearly. Amid the revolutionary fervour of our own time, the story of similar expectations and struggles in the 14th century offers not a guide for action, but a caution against over-simplification.

Superficial parallels can be found between almost any two periods, and historical analogies can be made to prove anything. In spite of obvious similarities between them, the 14th and 20th centuries are indescribably remote from one another. It is true that, in both, established values and institutions were being questioned with an uncommon ferocity, but it would be hard to find two periods in which the values and institutions had less in common. It is quite possible that the problems of the 14th century during the time of the Black Death are in no way parallel to the dilemmas and crises we face today. But in some ways one can earnestly hope that they are. An age that confronts annihilation needs to look somewhere for hope, and the men of the 14th century have shown that mankind can not only survive great and sudden disaster but can survive virtually intact. Some great contemporary Masters of War are convinced that the world can endure a nuclear conflict. It is not to their credit to think so, but they may be right. The experience of Europe after the plague would seem to offer the hope that men would rise, somehow, from the rubble. But the men who would endure and prevail would

almost certainly be intent upon eradicating forever those who ad-
ministered the disaster. The Black Death carries a warning for those
who trust too much in the gullibility and docility of ordinary men.
In the process of enduring suffering, men find their strength and it
is not the humility that their masters tell them they should find.
They discover that unsophisticated energy can make a mockery of
fastidious good taste, that vulgar humour is both truer and more
righteous than pious morality, that life is better than death. People
who have learned that will never be quite docile again. 'Therefore I
warn you rich . . .' writes Langland. And then: 'Overplenty feeds
the pride which poverty conquers.' And if one would know where
to look for the enduring values that could show the way in times of
widespread chaos, Langland tells us:

> God is often in the gorge of these great masters,
> But among lowly men are his mercy and his works. . . .

One need be neither a Maoist nor a sentimentalist to agree. To
assert that simple, traditional values persist among the unsophisticated long after they have become mere conventions to be given
lip-service by the privileged is only to say that the cultural-lag is
greater there, and that the mentality of the people lags behind that
of the more privileged classes both in growth and in decay. The
14th-century guardians of morality failed in a number of ways.
Their commitment to institutions and modes of thought that were
suddenly obsolete made them irrelevant. They were capable neither
of encouraging the energy and strength of the people nor of inhibiting their most dangerous vices. Their very wisdom clouded
their vision. When wisdom is confused, the ignorant mercifully see
more clearly than the wise. As Chaucer says,

> Now is nat that of God a ful fair grace
> That swich a lewed mannes wit shal pace
> The wisdom of an heep of lerned men?

Like the priests who deserted their parishes, and the bureaucrats
who deserted their offices, and the doctors who went to the country,
a great many learned men were simply somewhere else. And the
energy and simple virtues of the people filled the vacuum. Radical
new forms of thought and radical new priorities were needed; persistence in the real virtues of the past was needed. The traditional
leaders and men of learning could provide neither. In such a period
of political and spiritual anarchy, or in a decadent society whose

institutions and authorities are rotten with hypocrisy, there are two forces of endurance and purposeful change; the radical intellectual who can sense the values of the future and the unsophisticated who cling to the uncorrupted values of the past. A coalition of such forces is difficult to imagine and perhaps impossible to achieve. But the most powerful movements of reform in the 14th century—the Lollards and the Hussites—were the result of such a coalition. Confused and ultimately unsuccessful in bringing about the changes they hoped for, these 14th-century movements offer not so much a method and example as a reminder of the need for bold alliances.

Perhaps we should talk about the people less and talk to them more. Perhaps we should trust them. Perhaps we do not have to be afraid. In times of great trouble it is they who make history, hold together the fabric of society, and nourish the spirit of change. When the kings and presidents and popes and generals are dead and embalmed in books, simple men still sow and reap and marry and raise their children. They still drink and fornicate and put on new clothes. Any one rash enough to attempt to suppress the energy they embody, and any one presumptuous enough to appoint himself their spokesman, might listen and beware. Any whose faith in mankind has been eroded to cynicism by the hypocrisy of the mighty, can listen and take heart. The Black Death would seem to teach us that men will endure. Rough and vulgar, ignorant and sometimes violent, the mass of men will come through and will bring some good things with them: energy, humour, defiance—whatever it is that allows us to persist and even triumph, to fulfil the promise that he who endures to the end shall be saved. For all the horror it held for those who endured it, in the perspective of time the Black Death is a triumph of life.

A SELECTED BIBLIOGRAPHY

CAMUS, ALBERT. *The Plague.* Trans. Stuart Gilbert. London, 1948.

COULTON, G. G. *The Black Death.* London, 1929.

— *Medieval Panorama.* 2 vols. London, 1961.

CRAWFURD, RAYMOND. *Plague and Pestilence in Literature and Art.* Oxford, 1914.

DEFOE, DANIEL. *A Journal of the Plague Year.* London, 1722.

GASQUET, FRANCIS AIDAN. *The Great Pestilence.* London, 1893.

HAYS, DENYS. *The Medieval Centuries.* London, 1964.

HECKER, J. F. C. *The Epidemics of the Middle Ages.* Trans. B. G. Babington. London, 1844.

HOENIGER, R. *Der Schwarze Tod in Deutschland.* Berlin, 1882.

KLEIN, HERBERT. *Das Grosse Sterben von 1348/49 und seine Auswirkung auf die Besiedlung der Östalpenländer.* In: Mitteilungen der Gesellschaft für Salzburger Landeskunde, 1960.

LECHER, CARL. *Das Grosse Sterben in Deutschland.* Innsbruck, 1884.

LOPEZ DE MENESES, AMADA. 'Documentos acerca de la Peste Negra en los dominicos de la corona de Aragon', *Estudios de Edad Media de la Corona de Aragon,* VI (1956).

MANZONI, ALESSANDRO. *The Betrothed (I Promessi Sposi).* Trans. Archibald Colquhoun. London, 1952.

MARSARI, CESARE. *Saggio Storico Medico sulle Pestilenze di Perugia.* Perugia, 1839.

MICHON, L. *Documents Inédits sur la Grande Peste de 1348.* Paris, 1860.

NOHL, JOHANNES. *The Black Death.* Trans. C. H. Clarke. London, 1926 and 1961.

PERROY, E. 'Les Crises du XIVe Siècle', *Annales: Économies, Sociétés Civilisations,* IV (1949).

PHILLIPPE, A. *Histoire de la Peste Noire.* Paris, 1853.

PORQUET, LOUIS. *La Peste en Normandie du XIVe au XVIIe Siècle.* Vire, 1898.

223

PREVITÉ-ORTON, C. W. *The Shorter Cambridge Medieval History*. 2 vols. Cambridge, 1962.

RENOUARD, X. 'La Peste Noire de 1348–1350', *Revue de Paris* (March, 1950).

SAHM, WILHELM. *Geschichte des Pest in Östpreussen*. Leipzig, 1905.

SALTMARSH, JOHN. 'Plague and Economic Decline in the Later Middle Ages', *Cambridge Historical Journal*, 7 (1941).

STICKER, GEORG. *Die Peste*. 2 vols. Giessen, 1908–10.

INDEX

26194